THE MYTH OF THE TIGER

THE MYTH OF THE TIGER

WHAT YOU NEED TO KNOW ABOUT THE CHINESE WORK PSYCHE REVEALING THE CHINESE WORK CULTURE

Alexander Johnson

COPYRIGHT

WHY DRAGON VERSUS TIGER?

According to Feng Shui practitioner, Sally Painter, the Dragon and Tiger are symbols for the balance of power. Feng Shui aims to achieve a balance of Yang (male) and Yin (female) energy, or chi, which creates harmony in your environment, be it at home or at work.

For centuries, martial arts disciplines have used the Tiger and Dragon to symbolize conflict and long-standing rivalry between these two powerful forces. Both the Dragon and Tiger are required in order to maintain the delicate balance between male and female chi.

Symbolism of the Dragon

The Dragon is a celestial guardian in Chinese culture that has long opposed the Tiger. It represents the Chinese emperor and royalty who have claimed to have descended from god dragons.

Symbolism of the Tiger

The white tiger symbolizes the prosperity and luck of descendants in the West compass direction. A celestial guardian and protector, the Tiger is believed to ensure the continuation of a family's health and wealth, as well as the continuation of their bloodline.

When the Dragon and Tiger are at odds, the family's bloodline—and their future—is threatened. Therein lies the importance of balancing the two energies.

The Tiger challenges the Dragon's long-held power and energy, which is thought to belong to emperors. It seeks to destroy the hold emperors have on the world, and in doing so, leveling the playing ground. The Tiger seeks to restore the balance of power, and to diminish the hold of the emperors on the world.

Most Feng Shui students are aware of the irony of the Chinese emperor's power in contrast to the life balancing doctrines of Feng Shui, yet dynasties have ruled the world for centuries, creating imbalances in power and wealth. Even more ironically, only emperors were allowed to use Feng Shui, as the practitioners and masters in their courts closely guarded the principles. As such, the Dragon remained truly powerful.

Yin, Yang, and Balancing Chi

Martial arts masters used their role-playing movements to symbolically challenge the oppressing ideology. Martial arts depict the combat between the Tiger and the Dragon using opposite techniques, which were symbolic of the opposing Yin and Yang chi energies.

The Dragon versus Tiger ideology aims to achieve the optimal balance of Yin and Yang chi that can help restore balance to not only your home life, but also to your work environment.

ABOUT THE AUTHOR

Painting on wood
Emperor Qianlong, circa 1737 during the Qing Dynasty
(1644 – 1911) – Artist Unknown

Alexander Johnson was born in South Africa in 1967, where he grew up and completed his tertiary education to become a Professional Engineer. He is a partner in a consulting company, advising clients on project set-up, implementation strategy and project management.

His parents came to Africa from Europe in the 1960s in search of greater fortunes. Alexander was exposed to a European culture in the heart of Africa with its African traditions, which gave him a broad outlook and interest on the intricacies of the co-existence of very different cultures.

He and his family currently reside in Johannesburg, South Africa, where they have lived for the last 25 years. They share the house with a lifetime collection of books, an interest he attained from his well-read mother at an early age.

Alexander is also an amateur writer and film producer, artist, avid sportsman and life traveler. He has always thrived on adventure, having trekked through the Namib Desert, back-packed through Europe and the Middle East, explored the great expanses of Southern Africa on foot and by car, sailed up and down the coast of Africa and spent time working and living in various African countries. Alexander has traveled to numerous destinations around the word with his family, exploring the different cultures, their traditions and the local history.

While working for a Chinese organization in Africa, he became so intrigued by the cultural differences between China and the West that it compelled him to document the interactive behaviors between these two far-flung cultures, which ultimately culminated in his first published book.

DEDICATION

Dedicated to my family

CONTENTS

ACKNOWLEDGEMENTS

The journey of this book started quite unintentionally. Trying to understand my Chinese colleagues and my Chinese employer, I ended up having many debates with my Western work colleagues—while we all worked for the same Chinese company—analyzing the strange interactive behaviors between Western and Chinese work colleagues that we faced on a daily basis. The complex understanding of the 'Chinese' became so involved that I started making notes in order for me to piece together the intricate web of the Chinese psyche. More debates (with my Western colleagues) and many notes later, I concluded that I should write my thoughts, experiences, and interpretations into more than notes, and so the idea of this book was born.

That journey started back in 2013. While I tried to understand my Chinese colleagues better by engaging in vigorous debates, their interactions with me (and with our Western colleagues) generally did not reveal anything more about their deeper cultural psyche than what we could gather from the 'outside'. I was very much dependent on my astute observations, interpretations of these observations, and my analysis and plausible reasoning of these Chinese behaviors when I formulated my take on the Chinese psyche. I therefore acknowledge that some readers of this book might perceive my views—based on a Western interpretation of observations made—as bias, but I have made every effort to evaluate the Chinese psyche as objectively as possible, albeit from a Western perspective in most instances.

The first two years demanded much of my patience to try to piece together the different nuances of the intricate Chinese behaviors, which I was able to observe both in the workspace as well as at social engagements. Initially, many behavioral trends didn't make sense at all and didn't fit nicely together, and no obvious behavior patterns emerged. Chinese behaviors, reactions, and reasoning appeared to be highly random and disconnected. Over time though, the Chinese psyche puzzle started forming a picture; faint at first, but with time, it became clearer.

In 2016, after having spent some three years being deeply exposed to the Chinese business culture as well as observing first-hand the Chinese traditions and cultural aspects—at my Chinese employer, engaging with multiple Chinese supply companies and contractors as well as engaging socially—my understanding had matured and my book started taking shape. Over the last four years, I have read many a book on China to get a better understanding, initially, to enhance my work experience, but it also had the added benefit of preparing me better for writing this book. I also enthusiastically absorbed any news relating to China and read many articles on the Internet. My Yin and Yang started to make sense.

The two postscript chapters, 'Chinese Business Culture, Etiquette, and Behavior in the Work Environment' as well as 'Chinese Cultural and Traditional Revelations' provide insightful information, and further information can be sourced on the Internet. Wikipedia specifically hosts a wealth of information and I have referenced certain information from their websites. Other internet research also provided valuable insights. These websites confirmed many of my initial observations and deductions made. The majority of the book is however a rendition of my personal experiences. The supplementary postscript sections, obtained from my personal experiences as well internet research, have been added to provide the reader with a wholesome experience and better appreciation of the general Chinese behavioral, cultural, and traditional aspects, that can be widely sourced from many books as well as many Internet sites, but are not readily contained in one unified piece of writing.

I firstly would like to thank my wife and two daughters for allowing me the space, creativity, and enthusiasm to write this work. I spent many a night working right through, when my creative juices were flowing profusely, and I was unable to put my thoughts on hold or my pen down, emerging from my trance absolutely exhausted in the morning when the kids had to be taken to school and I had to ready myself for some 'real' work.

From an in-depth level of understanding, I owe a big thank you to my business partner and friend, Fred Spearhead, with whom I could debate the Chinese psyche for hours. We analyzed and re-analyzed their peculiar behaviors, trying to fit each puzzle piece of a newly discovered behavior into the picture of that mysterious place and its mysterious people; a place most people only know superficially as China. Fred critically read and reviewed my book, and I am thankful for his valued contribution on some of the finer details of my book.

I also owe a thank you to my mother-in-law, an avid reader, critic, and fan who dutifully proofread my book, pointing out many improvements on the use of the English language, and being more vigilant than Word Spell Check in correcting spelling mishaps.

I would have loved to have a Chinese critical eye sweep over this work from one of my many Chinese colleagues, but this would have been impossible. It would probably put the candidate into a serious predicament; the reason which you shall read about and understand better as you unfold the layers of the Chinese psyche when immersing yourself into this book.

FOREWORD

I had the privilege of joining a Chinese organization that was involved in one of the largest investments in Africa. My primary objective, apart from contributing professionally and constructively to the company, was to learn as much as possible about China as a country, its traditions, culture, and the people. It was a fascinating—but sometimes frustrating journey—, enveloping me completely in the mystique, that China was and is today. In the first few months, I went through a steep learning curve with new impressions around every corner. Slowly, I was able to piece together the intricate web of Yin and Yang, Dragon and Tiger and the forces in general that shape the modern Chinese psyche in the global village today. I made every effort to learn everything about the Tiger by immersing myself in literature on China, having read a number of books on this subject to date, researched the Internet, debated China with my Western colleagues, and made grave efforts to get to know and understand my Chinese colleagues better.

I found this journey so fascinating that I started capturing my impressions and learnings. Eventually, my notes became so comprehensive that I started envisaging writing this book. I hope that the fruits of my journey, captured herein, will give you not only pleasure but will also open your eyes to the unique world that is China, with all its nuances, and the complex world of interpersonal relationships shaping the memorable experience of interacting with the Tiger.

This book represents my perception of the Chinese world, and while it might offend some readers, this was my reality. It is written from the viewpoint of Western understanding and impressions. No doubt, Eastern cultures will have their very own interpretation of Western cultures and its shortcomings, in the eye of the beholder. I felt strongly about sharing my experience with others across all worlds—people with Western beliefs as well as people with Eastern values—in order for all to have a better chance of crossing the cultural divide still so vivid in the 21st century between East and West.

I am hoping that this book will benefit both non-Chinese as well as Chinese companies and people from all walks of life by equipping non-Chinese people to better accommodate Chinese cultural subtleties. Conversely, I hope it will help Chinese people better appreciate the Western perceptions of their culture and traditions. Building great relationships can be achieved through compromise from both parties, for without compromise and understanding one will forever be captured in one's own make-believe fantasy world.

I have not divulged names of organizations or names of affected persons where I share sensitive observations and findings in this book, in order to protect their identities as well as my own well-being.

PROLOGUE

A light sweet fragrance scented the air. The pavements and streets exuded a purple glare, as far as the eye could see. Pedestrians frolicked in the subtle warmth filtering through the purple urban canopy. Spring was in the air. Children with sticky faces were eagerly licking colorful ice-lollies. Bees started to emerge from their winter hibernation, attracted by the warmth and promising smells of nectar and pollen alike.

Tourists in buses made their way slowly down the streets. The city was a site to behold. This spectacle presented itself only once a year, precisely around springtime, and people came from afar to revel in it.

For the Chinese, the beauty of a blossoming spring flower has been etched in millennia of memories. Spring flowers exemplified the reincarnation of life itself. The smell, myriad of colors, sounds, and life all around made one feel alive again after a cold and dry winter. It reminded of home, of family and of memories. It eternalized the good over bad, the harmony of nature and the power of beauty.

Cars full of families rolled down the tree lined streets to take in this spectacle of nature—a spectacle of color, light, and smell—that enlightened the soul like a Chinese opera would enlighten the heart.

The Jacaranda—so profound in this city—once again presented a spectacle beyond one's wildest imagination and had been long forgotten since the last spring. It made one rejoice in life, in being alive, and in being part of a great nation, conquering the world.

CHAPTER 1

INTRODUCTION

*"By three methods we may learn wisdom: First, by reflection,
which is noblest; second, by imitation, which is easiest; and
third, by experience, which is the bitterest."*

—*Confucius*

Walking around any African capital city—especially in the last
decade or so—, one might be overwhelmed by the number of
Chinese people to be encountered. On every street corner,
one will find a Chinese grocer, fabric shop, cheap Chinese
imports shop, or some other Chinese paraphernalia shop.

Anything that one can think of is usually made in China
and is readily available, even in the remotest part of a country.
In short, the Chinese are everywhere. China Malls, exclusively
selling Chinese manufactured items, can be found in every
suburb and larger cities now boast a Chinatown. While the
West has had Chinatowns and Chinese immigrants for decades,
many having arrived in the 19th century, Africa is seeing a large
influx of Chinese migrants and workers now. They are arriving
in their thousands, offering services in industries as varied as
restaurants and science.

Before the current great Chinese immigration to Africa,
China was a faraway land with mysterious people about whom
we knew precious little. We could hardly pronounce their

names, let alone try to learn their complex language. When referring to a Chinese company or person, the best one could muster was to refer to 'the Chinese company' and 'the Chinese CEO'. The names were as foreign to our language and pronunciation as China was as a country. However, in the last decade the Chinese presence has become increasingly prevalent, compelling people around the world to memorize their names, learn something about their Chinese employers, and try to understand the culture better.

Who are these Chinese people? Where do they come from? What are their beliefs and rituals? Africa has suddenly found itself surrounded by Chinese people and the time has arrived for Africa and the world to better understand these people from a faraway land.

My first contact with Chinese people, where I had the chance to really get to know their psyche, presented itself through an employment opportunity, working for one of the larger Chinese companies currently venturing into Africa and heavily investing on the continent—one of the largest single Chinese investments to date. I took on this opportunity with the firm idea of learning as much as I could about their people culture, business culture, traditions, and language. China has become a huge global economic role player, but non-Chinese people understand virtually nothing about them. China is a current and future force that will dominate the world economy for probably the next two decades, having an insatiable appetite for internal growth and development as well as global expansion and economic globalization.

China is still one of the fastest growing economies worldwide, showing an average GDP growth of around 7% (6.7% in

2016). A percentage growth in the Chinese economy easily swallows up multiple country economies and many African economies in one fell swoop. It is a force to be reckoned with.

The faster we understand the Tiger, which is China, the easier it will be to work with Chinese companies and Chinese people, ultimately benefiting all and making the work experience overwhelmingly constructive. The West views the Chinese nation with fear and anxiety, as it seems to swallow up the planet in its insatiable appetite for more and more resources and commodities outside China. China, the Tiger, is gritting its teeth, as it prowls for any opportunity to satisfy its hunger.

Before my first work encounter with Chinese co-workers, a friend advised me on my prospects, saying, *"When working with people from another nationality, while the language is a barrier, the work ethics and business culture has a common threat and one soon moves constructively forward in achieving the same goals. But when working with the Chinese, it is like working with Martians."*

Chinese persons appear to be quiet, reserved, and sometimes even arrogant. It is difficult to interact with them and get through to them. Often, the conversation is stiflingly slow and facilitated by a translator. Communication in English is difficult to follow, and literal translations often obscure the intended meaning of the discussion. The pronunciation of words spoken by Chinese nationals in English is often difficult to understand. Similarly, Chinese people struggle to understand what Westerners are saying and to grasp English meanings; they would pretend to understand so as not to embarrass themselves. It is not uncommon for Chinese to nod their heads and agree to everything in the affirmative, only for one to realize days later that they did not comprehend a single word of what was being communicated. All this can lead to frustration and ultimately conflict, which challenges relationship building, a vital link in trying to effectively engage in business for or with Chinese companies.

The following chapters will give you a better understanding of what makes the Chinese tick in the workplace and provide you with the essential tools to better—and more constructively—engage in the work environment. I also aim to make you aware of the Chinese culture, which should give you the edge when engaging professionally and socially with Chinese people anywhere in the world.

Chapter 2 looks at China's historic and current role in Africa. Africa has become China's number one investment target over the last decade. Understanding China's motivation behind their Africa strategy will set the scene for the rest of this book.

Chapters 3 – 5 introduce to you the Chinese cultural behaviors that drive a nation. These behavioral traits need to be appreciated in order to better understand the psyche of the Tiger. Confucian Harmony, Mianzi (the act of saving face), and Guangxi (the act of maintaining relationships) have been fine-tuned by Chinese society over many millennia and form an integral part in the behavior and actions of modern China.

Chapters 6 to 12 capture my experiences, having worked directly for a Chinese company and having had the privilege to delve into the Chinese culture, meet Chinese people, and get to understand the Chinese psyche.

Postscript Chapters 1 and 2 give a concise description of Chinese 'Business Culture, Etiquette and Behavior in the Work Environment' as well as 'Chinese Cultural and Traditional Revelations' to give you a more easily referenceable overview.

The intent of the book is to help you try to understand the Chinese people, their business culture, their national culture, and their day-to-day behavior, as an outsider would experience it when working with Chinese nationals for the first time. It is how Chinese persons tend to behave in a business environment. Where possible, I have tried to explain or justify their behavioral traits, however, in some instances I was only able to observe their behavior, without being able to fully understand or explain it.

The following chapters do not try to justify or excuse the interpretations made by non-Chinese colleagues in the work environment. The observations and experiences are conveyed as they have been interpreted (based on the principle that 'my perception is my reality!'). I have no doubt that Chinese people find non-Chinese—and specifically Western—behavior as foreign as non-Chinese people often interpret their behavior. The book also does not analyze Western typical behavior and business culture in the work place, unless it is as a direct consequence of having engaged with a Chinese person or company, which has resulted in an interesting and peculiar behavioral outcome. However, some typical Western business culture is described and compared to Chinese business culture, where relevant, to give context to observations made.

As these two very opposite cultures are slowly getting to know each other, I have no doubt that over the next decade or two, interactions will become easier, and business cultures can be better integrated, which will ultimately lead to more constructive work output, teamwork, and greater success in the workplace and in closing better global business deals. For now though, the road of cultural integration ahead will still be somewhat bumpy and frustrating for both entities in the work environment. While Chinese businesses need to learn how to operate in a more modern and transparent manner in the global village, the global village needs to make every effort to better understand the Chinese business culture and psyche.

CHAPTER 2

CONQUERING THE LION

"Wheresoever you go, go with all your heart."

—*Confucius*

The world was there, beckoning, asking to be conquered. It provided all the needs of a vast nation that was hungry, ready to consume what was available for harvesting, be it perishables, consumables, raw materials, minerals or technology. China, with a surface area of more than 9.6 million square kilometers—similar in size to the United States—was quickly becoming too small for its billion plus nationals. They needed to be fed, housed, and given a means to a more prosperous life. The Tiger had awoken after the Cultural Revolution. The Chinese nation wanted more, needed more, and now had to burst out of its constraining chains into which communism had so effectively shackled the nation. A whole generation of Chinese was shielded from the world, fighting to survive in a repressive regime that did not allow individuality, ownership, self believe, or growth. The Tiger had to be fed, for the nation was anxious for change after years of oppressive rule. As had been done by many dynasties before the modern age, China was always considering its options to harvest the world far beyond its borders.

Conquering the world through trade and economic colonialization was nothing new to this vast empire. It had been done for millennia, by controlling the famous silk route skirting the Taklamakan Desert as well as crossing the oceans to trade with India, Malaysia, and even as far afield as Africa.

The last great dynasty to trade successfully with lesser nations was the Ming Dynasty, sending its famous court eunuch, mariner, explorer, diplomat, and fleet admiral, Zheng He (1371– 1433), to lead huge Chinese fleets to seek new countries with whom they could engage in trade across the oceans. Chinese dynasties have always seen themselves as the center of their known universe, viewing all other beings as inferior—not worthy of their acknowledgement or approval. What China really needed was raw materials, to keep their vast nation going in exchange for common goods, like china, gunpowder, spices, and tea.

After 1948, when the Communist Party of China, under the leadership of Mao Zedong, had eventually forced the Nationalist Party to flee mainland China for Taiwan, there existed two great communist countries, namely The Republic of China and the Soviet Union. Both countries were rather skeptical of each other and an immediate rivalry and competitiveness occurred as soon as the Nationalists had made it into their boats and left the hostile shores of China (Wikipedia, Quotations from Chairman Mao Tse-tung).

Russia had been a communist enclave since 1922 and thus had good practice at converting its people into communist submission as well as attempting to invade suitable target nations—prone to social inequality and injustice—having a willing target populace to take up arms against its oppressors and be liberated by socialist glory.

After the Second World War, Marxism, Socialism, and Communism were seen as a great threat after Stalin's annexation of Eastern Europe, which turned it into a communist frontline threatening the West. It became known as the now infamous Cold War, which lasted for half a century.

Territories—hot and panting for socialist revolt and Marxist change—were far and few between, but some hotbeds existed in third world countries that were still being exploited by Western colonial occupiers, who were greedily extracting the agricultural and mineral wealth of these countries. They used the local labor, paying them a pittance—the indigenous people could barely keep their heads above water. Socialist overthrow talk thrived in these conquered communities, soon leading to resistance—and freedom fighter movements that, before long, scratched, tucked, and clawed at the colonial regimes, making life in the colonies for the dominating European masters a rather living hell.

This created the perfect environment into which the Soviets could clandestinely insert themselves, preaching Marxism, Socialism, and Communism, training the resistors in guerrilla warfare, and distributing light artillery and weapons including the most famous liberator—the Kalashnikov AK-47, which was probably single-handily responsible for killing more people in Africa in fifty years than perished in World War 2.

In the first two decades of Communist China, the nation went through a tumultuous upset, as the communists imposed their doctrine, thought processes, and views on a liberated nation. The thought was inward, and the world effectively ended at China's borders. The Chinese people had to be re-educated after millennia of dynasty rule and subordination.

China was self-absorbed, and selfishly reinvented its new socialist identity. The world for China was China itself, not that anything had fundamentally changed in the Chinese mentality since the dynasty days. China had always seen itself as the world. While the communists had replaced the dynasties, there was still one emperor, one ultimate supreme leader with the power of life and death over a whole nation.

By the 1960s, the Communist Party of China or CPC had stabilized the Chinese nation into a singular body of thought, behavior, and belief. All the non-believers, capitalists, nationalists and any other non-converters had mostly been crushed, killed, or flushed out of the system. This allowed China to turn its thought once again to the need for raw materials to feed the hungry mouth of the Tiger. But China had been shunned from the global arena—the world having turned against it and the mistrust having entrenched itself to a critical level (Wikipedia, Communist Party of China).

China was isolated. Not even its gigantic neighbor, the Soviet Union, trusted them for it feared the Chinese appetite for wanting to expand its territories to the North; something the dynasties had done for the last 3000 years. China had few friends left in the world.

This left China with few choices however, they identified one opportunity—Africa. In the late 1950s and early 1960s, Africa was in the throw of independence wars against its colonial oppressors. In a matter of a decade, over 90% of African countries would achieve their independence. This was the perfect breeding ground for anti-capitalist and anti-democratic repertoire and action, already eagerly supported by the Russian Bear. In any case, China had only the Soviet

Union to compete with for territorial expansion in Africa, in light of their philosophies and idiosyncrasies overlapping on many levels; making them communist rivals of the highest order.

China sent observers to Africa, supplied armory, and accepted African students to Chinese universities, but other than that, it had little influence on Africa's liberation. The Soviet Union had a head start and were well entrenched in supporting various liberation struggles throughout the vast African continent. Also, the Chinese nation always saw themselves as a superior race and found it rather difficult to work side by side with their African comrades.

During the liberation struggle years, Africa also had little to offer, with most raw materials ending up in Western factories and markets. Yet again, China's focus turned inward when Mao Zedong's Cultural Revolution gripped the nation in fear and trepidation in the 1960s and 1970s.

China's true economical liberation came after Mao Zedong's death in 1976, which resulted in Deng Xiaoping becoming the paramount Communist Party Leader. Deng Xiaoping introduced the Reform and Opening Policy to create a socialist ideology with a distinct Chinese identity. In reversing some of Mao's extreme-leftist policies, Deng Xiaoping created an environment in which a socialist Chinese state could make use of the global market economy without itself becoming a capitalist state (Wikipedia, Communist Party of China).

This was the birth of Chinese capitalism—a hungry belly of 1.4 billion people anticipating change, growth, and materialistic liberation. Over the half century up to this point, China had effectively self-destructed, introducing numerous purging campaigns, including what I like to refer to as the Industrial Revolution, Agricultural Revolution, and Cultural Revolution. In addition, this led to the destruction of much of the country's knowledge, culture, history, and intellectual property. China was left with a vast uneducated population of mainly peasants who had been suppressed for years.

THE REVOLUTIONS

The purging campaigns in the last century had a profound effect on the Chinese population. It left an indelible psychological mark on society. It also brought out their creative thinking, as many people had to improvise food sources, tools, and subdued forms of entertainment that would not attract the attention of the Communist Party.

These periods became known as:

Preferred Description	Official Name	Period
Industrial Revolution	Great Leap Forward	1958—1961
Agricultural Revolution	Great Chinese Famine	1959—1961
Cultural Revolution	Cultural Revolution	1966—1976

A common threat throughout the three periods was that the paramount and esteemed leader, Mao Zedong decided on a new course of action, instigated its implementation by brutal means, forcing the general Chinese society—irrespective of status, class, or intellect—to follow and subjugate to the draconian measures enforced upon them. The consequences were devastating, with many murders committed, ultimately resulting in a re-educated society that was far worse off and profoundly traumatized. It took decades to recover once Mao Zedong's callous hold on the Chinese people had been extinguished for good upon his death in 1976.

This failed outcome of each revolution resulted in Mao brooding upon the failures, then deciding on a new course of action and policy, even worse in design, and certainly impacting more ferociously on his people. The circle of self-destruction turned once more and continued its overlap with the next revolutionary circle. A frightened society obeyed vigorously by obeying the demands of the leader—no matter how absurd—inflicting lasting destruction upon themselves as a people and a culture that has been around for nearly four millennia.

It is in the Chinese DNA, from millennia of autocratic emperor rule that Chinese people in general conform unconditionally to authority. Throughout history, this has allowed Chinese leadership to introduce new policies, rules, and behavioral requirements with comparative ease. The ease of introducing and enforcing the 'one child policy' is a good example of this Chinese behavioral phenomenon.

The Industrial Revolution

Not long after the creation of the People's Republic of China in 1949, Mao Zedong introduced the Great Leap Forward, a campaign to massively overhaul the Chinese economy and society. The aim was to rapidly transform the country from an agrarian economy into a socialist society through rapid industrialization and collectivization (Wikipedia, Great Leap Forward). Farming communes were established, forcing peasants to collectively manage state-owned land and having to give one third of all produce to the government granaries with the intent to be used to feed urban dwellers. In parallel, the Communist Party of China planned to revolutionize the steel industry by opening a number of new steel mills in the bigger urban centers, for which they needed labor, which was sourced from the rural areas. Millions of peasants were uprooted and sent to work in the steel mills. This had a dual impact; firstly, the peasants were no longer tilling the earth, thus considerably affecting the National agricultural output, and secondly, they had no experience of how to operate steel mills. Although Chinese National steel production initially increased, it quickly became apparent that it was not in line with Mao's very ambitious vision to be on par with Britain's industrial output within a decade.

Hence, a further socialistic initiative was started, encouraging people in the rural areas—mainly peasants—to build what became known as backyard furnaces to produce more 'high quality' steel. In order to achieve set production outputs, the peasants were compelled to melt down anything of a metallic nature; pots, pans, cutlery, and anything else with metal in it was smelted. The backyard furnaces were stoked with the meager possessions of the peasants, using their furniture and other personal combustible items.

Only a low quality metal alloy, known as pig iron, could be produced in these low-temperature backyard furnaces. This low-grade pig iron could not be used directly for steel production purposes, requiring further processing. The backyard furnace initiative had a further double impact on society, namely that the remaining rural peasants were now not ploughing the land, reducing National agricultural output even further, and secondly, that people could no longer feed themselves, as they did not have enough food, but also had no utensils or indeed homes to go back to.

The Agricultural Revolution

The Great Leap Forward impacted directly on the well-being of society and resulted directly in the Great Chinese Famine. In order to feed the bulging urban populations made up of peasants, now working the steel mills, the remaining peasants were expected to produce even higher agricultural yields year after year. In order to be able to keep on giving one third of the production to the government granaries, they were forced to dilute their own grain reserves, and it did not take long before the peasant grain reserves were depleted.

Desperate measures were introduced by the Communist Party to boost grain production, but to no avail. Grain production numbers were improvised to give the impression that year-on-year production had increased. Grain was transplanted into dense patches to fool the communist cadres into thinking that higher yields were being achieved. Propaganda material showed children standing atop wheat fields, implying that wheat fields were now cultivated so densely that one could walk on top of them.

New agricultural methods, based on the now-discredited Soviet agronomist Trofim Lysenko (Wikipedia, Trofim Lysenko), were introduced, including close cropping and ploughing deeper, but to no avail; the crop yields did not increase, but declined instead.

Peasants were forced to work the fields continuously, having to sleep in the fields. The communist cadres destroyed the peasants' empty houses (those not yet demolished to be fed as fuel into the backyard furnaces) to prevent them from sneaking back into their houses at night, and so that the houses could be used as fertilizer on the fields. The combined actions of the Great Leap Forward and the Great Chinese Famine resulted in some 30 to 55 million people dying, not only from starvation but also from torture, beatings, and being buried alive by government representatives and the militia. In order to achieve better agrarian and industrial output, at least 2.5 million people were beaten or tortured to death, and it is estimated that up to 3 million people alone committed suicide during this period due to the harsh conditions. People were beaten or killed for reporting the real harvest numbers; for sounding alarm; for refusing to hand over what little food they had left; for trying to flee the famine area; for begging for food; or for as little as stealing scraps of food, which angered officials. The Great Leap Forward was the deadliest famine in the history of China, as well as in the history of the world (Wikipedia, The Great Leap Forward).

The Cultural Revolution

Not even a decade later, Mao Zedong initiated the Cultural Revolution to affirm his control of the Communist Party, after the embarrassment of the failed Great Leap Forward and the consequential Great Chinese Famine. The stated goal was to preserve 'true' Communist ideology in the country by purging remnants of capitalist and traditional elements from Chinese society, and to re-impose Maoist Thought as the dominant ideology within the Party (Wikipedia, Maoism). Initiated by Mao, and supported by the Red Guards, a systematic purge of anything considered bourgeoisie, was initiated. The political elitists called for the destruction of the "Four Olds"; namely, old customs, culture, habits, and ideas. The Red Guard onslaught was particularly destructive, especially in the realms of culture and religion. Historical sites in every part of the country were ransacked and destroyed (Wikipedia, Cultural Revolution). Historical artifacts, museums, tombs, palaces and art were destroyed across the country.

It was during the period of iconoclasm that Beijing Normal University's Red Guards desecrated the cemetery, which included tombs with artifacts belonging to several historical figures, including that of Confucius. Corpses were removed from their graves, and hung from trees that stood in front of the Temple of Confucius (Wikipedia, Cemetery of Confucius).

They destroyed libraries containing foreign and historical literature. Cemeteries, monasteries, mosques, churches and temples were closed down, converted to other uses or looted and destroyed. Tibetan Buddhists were held at gunpoint and forced to destroy their monasteries (Free Tibet, Tibet's Monasteries). More than ninety percent of the Tibetan monasteries were destroyed. Buddhism was depicted as a superstition by Marxist propaganda, an instrument of the 'ruling class' and therefore considered a means of hostile infiltration. During this time, religious teachers were arrested and sent away to camps. Methodically, intellectuals were rooted out, humiliated, tortured, sent to correction camps, and sometimes killed.

Since the Cultural Revolution halted the majority of China's economic activity, it affected the lives of the entire population as Mao Zedong Thought influenced the way forward. Maoism is a political theory based on the teachings of Mao Zedong (1893-1976), probably the most influential Chinese political leader of modern times (Wikipedia, Cultural Revolution; History.com, Cultural Revolution).

Maoism was the political strategy and military ideology that guided the Communist Party of China (CPC) from the early 1950s. It also influenced revolutionary actions on a global scale.

Maoism was similar to other forms of Marxism, with one basic difference. Mao believed that the peasants, rather than the industrial working comrades, were ideally placed to revolutionize China's socialist society (Wikipedia, Maoism).

Sizable numbers of Red Guards were brought to Beijing at the start of the Cultural Revolution. The government funded this campaign to destroy all remnants of the 'Four Olds' and replaced it with the corresponding 'Four News'. Changes included destroying ancient artifacts, paintings, buildings, temples, cultural treasures, to name a few. Names of buildings, streets, and people were changed and they even cut off people's hair. These actions destroyed the status of traditional Chinese culture, which weakened the practice of traditional customs.

The Red Guards possessed more authority than the army and police; they were essentially above the law. They encouraged the public to ignore or attack traditional Chinese ideas and arts in favor of Mao, to question their teachers and parents and to criticize cultural institutions. Traditional Chinese culture strictly forbade these behaviors in the past.

Police and local authorities covered up many deaths during the Cultural Revolution and scores more went unreported, so we may never know the true number of people who died or were persecuted during this era. However, it is widely estimated that between 400,000 and 3 million people may have lost their lives (Wikipedia, Maoism).

The true cost of the Cultural Revolution was the immense psychological impact it had on society as a whole. That was what shaped the behavior and character of the modern Chinese citizen to a large extent.

CHINESE COMMUNISTIC CAPITALISM IN AFRICA

The Communist Party eventually acknowledged the impact the 'revolutions' had on Chinese society as well as the Chinese economy. It introduced reforms and a new way of thinking as soon as Deng Xiaoping took the country's helm after Mao Zedong's death in 1976.

A radical change was required to stir the Tiger's belly. The country needed to be re-educated, re-industrialized, and re-agriculturalized and the Tiger needed to be fed. After Maoism, raw materials were in scant supply. The Communist Party, to keep its doctrine alive, had exhausted the country's riches and natural wealth. The raw materials had to come from somewhere else. And what better place to get these raw materials than from Africa, a former playing ground and well known to China.

Africa—at that point—was largely a continent of some fifty-odd independent countries, par one or two that were still going through a liberation struggle. The continent had a young, free society, compared to the rest of the world—especially the Western World—and democracy, independence, and freedom came at a huge price. This young democracy had no clue how to govern itself; governments were mostly inexperienced, which meant that self-empowerment and self-enrichment were the order of the day. Better yet, many African countries were striving for socialism, communism, nationalization, and one-party rule.

This was the perfect scenario for Chinese neo colonialization—a new form of economic colonialization (something the West had practiced for decades). Africa, slowly self-destructing after independence, was willing for anybody to become their partners and advisors, as long as the dollars flowed freely into the appropriate Swiss bank accounts. This created the perfect environment for China to impregnate the African belly.

The Chinese dynasties were masters at economic colonialization. They had been doing this for centuries. In exchange for fabricated, cheap items, they secured raw materials and rights to mineral concessions at political level. This created immediate leverage, and made millions of government riches available for palm greasing, individual reward, and funding of government projects. As a result, China became far superior to Western countries, who attempted to gain economic empowerment in African countries through private or listed companies, but seldom at government level. This was a world competition between East and West, trying to win the heart of Africa. However, several orders of magnitude placed China firmly in the lead.

Since the Bronze Age, mining output would be beneficiated at or near the mining source and the manufactured items—

mainly metallic items such as weaponry (spear tips, swords, lances)—could be traded with other clans, empires, or even countries in exchange for agricultural products, clothing, and livestock.

China, with its advanced civilization and technology, could manufacture many sought after commodities such as gunpowder, porcelain, mirrors, and china, which it could then trade in exchange for raw materials, especially minerals and metals. These items were used back in China to manufacture more advanced goods for further trade with countries producing mining commodities. Goods could be manufactured significantly cheaper in China, which eventually led to mass production. Manufactured goods could then be sold back to countries where the raw materials came from at a relatively cheap price, initially in exchange for more raw materials, and later for hard currency and in modern times in exchange for rights to mining concessions.

Raw material suppliers were unable to compete with China in manufacturing goods cheaply and quickly, especially the third world countries.

Cheaply fabricated items from China broke the mining-beneficiation link, resulting in a steep decline of most manufacturing sectors in many African countries. The African governments would rather get easy and quick money in exchange for a mining concession acquisition or mining license, allowing the new owner of that concession to again take Africa's mineral wealth offshore, similar to the colonization practices employed by the Europeans from the late 17th to mid 20th century.

In the first years after independence, Western ex-colonial

powers still played a key role in the mining sector of newly independent African states. However, internal strife, civil war and a deteriorating economy often drove Western mining companies to abandon their African operations. While many Western companies were still operating in Africa at the end of the 20th century, the true potential of Africa's mineral wealth was never fully realized. Countries such as the Democratic Republic of Congo (formerly Zaire), still held between 4% and 45% of worldwide copper and cobalt reserves respectively, as well as the world's largest reserves of coltan, which have hardly been exploited due to ongoing internal strive since independence in 1960. While some mining companies have dared to venture into the volatile region to get their hands on these lucrative metals, as well as gold and diamonds, many have not succeeded. They had to abandon their operation due to the local political turmoil, or were unceremoniously kicked out of the country for failure to pay their fair share of palm greasing monies to the political factions of the day.

The first president of an independent Ghana, Kwame Nkrumah, first coined the term neo-colonialism or neo-imperialism; it constitutes the use of capitalistic methods, economic globalization, and cultural influence by a 'dominating' country or economy to benefit from a weaker, developing country's raw material wealth, use its people as cheap labor, and to manufacture goods destined for the Western market cheaply. It is a means to establish military bases, or to exert direct military control and hegemony.

While neo colonialism has been dominated by Western powers from 1960 to around 2000, China has now moved handsomely into this space, dominating economic as well as political influence, especially in Africa. Due to Africa's disastrous experiment with independence, resulting in the economic and political failure of many countries, the prospect of getting a new and willing economic partner on board became too good to resist. African governments were more than keen to accommodate a partner like China to enter this arena, with lucrative promises of financial aid, economic upliftment, infrastructure upgrades, and employment opportunities for the local populace on grand scale construction projects.

While no different to neo colonialism, it was not a forced marriage out of economic desperation, but rather colonialization by invite, which perhaps could be referred to more aptly as Sino colonialization. The only difference this time around is that the mining sector no longer supports—or is forced to support—other critical sectors such as manufacturing and downstream beneficiation of raw materials. It is in China's ambitious interest to sell cheap and low quality goods—made in China from the very raw materials extracted from Africa— back to Africans, creating an economic dependency not unlike the imperialists or neo colonialists of yesteryear.

CHINA'S SECOND HOME

China's road into Africa has been and still is to home in on countries that present agricultural and mineral wealth that would benefit China. African countries, vulnerable and hungry for cash inflow, are more than willing to receive Chinese delegations at government level with immediate promise of bilateral trade. In exchange, China only wants access to agricultural land and rights to mineral concessions, with the promise of large scale Chinese investment into these sectors but also the local market in general, especially infrastructure.

This glorious opportunity holds a promise that few African countries can resist, especially countries where the GDP growth is often non-existent and inflation is rife, with a poor and unsettled populace eager for jobs and an income. Much like the European colonial model, which enforced imperialism onto undeveloped regions around the world, there is one major difference. While European colonialists forced their way militarily and then economically onto African soil, China is now preying on African government's self-enrichment ideologies.

While it appears that China is in Africa to help African countries realizing their untapped potential, it must be noted that China is purely in Africa to secure strategic commodities, to keep the Tiger's belly from running empty when global commodities become scarce. The first hunger pangs are predicted to occur around the world as early as 2030.

While lucrative investments in Africa appear to be for the benefit of the indigenous regions, closer inspection suggests that investment projects are strategic in order to be able to access commodities in the most effective manner and to transport products to ports and then to China in the most efficient way. There seems little promise of economic development that would benefit the local economic environment in parallel. Sadly, the new economic gears in African host countries are being firmly turned by the Sino colonizers, and benefit only the few African political cronies who are quite willing to ignore any negative afflictions in return for personal monetary enrichment stemming from these schemes. Unfortunately, no African country is prepared to or even capable of predicting what will happen once the mineral wealth is stripped, and they no longer are of use to the Tiger.

Although China has had a noticeable economic presence in Africa since the early 1990s, particularly in Zambia, in the first decade of the 21st century, Africa has really seen the Tiger step onto African soil, making itself at home, bringing along its children, and in the process displacing the mighty African lion, weakening his roar and taking his territories. Africa, yet again has been colonized—this time not by Christian missionaries and military force, but by the lure of money and economic promises.

As of 2016, it is estimated that some one million Chinese people are now on African soil, building their African empire across the continent with a presence in at least two thirds of African countries. In many African countries, Chinese nationals now outnumber many minority groups. In 2016 it was thought that Namibia had as many as 230,000 permanent Chinese residents compared to some 145,000 whites, which means that the Chinese constituted around 10% of the total population of 2.3 million. China has become Africa's biggest trading partner, investing between US $160 and $200 billion annually. Africa has become a hotly contested property for its commodities, a race that China has won handsomely, and the rest of the world has failed to cash in on this opportunity.

China's drive is not only for metals in the ground, but also for agricultural lands. China is likely to have a water shortage by as early as 2025 and therefore agrarian as well as livestock produce generated on foreign land will alleviate the demands of China's growing middle class, anticipating a more affluent lifestyle.

Africans at grassroots level are not always delighted with the influx of Mother China, as they see their lands being gobbled up by Chinese farmers, who enter into long-term lease agreements at government levels. While Africa has a poor environmental and conservation record, Chinese companies have even less regard for environmental damages caused by their presence. An underground network of sophisticated wildlife poaching has developed, fueled by the insatiable demand by Chinese nationals back in China for exotic meats, animal products used as aphrodisiacs, and plant products used for medicinal purposes.

Poor African peasants are easily influenced for a few dollars to commit environmental crimes. Africa's elephant population has decreased by 30% over the last decade (2005 – 2016) with about 100 animals now being slaughtered daily by poachers seeking ivory, meat, and body parts, with only an estimated 400,000 elephants remaining. The rhino population—already decimated in central and northern Africa—is on the verge of extinction in Southern Africa, where the last remaining significant number of rhinos can be found. At the rate of 1,500 rhino killings per year, rhinoceroses will disappear well before 2030. Lion bones are used to ferment lion bone wine while thousands of live pangolins are transported by ship to the East—their meat considered a delicacy and their scales being pulverized into yet another aphrodisiac (NPR.org). The list goes on and on, and with the Chinese middle class growing fast, the demand for more and more rare products will only increase.

Africa, having gone through half a century of freedom

struggles, socialist and communist governments, corruption, and general despair, is ready to embrace a transparent and democratic society with better human rights for its citizens. Unfortunately, totalitarian China is not there yet. It continues to treat its citizens as an extension of its Communist policies and prefers to deal in Africa at Government-to-Government level. And African governments have a poor record of working in the best interests of their citizens.

For now, it appears that China has little political ambition in Africa; that she is really only interested in the raw materials to feed the Chinese Tiger. A natural spin-off of this is that China will establish pockets of Chinese communities in Africa, but only to operate and administrate its interests.

China is a shrewd business partner, cleverly attaining first rights on commodity deposits in exchange for infrastructure upgrades. It needs to be seen what China's long term ambitions in Africa are—in light of commodities—anticipated to go into a worldwide shortage by 2030, and China is the only country in the world to strategically position itself to have access to a wide range of commodities beyond 2030.

WHY AFRICA?

The historical link between China and numerous African countries is not necessarily the primary reason for China having singled out Africa as its primary investment destination. China has invested heavily in the USA economy, however, an economic cat and mouse play is always present between these two superpowers. Investments are in the form of bonds and beneficiation factories using raw materials supplied by USA-affiliated companies. What China really needs is raw materials to supply its own factories back in mainland China. The internal consumption of beneficiated goods has increased multi-fold over the last 25 years and the export market for fabricated goods has been growing steadily.

While China does have some raw materials, it does not suffice to push the economy along at an average 7% GDP growth rate. Further, China has limited arable land (only 10% of China's surface area is suitable for agricultural purposes) and water resources are reaching its maximum output levels in less than a decade from now. It is likely that China will have no reliable supply of potable water left by as early as 2025. Furthermore, the world has been consuming its finite supply of raw materials at an alarming rate and it is estimated that by 2030 the global village will start to experience the first significant commodity shortages (Moyo, 2013).

What China has been seeking is a willing strategic partner where raw materials are readily available for further exploitation. Further, raw materials supply had to be guaranteed. At the same time, arable land and water resources would be needed for China's expanding agrarian needs.

Africa has the perfect credentials for such an undertaking. It has significant deposits of untapped commodities, including copper, cobalt, iron ore, coal, and oil. It also has the largest swaths of unused arable land in the world. In the past, African governments have never benefited directly from mining enterprises. Many African countries were considered unattractive investment destinations due to ongoing internal wars and political volatility. And here was a new global partner who was prepared to form strategic investment partnerships with marginal African countries that would directly benefit African governments. Further, red tape could be easily bypassed by forming partnerships directly with governments. Africa hadn't seen proper investments for decades and so this presented the ideal opportunity for them to get their greasy hands on some hard currency without too much effort.

China is the only country in the world to position itself strategically in order to secure and have access to a broad variety of commodities beyond 2030, when it is expected that commodity shortfalls could lead to significant commodity wars. While Western governments focus on short-term economic drivers and foreign affairs (military superiority), China seems to be strategizing a long-term sustainability plan. China uses state capital, directly supported by the Chinese government, to invest in identified commodity deposits. China is also typically prepared to pay a premium for these deposits, which many Western companies cannot afford or are not willing to expend (and they certainly are not getting full government support), which assures the Chinese government of a guaranteed buy.

Chinese firms are already acquiring or exploiting many minerals that, from a Western viewpoint, are not financially viable. It only makes sense to exploit such deposits if it is for strategic gain, as in some cases the product can be obtained cheaper in open trade. For some commodities such as copper and coal, China has become a monopsony trader, as it has become the major buyer of these commodities and is therefore able to dictate pricing. It would then make sense for African governments in countries rich in these commodities to enter into exclusive agreements from which they could benefit as well.

THE ART OF BLENDING IN

In light of China having lived in isolation for centuries and having considered themselves to be the center of the universe for millennia, Chinese people find it hard to integrate with other cultures. They have rigid traditional beliefs and customs and consider many other cultures as being benign.

Of course, any prejudicial behavior towards another race is considered racism. The Chinese do display traits of racial intolerance towards Africans. This racism manifests in many forms, ranging from underpayment to long working hours, to physical abuse as well as Chinese nationals keeping to themselves by living in their own 'Little China' communities in the middle of Africa.

Howard W. French, an American author who traveled through various African countries around 2013, captured this first-hand experience of Chinese attitudes and actions towards Africa and Africans in his book, *China's Second Continent* (French, 2015).

He describes typical encounters between these two ancient cultures in the modern twenty first century era in remote corners of a desperate Africa, where human life comes cheap and human rights have no place. He repeatedly encountered Africans who found themselves in an abusive work situation, under the management of draconian Chinese bosses.

There are no work contracts in place. Africans are paid less than their Chinese counterparts are paid for the same jobs. Africans will get no personal protective clothing and equipment (PPE) on an industrial site, while their Chinese colleagues get brand new PPE. Salaries are paid out in cash, but subject to on-the-spot scrutiny, the Chinese representative deciding in the moment what he should be paying the African laborer based on his apparent performance. In some instances, salaries are withheld completely.

Because Africa generally has a huge unemployment problem, these African workers are obliged to accept these poor working conditions and make do with below par salaries or face ongoing unemployment. In rare cases where an African laborer does take his complaint to the Labor Department, complaints are never successfully resolved. Department officials who handle such cases are easily bribed by the Chinese employers to make issues go away.

Due to the favorable Afro-Sino relationship at government level, Government officials show little enthusiasm to challenge Chinese operations that do not comply with labor regulations. It is a vicious circle where the only loser is the African population itself; it has to survive in a corrupt system that only favors people and companies with political ties.

It is difficult to believe that in today's Africa this type of racism is tolerated when Africa fought so hard to rid itself of the colonial shackles. Chinese will openly ridicule the inability of Africans, their low intellect, and inability to manage their own affairs.

Chinese-owned hotels in certain African cities will only cater for Chinese, will accept Westerners, but would refuse black patrons. Where black patrons are allowed to stay at the hotel, typically no towels are provided, as Chinese people visiting from China would not want to use a towel that might have been used by a black person. Chinese visitors would know to bring their own towels. A Chinese doctor who runs a clinic in Liberia openly confessed that he would not hire locals because they were dirty, lazy, and prone to stealing. These are but a few examples of Chinese prejudice existing and being practiced in the host country. As Africa is attempting to streamline itself with best democratic practices and govern their countries more transparently, the onus will be on the Chinese entrepreneurs to adapt and blend in better with these new cultures and traditions.

During my tenure with a Chinese company, some acts of racism were certainly visible on the ground. Chinese organizations were obliged to hire local labor so Chinese laborers, experiencing Africa for the first time, were forced to work alongside African laborers. Having a pre-conceived opinion of Africans, on rare occasions some black laborers from the host country were humiliated in the work environment by derogatory acts. This included physical prodding, burning with cigarettes, females being groped, and individuals' teeth quality and arm muscle size being mockingly assessed. Fortunately, the specific host country in question exercises stringent labor practices and put a quick end to these subjections. In one case, wheelbarrows imported from China without leg supports were supplied to prevent African laborers from putting down the wheelbarrow during working hours in order to be able to take a rest. Of course, HR (the Human Resources Department) immediately stopped this practice and the wheelbarrows were modified to serve their original functionality.

Our Chinese colleagues in the office environment very much kept to themselves, not only during work hours, but also certainly after hours. Bridging cultural divides was not easily achievable. In the work environment, the Chinese stick rigidly to their cultural work practices, not taking cognizance of local best practices. This could result in their undoing in the long term as their attitude comes across as arrogant and aloof, since they don't incorporate the ideas of their locally sourced employees who possess local knowledge. Very little pragmatic knowledge transfer occurs between Chinese colleagues and their non-Chinese counterparts. After all, being seen to not know something could bring shame onto the Chinese colleagues and thus pretense is kept up at all times that only their Chinese way is the right way.

China could also find itself exposed at government-to-government interaction level, as African governments are often aligned to a specific ethnic group that enriches itself by looting the state coffers and country's riches. African governments do fail epically, and any associated conspirators and partners could await the same fate. Africa has always been—and still mostly is—a minefield of hope and opportunities, but also of pitfalls in perpetual motion of change. One day, Africa can be good to you and the next you have a mob of disgruntled citizens destroying everything in their path.

Africa is not for the fainthearted. It takes guts and determination to be successful in Africa's ever-changing political landscape. The Chinese state saw this opportunity and to date has probably been the most successful country to try to establish a working relationship, albeit strained at times—especially at grassroots level. Most Western countries have not had successful interactions with African governments since former colonies achieved independence. And Western companies have come across as being exploitative and greedy, not leaving any spoils for the host country. The big difference with the Chinese investors is that the African governments receive huge benefits from the Chinese investments. Sadly though, not much of that money filters back into the upliftment of the local populace, which could likely lead to the ultimate undoing of not only the African governments of the day, but the Chinese long term investment strategies all over the African continent.

ONE BELT, ONE ROAD

The Chinese government in 2013 launched the latest Chinese economic initiative, known as One Belt, One Road. It plays an important role in China's global investment strategy, which will also positively affect Africa in the long term. According to Wikipedia, the *One Belt, One Road* economic initiative suggests that Africa is certainly part of China's long-term investment strategy.

Xi Jinping, current paramount leader of China, proposed the One Belt, One Road initiative, which is also known as the Silk Road Economic Belt, the 21st-century Maritime Silk Road, or the Belt and Road back in 2013. According to Wikipedia contributors, it became the most-frequently motioned concept on People's Daily in 2016. Premier Li Keqiang promoted the initiatives during his State visit to Europe and Asia. The initiative focuses on fostering connection and cooperation, specifically between China and Eurasia. The Maritime Silk Road (MSR) and land-based Silk Road Economic Belt (SREB) are the two main components of the initiative, which underlines China's campaign to increase its role in global affairs and its desire to obtain priority capacity cooperation in industries such as steel manufacture (Wikipedia, Belt and Road Initiative).

The Belt infrastructure primarily covers approximately sixty countries in Asia and Europe, as well as East Africa and Oceania and it is expected that the cumulative investment may reach US$ 4-8 trillion over an indefinite period. The One Belt, One Road initiative is in contrast with the Transatlantic Trade and Investment Partnership and the Trans-Pacific Partnership, two USA-centric trade arrangements from which the US has extracted itself in early 2017. This paves the way for China to incorporate Africa into the One Belt, One Road initiative.

The Maritime Silk Road aims to foster collaboration between Southeast Asia, Africa, and Oceania across the Indian Ocean, South Pacific, and the South China Sea. Most countries in this region that have joined the Silk Road Economic Belt initiative have already joined the Chinese-led Asian Infrastructure Investment Bank.

The Wikipedia source states that Zanzibar and other East African countries will play a major role in the MSR once the modernization of their rail link and construction of local ports has been completed.

An agreement was signed between Premier Li Keqiang and the Kenyan government in 2014, which initiated the construction of a 2,700 km (1677.70 mi.) long railroad between Nairobi and Mombasa at a cost of US$ 250 million.

In addition, a cooperative memorandum of understanding was signed between China's Sinomach and General Electric in 2015 to increase the number of consumers in sub-Saharan Africa, promote clean energy and to build wind turbines.

CHAPTER 3

CONFUCIAN HARMONY

"To put the world in order, we must first put the nation in order; to put the nation in order, we must first put the family in order; to put the family in order; we must first cultivate our personal life; we must first set our hearts right."

—*Confucius*

In order to better understand the Chinese psyche, one needs to delve back into three thousand years of history. While it is a common belief by Westerners that the Chinese psyche was formed in the last seventy years of communism, this is a fundamental misconception. The Chinese psyche has formed over many centuries, since the first Chinese history was engraved on the 'oracle bones'. According to author of *The Great Wall*, Julia Lovell, this afforded insights into a society three and a half millennia old; a society whose fundamental beliefs and concerns have shaped the Chinese people ever since (Lovell, The Great Wall, Page 29).

The first dynasty, The Shang kingdom (circa 1700 – 1025 BC), commenced the development of a complex society, ruled by numerous dynasties. The Nationalist movement disempowered the last, the Qing Dynasty (1644 – 1912), in 1912. In essence, the dynasties—while being ruled by various ethnic groups, ranging from Kublai Khan's Mongolians to the

Manchurians—entrenched a deep-set Chinese way of living and culture; a cohesion and cooperation of different regional cultures and ethnicities, not achieved in Europe until 2,000 years later. While China was recording their history with a complexly written language and producing gunpowder, many European areas were still run as individual fiefdoms that survived by raiding and annihilating each other.

CONFUCIUS, THE PHILOSOPHER

The largest single influence by any person on the Chinese culture was from a philosopher, living in the sixth and fifth century BC, called Confucius. While Mao Zedong created a populist political cult culture, even he prescribed to the Confucian values. Confucius (551 – 479 BC)—posthumously enshrined by the Former Han Dynasty (202 BC – 8 AD) as imperial China's pre-eminent philosopher—preached political unification. Nostalgic for a long-lost mythical ideal of Chinese unity and virtue nurtured by the Eastern Zhou Dynasty (771 – 256 BC), Confucius hoped to end the conflict of fragmentation of his own era through a moral revival. He believed that if everyone conducted himself with humane benevolence, the country would be peacefully reunified. The social code that held together Confucius' injunctions to be good, was the correct performance of ritual, loosely understood as encompassing all forms of public and private behavior: bowing, mourning parents, wearing the correct color of lapels, playing the correct kind of music, worshipping the correct mountain, and hiring the correct number of dancers. Confucius' great, popularizing innovation was to break down his political philosophy into a manageable, bite-sized analogy of family relationships. Confucius equated the bond between father and sons with that between ruler and subordinates or subjects. Good father and son relationships made good rulers and subjects. Good rulers and subjects would bring China back to its rightful state of peaceful, prosperous unity (Lovell, The Great Wall, Page 48, 49).

According to China-Mike, Confucianism is built upon a complex system of social and political ethics based on filial piety, kinship, loyalty, and righteousness. The teachings of Confucius encompass a broad spectrum of behaviors, ranging from the ways in which a 'true gentleman' should behave in every aspect of his daily life to the ethics that a ruler should practice in governing his subjects with benevolence (China-Mike, Confucius 101: A key to understanding the Chinese Mind).

Confucian harmony plays a key role in the psyche of modern China. Predictably, it has always been a key driver of Chinese behavior both in their personal lives as well as in business, since Chinese history has been recorded. In the modern Chinese work environment in a Western setting, the subtleties of this paramount behavioral trait are initially difficult to recognize, but over time it becomes apparent how much Confucian harmony drives the day-to-day behavior of Chinese co-workers.

HISTORY DICTATES

While Confucius' philosophies were not widely adopted in his own lifetime, the first Qin emperor (221 – 206 BC) unified China's political institutions, loosely based on Confucius' philosophy. Confucian philosophy was thereafter enshrined into dynasty culture and politics, creating a nation living in a state of Confucian harmony. The Confucian concept of living in a world in harmony with your fellow countrymen, colleagues, and family has largely shaped the Chinese nation into what it is today.

In the early 1900s, as the imperialistic system started to implode, Chinese intellectuals blamed Confucianism for China's antiquated feudal system, which left the country lagging behind in development when compared to other countries. This allowed foreign powers to colonize parts of China.

Mao Zedong officially despised Confucius and Confucian values that represented the values of an Imperial China, which was no more. The blind following of Confucian values had kept China shackled in a feudal system for two millennia. Privately, Mao did practice some of the Confucian teachings.

With the modernization of China's economy and political system after Mao's death, Confucianism slowly came back into mainstream Chinese cultural values. It also fits in with the values of the modern Communist Party of China (CPC), emphasizing national stability and social harmony. Confucian teachings have become popular again with over 100 Confucius Institutes being established worldwide, offering Mandarin, and Chinese culture lectures. The Chinese government is firmly planting the seed of Chinese culture into other nationalities, and imprinting the Tiger's claw around the globe.

HARMONY IS PARAMOUNT

The concept of a harmonious relationship in the workplace or at home plays a pivotal role and underlines the behavior and culture of modern China. When doing business with Chinese companies, it becomes apparent how Confucianism affects business practices.

My first experience with Confucian harmony occurred even before I joined the Chinese organization. Prior to even an employment offer being made to me, the head of the Chinese company approached my previous employer directly—without my knowledge or consent—and enquired whether he would be happy for me to join the Chinese organization. This compromised my position and potential future career at that employer, and it appeared to minimize my negotiation leverage with the Chinese organization, with whom I had to yet agree contractual terms. Confucian harmony and harmonious relationship preservation manifested itself in its raw form.

The twist in this tale was that my previous company was already providing services to my imminent employer. It was a delicate matter, and as the Chinese company's potential employment prospect would offer me a once in a lifetime opportunity, I needed to handle this very delicate situation with utmost diplomacy. I prepared a well thought through strategy to break the news of my potential departure with my boss. However, my future Chinese CEO beat me to it, without my knowledge.

He evaluated the situation at a completely different level of consciousness. He already had established a harmonious relationship with my previous boss, as they were doing business together. The last thing he wanted to do was to destroy the business relationship by an action that could create mistrust. The Chinese CEO had to first get the agreement and blessing of my previous boss before he would even consider making me an offer. Of course, in the Western corporate environment, one would first have an offer on the table before breaking the news in order to prevent negotiation leverage from being compromised both ways.

EDUCATION

"If you do not study hard when you are young, you'll end up bewailing your failures as you grow up."

—*Chinese proverb*

Confucius' influence on Chinese education has dominated Chinese society since he philosophized the need for stringent educational requirements by Chinese citizens in order to be able to master Confucian Harmony. Confucianism resulted in the Imperial examination system being implemented by the Former Han Dynasty (201 BC – 8 AD) around 124 BC (China-Mike, Confucius 101: A key to understanding the Chinese Mind).

Confucius' intent was to replace the hereditary rule by the aristocracy with a system based on education (meritocracy). This examination was required if one wished to enter the civil service as a government official, which would bring with it wealth, affluence, influence, and face (Mianzi – See Chapter 4).

This exam provided the only opportunity to attain a higher employment position and move up the societal ranks. The exam required the long hours of learning with heavy focus on memorization of Confucian writing and classic works of literature. Confucian education focus remains a pivotal part of the modern education system in Chinese speaking Asia, including countries such as South Korea and possibly in North Korea (although I could not verify this), Japan, Taiwan, and Singapore.

But, as is typical in China now as it was then, it was possible to get around the educational requirements with the right Guanxi (relationships – see Chapter 5). The people in higher government positions as well as the wealthy were always able to bypass the system, allowing their offspring to benefit without having to achieve the necessary educational requirements. It is common practice in China today for children of well-connected parents to get into the most exclusive universities, not necessarily having achieved the required pass rate. I will discuss the modern Chinese educational system in more detail in Chapter 8: Education.

Chinese colleagues are quick to emphasize their qualifications to their non-Chinese colleagues. After all, educational achievement sets people apart and slots them into a higher cultural, corporate, and political rank. Typically, they will not boast about their own qualifications, but one of their colleagues will subtly advise non-Chinese colleagues about the qualifications of their peers. Emphasis is placed on Master degrees and doctorates. Chinese colleagues with doctorates will introduce themselves as Doctor, so Li Gang would refer to himself as Dr Li. The use of the correct title is important in the Chinese business culture.

RANK IN SOCIETY

Confucius prophesied that harmony would be achieved if everybody understood his or her place in society. Every rank in society required a certain behavior that one needed to be taught and society as a whole needed to clearly understand these societal rankings. This would allow man to be in harmony with the whole universe.

Rank has to be respected. Social order would be under threat if people did not adhere to these pre-determined behavioral requirements and not respect people according to their ranking. Confucius came up with the system of interdependent relationships. Lower level people always respect higher ranked people. Behavior towards higher ranked people needs to be obedient and courteous. These behaviors start at close family unit level, all the way to interactions at government level. Thus, it is typical to notice that Chinese society tends to revere age and authority. The reverence may not always be sincere in today's modern China (China-Mike, Confucius 101: A key to understanding the Chinese Mind).

China-Mike explains that Confucius believed that the only horizontal relationship was that between friends and all other relationships were built on moral behavior. He defined five primary relationships that proved that moral behavior stems from fulfilling traditional roles. The five primary relationships include that between:

- Friend and friend
- Husband and wife
- Brother and sister
- Parent and child
- Rulers and ministers

In Western egalitarian culture, individuals have equal standing and access to opportunities in a society. While Confucian ethic is somewhat egalitarian too, equality is found in social rank.

Modern Chinese roles are less narrowly defined today than they were in the past, yet they continue to respect hierarchical differences in status more than Westerners do. Rank status was evident in the workplace, with groups of Chinese colleagues working within their rank hierarchy. While these rank bands tended to fall into the 'Friend and Friend' category, people would not make decisions or indeed agree to decisions unless clear instruction was received from a higher-ranking employee. It became apparent that non-Chinese work colleagues were not rank categorized by their Chinese colleagues, but rather seen as Outsiders without any rank influence. More on this below, under 'Family Relationships', as well as in Chapter 4: Mianzi, and Chapter 5: Guanxi, where this phenomenon is analyzed in more detail.

While Western business culture promotes egalitarianism, one will not see higher-ranking Chinese people enter into social chatter with lower ranking people. The hierarchical chain of command is widely respected in Chinese society to this day. Interestingly, it is suggested that any issue should always be addressed with the highest-ranking business col-league possible, if one is to have any chance of having it addressed and sorted out. A lower ranking superior will not take up the issue with a higher-ranking superior on your behalf and typically, the Chinese leader makes all decisions. The Chinese leader will typically find out about issues from the lower ranking Chinese people in his or her organization via a network of 'unofficial' communication routes. If the Chinese leader is unaware of an issue (he or she never enquired about it), then the issue does not exist for lower ranking team members. Also, if the Chinese leader believes the issue is minor in nature, then it is minor, regardless of one's facts or experience.

FAMILY RELATIONSHIPS

Since Confucian times, there has always been a significant focus on the family unit, including extended family, making up the primary social organizational structure. In a Confucian society, one showed a great deal of 'filial piety', which is still noticeable in modern China society to this day. Originally, this was conceived as devotion and obedience towards one's parents, especially the father. In modern China, this devotion is extended to the broader family and clan, which could include family members one reports to in the workplace—such as a nephew and uncle relationship—equating to subordinate and manager role in the workplace. Chinese corporate teams certainly include family relations and it appears to be common practice for extended family teams to work together in a specific department for a specific company. This also explains why, in many instances, a Chinese subordinate will never challenge his Chinese superior.

This focus on devotion within the family has the required individuals to show proper behavior and conduct themselves honorably. And individual's successes and failures affect and belong to the whole family. The Confucian concept of family identity sharing success, shame, and face has resulted in Chinese families being stereotypically overbearing; getting involved in individuals' every aspect of life from the way you dress, to the way you look, to the way you behave.

With the focus being on the family unit, Chinese do view the world according to relations (Guanxi – see Chapter 5), creating a personal and professional network emanating from such a family unit (the Insiders) with everybody else (the Outsiders) being considered with depredation. For an Outsider to instruct, challenge, or question and Insider in a forum of people would be considered rude, cruel, and even sacrilegious. Any relationship in place could be at serious risk of instant discontinuation. It is not about the Insider's pride that may be tarnished, but about his or her humiliation in front of the Insider group. It is thus the duty of the remaining Insiders to defend the honor of the threatened Insider.

The situation reversed is rather different. An Outsider can be challenged by the Insiders without any consideration as to how that might affect his or her honor. After all, he or she is not part of all the Insider inter-relational family unit, which has been brought together by fate, and therefore maintaining Confucian Harmony with an Outsider requires no further consideration of any potential impact on harmony (Confucian Harmony), face (Mianzi), and relationship (Guanxi).

The Chinese are highly averse to conflict, and therefore maintain proper demeanor, in order to preserve 'face' within the family unit. The concept of maintaining and losing face is discussed in more detail in the next Chapter (Chapter 4, Mianzi).

INDIVIDUALISM VERSUS COLLECTIVISM

"No matter how big, one beam cannot support a house."
—*Chinese proverb*

Western culture tends to focus on the person, instead of on achievements or their affiliations with certain groups. It encourages and reinforces individual expression from a young age.

The Confucian society, on the other hand, focuses on collectivism. The individual's desires are less important than that of the group. Individuals are defined by their relationships within the group and individual expression is sometimes considered immoral (China-Mike, Confucius 101: A key to understanding the Chinese Mind). This behavioral trend transpires throughout the Chinese population to this day.

Chinese people are conditioned to suppress their personal thoughts and needs and focus firstly on that of their families, their communities, their clans, and their nation. However, some subtle changes are happening as the Chinese culture is becoming more 'Westernized'. American pop culture leads the way for cultures from around the world, however, despite Westernization, some Asian cultures continue to center around humility and modesty. The Chinese still shun boasting and individualism (China-Mike).

COMPLIMENTS

Giving compliments is a courteous tradition in Chinese culture and can be compared to giving gifts. Chinese people are generous with compliments. They won't hesitate to compliment you on your 'excellent' use of their language, even when you barely managed greetings. Westerners are initially overwhelmed and touched by being showered with numerous compliments from their Chinese colleagues; however, it does not take long before the compliments become somewhat annoying and overbearing. Compliments are typically dispensed for trivial issues such as looks, intellect, or Mandarin competency. What quickly becomes apparent is that the Chinese compliment givers are gratifying their non-Chinese colleagues, rather than genuinely complimenting them.

While they are gracious compliment-givers, they are modest, too. Instead of thank you, they will dismiss a compliment given to them by saying *"Nali, nali."*—*"Where? Where?"* As if asking, *"Where is the person you're referring to?"*—instead of *"Thank you"* (China-Mike, Confucius 101: A key to understanding the Chinese Mind).

Compliments are however given very sparingly by the Chinese leader and then only to certain people worthy of such veneration, while some team members will never receive a compliment regardless of their superior performance and beneficial contribution to the company. This aligns well with the principles of reinforcing societal rank.

THE INSCRUTABLE NATURE OF THE CHINESE

While Western cultures encourage individual expression, the Chinese are inscrutable. Their devotion to hierarchy and authority, as taught in Chinese culture, promotes a more unbiased, expressionless, rank-based behavior. Many Westerners interpret the lack of open and transparent communication as deviousness, not creating open communication channels that make it difficult to manage inter-cultural teams.

People in a Confucian society are encouraged to act according to their ranks and avoid the urge to express their own opinions. Obedience and reverence are more than just acts of politeness. It is indeed crucial to preserving social harmony. In traditional Chinese society a wrong utterance towards a person in power, and an emperor especially, could well have resulted in one's death. Even in modern China, people tend to retain a neutral expression, particularly in the workplace when dealing with customers and authority figures. Failing to retain your composure could cause you to lose your job and your standing within society (China-Mike, Confucius 101: A key to understanding the Chinese Mind).

Chinese leaders will initially create an impression of employing Western communication principles pertaining to openness, transparency, and freedom of expression. This encourages Western team members to share experiences, opinions, and concerns, not unlike working in a Western corporate environment. The Chinese leader will create this behavioral relationship management with multiple Western team members simultaneously. Team management levels might be bypassed, and the Chinese leader may engage directly with lower ranks to discuss company issues. This is precisely the intent to receive multiple opinions about issues at the same time in order to formulate opinions about each employee's value to extract information as well as ascertain problem areas, which other employees or indeed functional managers might not want to share openly. The relationship intensity and sincerity are regulated entirely by the Chinese leader, and once he or she decides to terminate this engagement, the relationship is subdued or even over. Many a Western colleague has been trying to maintain relationships, to no avail, with their Chinese superiors for months on end, only to discover that the 'temporary' relationship had been over months earlier—as soon as the Western subordinate was no longer a useful, yet unintentional, informant. Chinese relationships with non-Chinese team members are typically temporary and functional.

To demonstrate one-sided rank based relationship management, the below example is typical.

At assignment commencement, the Chinese leader engaged frequently with the team and would seek out specific Western individuals with whom he would establish a 'close' relationship, being overbearingly friendly and overly courteous, treating the Western colleague with utmost respect. Such individuals were frequently summoned for advice and their opinions. They would be invited to meetings regarding issues that fell outside of their job descriptions. They would be invited to Chinese dinners, sometimes on a one-on-one basis with the Chinese leader only. Often, the direct manager of such a Western individual would be bypassed completely during these engagements. The stature and importance of the Western colleague's contribution to the Chinese organization was assured, or so it appeared.

This Chinese relationship management behavior was ascribed to Chinese business culture principles, and Western functional managers who were being 'side-lined' dismissed it as a concern. But as the assignment progressed, the leader consulted the selected Western team members less frequently and invites to Chinese dinners became less frequent. Face-to-face engagements remained courteous.

As the assignment ended, this relationship completely faded away; the Western colleague was ignored and any attempts to engage directly with the Chinese leader were directly dismissed. Constructive opinions and suggestions were purposely ignored. In fact, the Chinese leader would deliberately argue and not agree with anything the Western confidant said, to such an extent that the Western colleague was asked for his or her advice in a meeting forum just for the Chinese leader to argue and disagree with the answer received.

Clearly, the need for the Western colleague in the Chinese organization was waning quickly and the end game was approaching fast. It is important to recognize such signs as this behavior is typical when the services of a Western team member are about to be discontinued. These signs include relationships becoming more formal and distant, faultfinding, blaming, and non-support by other Chinese colleagues. The Chinese organization needs to create a reason for justifying your imminent dismissal.

CHAPTER 4

MIANZI

"Silence is a true friend who never betrays."
—*Confucius*

Selected sections of this chapter have been compiled with researched information obtained from knowledgeable sources, including China-Mike, *Mianzi*.

Saving face is a common concept across many cultures, but few take it as seriously as the Chinese. Lin Yutang (1895—1976) was a famous Chinese inventor, linguist, writer, and translator who stated, *"Face cannot be translated or defined"*, but loosely translated, it could be associated with prestige, dignity, and pride. According to China-Mike, Lin Yutang did define it as an "abstract and intangible" concept that underlined the most delicate standard by which Chinese people regulate their interpersonal relationships (China-Mike, Mianzi).

For the Chinese, managing 'face' is about much more than just protecting a person's ego or managing other people's impression of you, as is typical in Western societies. For them, it is about honor.

My first encounter with the concept of Mianzi presented itself in the workplace when a Chinese colleague started questioning the integrity of one of my Western colleagues' work output in a formal meeting. The engineer, confident in his design, defended his work and questioned the Chinese colleague's calculation accuracy in front of a large audience that included many Chinese colleagues. Soon, the meeting erupted into a raucous argument and counter-argument, and the meeting organizer had to interject. This was Mianzi in motion, except for the fact that none of the Western colleagues even began to understand what was being played out. In its simplest form, Mianzi is the concept of maintaining a harmonious relationship by keeping face.

In essence, when a relationship has been built, one does not challenge each other, as that could compromise the relationship. More importantly, one does not challenge the person in public, as this could humiliate him or her and he or she could be losing respect or 'face' in front of his or her colleagues—especially the Chinese colleagues. And more, a single Chinese team member losing face could tarnish that of the entire Chinese team. The honor of the entire team was in the hands of each individual team member. In this example, a more subtle manifestation was the fact that the Chinese colleague challenged an Outsider, which is quite acceptable in Chinese culture. The fact that the Outsider challenged back was however, the proverbial hair in the ointment; the Chinese colleague's face was tarnished in front of his Insider clan.

In the Western world however, one typically would interpret the challenge of one's work simply as a challenge of professional capability; one would feel compelled to defend one's position, if one feels strongly about the accuracy and correctness of such work. In Western business culture, it has nothing to do with pride or humiliation, but everything to do with professionalism in the work place.

The key factor in a Chinese business environment is to establish a harmonious relationship and this harmony must be maintained at all costs to prevent the relationship bond from being broken. Harmony must be maintained, even at the cost of getting the job done. In Western culture, 'getting the job done' trumps many other factors, including maintaining a relationship—especially a relationship with a person who is not 'getting the job done'.

Once a Western-Chinese—or for that matter, Chinese-Chinese—relationship has been broken, it is most difficult to re-establish the relationship again. One finds oneself in a very tight corner of maneuverability; you—the Outsider—can be subjected to losing face by your Chinese colleagues. At the same time, you are expected to maintain a state of Confucian Harmony by not retaliating or challenging your challenger; otherwise, the relationship (Guanxi) could be affected nega- tively, and probably forever. Balancing the ternary cornerstones of harmony, face, and relationship between Insiders and Outsiders is doomed for failure by the very nature of its expectations from opposing cultures, each having a very different value system.

The Chinese are very formal and appear conservative in the work environment. It requires much effort to build a relation- ship with a Chinese colleague, as it could take years to build the necessary trust. And even then, a non-Chinese colleague will never trump a Chinese in the relationship hierarchy. Insiders will always take preference over Outsiders.

When a Chinese colleague interprets your challenging questions as him or her 'losing face', the relationship could be very easily destroyed in the blink of an eye—you will not even realize that the relationship is over. It will be rather difficult—even near impossible—to ever build a true and lasting relationship between Insiders and Outsiders. This was never the intent of fate that one is born into, either as part of the Insider clan or forever an Outsider. Rather, Insider-Outsider relationships are temporary and superficial and are destined to dissipate into thin air as soon as the purpose of engagement is achieved. The only way for a relationship to become permanent is if the Insider clan believes an Outsider is worthy enough to join the Insider clan, which would then constitute a permanent relationship arrangement until the mortal end. But this certainly is a rare occurrence—one I have never witnessed. Mostly, Outsiders in a public, private, and work environment are made to feel like Insiders to get them to open up and be used until the day arrives that they realize they are just Outsiders.

Once a strong relationship has been built, it is challenging to break it. However, as soon as a partnership starts to become less harmonious, the relationship bond is broken and it is very difficult to re-establish it again. This type of partnership or relationship the Chinese seek is commonly referred to as Guangxi (see Chapter 5). It is a feeling of trust that the Chinese have with another person, and it is typically developed over a long period. Thus, to consider escalating any relationship issues with the Chinese is to always go against the idea of Guangxi, as the relationship would no longer be in the state of Confucian Harmony.

In the example highlighted above, the advice I gave to the engineer was to prevent an open confrontation at all costs. Instead, I recommended that he arrange a face-to-face, private meeting to understand the concerns raised by the Chinese colleague, rather than to present his own findings, and then to agree a solution. This solution was to then be reported back to the meeting forum. The engineer initiated my recommendation, which resulted in his design being accepted by the Chinese colleague; they reported their agreed-upon way forward to all the meeting participants. The Chinese colleague probably felt as though he was part of the solution, which may have been instrumental in moving the issue forward much faster.

Chinese colleagues will argue and stick together even if their solution is obviously wrong, just for the sake of maintaining Mianzi. They cannot at any cost be seen to have given in to an Outsider, especially in the presence of other Insiders. In fact, the Insiders will side with the "incorrect solution" in support of their own Insider colleague.

The concept of 'face' incorporates the idea of maintaining 'good reputation', 'respect', and 'honor'. One must learn the subtleties of the concept and understand the possible impact it could have on your doing business in China or with Chinese companies.

There are five categories of losing and giving face, namely:

- One may **lose face** through their involvement in an action or deed that is exposed. In this case, losing face is not the result of the action, but rather the fact that it's being made public knowledge
- One may **give face** to others through compliments and respect
- When one shows wisdom in action by avoiding mistakes, their face is increased. One **shows face** through experience and age

- Other people who compliment you to third parties will cause you to **increase face**
- Your face is increased when you successfully cause an Outsider to lose face

It is critical that you give face, save face, show face, and increase face when doing business in a Chinese business environment (World Tourism Summit). Non-Chinese colleagues, especially in the workplace, must take the relevance of Mianzi in Chinese culture seriously. Non-Chinese colleagues mostly don't grasp the importance and sensitivity around Mianzi, but for their Chinese counterparts it presents a critical relationship factor, which determines the longevity and outcome of a business arrangement between a Chinese and Western organization. Crossing the etiquette lines of Mianzi acceptable behavior often leads to the abrupt ending of a seemingly good relationship—much to the dismay of a non-Chinese colleague (China Mike, Mianzi).

From a Western perspective, Chinese people are considered to be over sensitive to any situation being perceived as having caused a Chinese person to lose face. This cultural phenomenon reverts to the primary Confucian concept of creating social harmony above everything else. While in a Western business environment constructive criticism and challenging of ideas is openly encouraged, it would be counterproductive in a Chinese business environment. Interestingly though, Chinese colleagues will openly challenge their Western colleagues in a forum. Why this paradoxical standard? It comes down to relationships (Guanxi) that determine whose face is worth preserving.

Chinese culture is of the opinion that you are born into

relationships with people whom you will engage with for the rest of your life. Any Outsiders will remain Outsiders and never have a true relationship, but rather a relationship of temporary convenience with their Chinese counterpart. Thus, such a temporary relationship does not have to fall within the framework of social harmony and thus it pays little dividends to preserve face. On the other hand, if the Outsider challenges any of the Chinese people in the inner relationship circle into which you are born, then all members of the inner circle would feel aggrieved as one of their own has lost face, making them all look foolish. The subsequent shame would then befall them all and this situation can have serious long-term consequences.

Being direct, challenging, and frank—as is typical in a Western business environment—would be seen as overbearing, rude, and uncultured in China. Showing disagreement, raising questions, and proposing an alternative solution in the Chinese corporate environment would be seen as a serious face-losing situation, not only for the subordinate being challenged, but also for all Chinese colleagues including the manager and even the Chinese company and the country as a whole. The Western colleague could be singled out and considered an undesirable element, or even an enemy.

The honor of the Chinese colleague is often avenged by not supporting the Western colleague in the work environment; ignoring his or her request for assistance or information; not processing travel bookings or disbursement claims; delay tactics; and sabotaging work output—these are all acceptable means to discredit him or her. Ultimately, the undesired Western colleague could be framed for a situation, which was not his or her doing in the first instance, resulting in his or her immediate dismissal. This will all be done without the non-Chinese colleague even being aware of the fact that he or she is being set up to fail.

WESTERN FACE VERSUS CHINESE MIANZI

In Western culture, preserving face is about the individual or inwardly focused, while in the Chinese culture the preservation of face is about a group of people and the relationship between these people or the outwardly focused relationship.

Mianzi is not about one's individual pride and ego being preserved, but more about how other people see an individual. In Chinese culture it is everybody's social duty to ensure that one of their own is not seen to lose face. Mianzi allows face to be given to an individual or group of people if they have earned it. At the same time, face can be taken away at an instant, for example if the manager ridicules or humiliates an individual or group of people in front of others. When face has been lost, it is notoriously difficult to win it back again.

Yvonne Chang from the University of Texas completed a study entitled *Cultural Faces of Interpersonal Communication in the U.S. and China* in 2008, in which she explained that face can be "communally created and owned". She goes on to explain, *"Deeply rooted in the Chinese concept of face are conceptualizations of a competent person in Chinese society: one who defines and puts self in relation to others and who cultivates morality so that his or her conduct will not lose others' face. This contrasts with the American cultural definition of a person who is expected to be independent, self-reliant, and successful. The end result is that a Chinese person is expected to be relationally or communally conscious whereas an American person is expected to be self-conscious."*

SHAME-BASED CULTURES VERSUS GUILT-BASED CULTURES

Confucius believed that people would work together harmoniously if they were led with excellence, and if they were 'put in their place' through ritual practices, roles and assisted in developing a sense of shame. He taught that a person should avoid shame in order to gain honor, which led to the development of a shame-based culture in China. Western cultures are more conscience and guilt based, whereas Chinese people followed a set of 'proper behaviors' in order to avoid losing face and being shamed. This 'proper behavior' does not stem from the fact that they might feel guilty about their actions, but rather because it will cause them to lose face, bringing shame upon their family, clan, colleagues or even company, according to China-Mike's work *Cult of Face*.

For the Chinese, shame is much more than one person's emotional reaction to a blunder. It is an inter-relational issue that helps the community exert social control. Most often, a shameful event in a family or clan-kinship is covered up and never spoken about in private or in public. This is in stark contrast to Western Culture, where much of a family's private business is completely socially acceptable (China-Mike, Confucius 101: A key to understanding the Chinese Mind).

RELATIVE ETHICS

Western cultures value the importance of being right and innocent. They value facts and objectivity and the laws apply equally to everyone. Our behavior is directed by our conscience. In a Western world, they save face for the purpose of personal integrity and morality. They value people of integrity—those who face the objective truth even in the face of negative outcomes. An apology can go a long way towards restoring respect. Society will typically forgive one's shortcomings if one takes responsibility for one's own issues (China-Mike).

Chinese people, on the contrary, would view this as a terrible loss of face. Society functions on the premise that personal relationships matter more than objective laws and customs. Rules are arbitrary and only made to serve the authorities.

Confucian teachings recommend that people should be treated differently according to their relative statuses. As such, Chinese ethics are situational in nature, while Western ethics are about what's right and wrong. Often, the 'truth' is determined more by what the relationship or situation calls for, rather than the actual truth (China-Mike, Confucius 101: A key to understanding the Chinese Mind).

Saving face is what's most important to the Chinese people and they will go to great lengths to protect their collective face. The Chinese will often assume that Westerners know when they have re-packaged the truth in order to save face (China-Mike, The Cult of Face).

Western colleagues often struggle with this re-packaging of the truth, since this tends to point a person out on their lies. However, open confrontation of a Chinese colleague is usually best avoided as it is considered rude and even cruel. If you must, rather talk to the individual privately, and always leave them with a way out of a situation that may cost them face. When talking to them, avoid assigning blame. Rather use flattery to let them know that there is a problem and ask for their wise guidance in resolving the issue. Suffice to say, Chinese colleagues are quick to challenge a Westerner's honesty and commitment, because the individual Westerner is considered an Outsider and therefore it is less important to keep his or her face.

SHY CHINA

Westerners will typically interpret the way in which Chinese colleagues avoid them as shyness, or perhaps assign it to the fact that they don't speak good English. However, that's a small part of it. The main reason why the average Chinese person avoids foreigners, is because they are afraid of appearing incompetent—especially before the boss or other employees—and losing face as a result.

Even in China, locals feel that they are expected to speak good English to foreigners, especially in the work place. As such, they tend to avoid situations where they may be humiliated for their pronunciation (China-Mike, The Cult of Face).

For Chinese dealing with other Chinese people is easier, because they know the rules of saving face. But who knows what might happen when they encounter a loud, emotional and unpredictable 'laowai' (a foreigner). Sadly, many Chinese people view Westerners as angry individuals that are incensed by the slightest provocation. Perhaps they have firsthand experience of a foreigner who had an emotional outburst that led to large-scale loss of face.

Many Chinese people are afraid of being apprehended on the street by a foreigner. When one does need directions, make your conversation polite, quiet, and to-the-point. Try to avoid attracting too much attention and don't gesticulate with your arms, a practice considered rude in Chinese culture. As John Wayne said, *"Talk low, talk slow, and don't talk too much"* (China-Mike, Cult of Face).

Effective communication during my employment with a Chinese organization was a serious inhibitor to progress. The Chinese management flatly ignored a request for a Sino-Anglo translator, because that would have clearly resulted in many of the Chinese colleagues losing face. After all, the primary reason for their transfer from the mainland China Office to an offshore country was surely their command of the English language. A potential Mianzi scenario bears much more weight than introducing a mechanism whereby the project delivery and office efficiency and general functionality could have been increased significantly.

PRESERVING NATIONAL FACE

Understanding the concept of face is the golden rule for making sense of the Chinese nation and their history (China-Mike, The Cult of Face).

In China, children learn the CPC's version of history, with the result that they are aware of their humiliations from a young age. Chinese people grow up with a strong sense of nationalism. This causes them to be highly defensive of their history and traditions and sensitive to any comments they might see as criticism, according to China-Mike. Avoid discussing Chinese politics, the CPC, or any other sensitive matters concerning China e.g. environmental damage, climate change, poaching of endangered species for the Chinese market, and other discussions that are likely to result in a face-losing situation. Typically, when entering into such discussions the Chinese counterpart will avoid voicing his or her opinion and will make every effort to extract him or herself from the discussion. The Chinese individual will not only lose face, but will be seen by his or her colleagues as having shamed the Chinese country, its people and the nation's values as a whole. It is also highly unlikely that a Chinese colleague will want to discuss the local politics and country issues or indeed Western politics. This is just not done in Chinese society.

HOW TO GIVE FACE

Tips by China-Mike, *Cult of Face.*

- Praise someone in front of his or her boss or elders
- Give them an expensive, imported gift
- Be generous with positive reviews, evaluations, or customer evaluation forms
- Show your appreciation with food. Chinese society and business runs on expensive meals and banquets
- When you're treated to a meal out, be sure to shower your host with compliments that show how much you are enjoying and appreciating it

HOW TO AVOID LOSING FACE

Tips by China-Mike, *Cult of Losing Face.*

- Never openly disagree, deny, challenge, or criticize someone
- Never interrupt someone who is talking
- Never be angry with someone, as it will cause you both to lose face

- Never turn down an invitation outright
- Never be late, as it shows disrespect
- Never call someone out on a lie
- Never fail to show proper deference to superiors or elders
- Never reveal a person's weaknesses
- Never fail to enthusiastically partake in drinking bouts at dinner engagements (unless you have a good medical excuse)

CHAPTER 5

GUANXI

"Do unto others what you want done unto you."
—Confucius

Selected sections of this chapter have been compiled with researched information obtained from knowledgeable sources, especially from China-Mike's articles, *The Cult of Face, Confucius 101: A key to understanding the Chinese Mind, Guanxi,* and *Chinese Etiquette Tips for Travelers.*

One of the key observations I made while working for a Chinese company is that the Chinese team has pre-existing relationships that date back years or even decades. They all seem to know each other, tend to live together in Chinese Communes, and work requirements are actioned silently without too much ado or communication. Everyone seems to know exactly what he or she needs to do and whom they need to do it for. This seemingly well-coordinated Chinese organizational structure comes down to the Chinese concept known as Guanxi. Guanxi in its simplest form can be interpreted as interpersonal relationships.

Guanxi ('gwan-shee') translates into relationships or social connections, but there is certainly more to this. The phrase *'It's not what you know, it's who you know'* has more relevance in China than perhaps any other country around the world.

China's success as a country is built on Guanxi—everything revolves around it. To them, Guanxi trumps all the factors other nations value, including wealth, ambition, talent, intelligence, and knowledge. You need the right Guanxi to get ahead in China, and without it, those with better Guanxi can thwart your ability to get ahead (China Mike, Guanxi).

Bureaucracy is strong in China, and you will have to navigate through businesses, agencies, and public officials to achieve the simplest of things. Guanxi applies to more than just politics and business. It extends to every aspect of life, including meeting a spouse, finding an apartment, and everything in between. Guanxi is the fuel on which society, commerce, and politics in China runs.

A WEB OF MUTUAL INTERDEPENDENCE

Relationships are based on mutual independence, and therefore, Guanxi is a mutual obligation that is deeply embedded in Chinese culture. It extends across social divides (China-Mike, Guanxi).

But Guanxi is not about your own contacts or influence, but it also extends to other people you encounter. It's about social debts. It's as though every Chinese person keeps a mental score, remembering the favors they've done and the debts owed to them.

Chinese people typically view relationships as lifelong commitments. Even after losing touch with someone for decades, they can contact you unexpectedly to call in a favor. Failing to return the favor would be considered a major transgression—a mortal sin.

If you gain a bad reputation in terms of returning favors,

you can be excluded and your Guanxi can evaporate instantly.

WEST VERSUS EAST

Sometimes, Westerners may view Guanxi as an underhanded—somewhat nepotistic—method. It appears to be slanted against Western nature to take personal responsibility for one's actions, successes and failures. Many Westerners feel that using connections to achieve goals in business and in life does not show a strong sense of individualism and independence (China-Mike, Guanxi).

Then again, despite the fact that little has ever been fair in Chinese society, it's unheard of to hear a Chinese person complain about life being unfair. Instead, the belief that 'might equals right' is heavily ingrained in their culture.

Over the centuries, personal freedom was limited. Instead, the common person had to follow many rules. There have never been inalienable rights that protected the ordinary people from the power plays of those in power.

The Chinese bureaucracy was fine-tuned over thousands of years and nobody ever expected to get anything because it was their right. The laws served those in power, and were changed at will by the dynasty or egomaniacal emperor in power at the time.

Western societies were generally developed based on the law, while capricious rules of emperors controlled Chinese society. This unwritten mantra still applies in modern China today, being practiced behind a dark web of secrecies, not readily visible to the unschooled eye.

GOING THROUGH THE BACK DOOR

As a result of the society's dependence on Guanxi, the Chinese have had to improvise in order to get their way. They are open to using behind-the-scenes methods to make the Guanxi work in their favor. Relationships built on 'hou men' (back door) take on significant importance. For the most part, real relationships command more respect than the artificial rules of society—which is why the Chinese have little trouble flouting the rules (China-Mike, Guanxi).

THE COST OF DOING BUSINESS IN CHINA

The Chinese—with their emphasis on connections or Guanxi—view Western business methods as ineffective, rude, and even arrogant. Foreign business people looking to do business with Chinese companies must cultivate Guanxi quickly because navigating the Chinese bureaucracy through the 'official' channels is futile.

A person with the right connections can easily bypass official regulations, whereas a person without Guanxi will for instance find it near impossible to get a simple rubber-stamp on an application.

Your best bet when doing business in China is to find a Chinese partner with Guanxi. People will often hire a relative of a powerful local official in order to move things along smoothly (China Mike, Guanxi).

A WORD OF ADVICE

Expats and foreign business people must not underestimate the power of Guanxi. The Chinese don't do favors to 'be nice', and you must understand that you are party to an implicit understanding or agreement that you will reciprocate when the time comes. Be clear on what you are getting yourself into before accepting any favors.

A Chinese person may well assume that Guanxi applies where you are from, and that you are in a position to return the favor in the future. Beware of being caught up in a never-ending cycle of obligations and returning favors. It may be a good idea to adopt the motto of 'There's no such thing as a free lunch', when it comes to developing long-term working relationships with the Chinese, according to China-Mike.

THE DRUNKEN BANQUET—A TIME-HONORED CHINESE TRADITION

It can take a lifetime of effort and energy to build a network and extend influence. One of the most common ways in which the Chinese cement new relationships, is through hosting banquet dinners. When a businessperson uses a member of his network for an introduction to a local official, he will treat the new acquaintance to an elaborate dinner with plenty of alcohol. The dinner might well be followed by a stop-off at a karaoke bar, where more favors can be expected (China-Mike, Chinese Etiquette Tips for Travelers).

A Chinese banquet is the all-purpose experience and the primary social gathering favored by the locals. It is not only used for repaying favors, but also for keeping up relationships with old friends and bonding with new ones. While friends take turns to host banquets (the host being referred to as the '*qing ke*'), older relatives are usually expected to entertain younger patrons.

WEDDINGS

Since Chinese work, public and personal lives are heavily interwoven, it is prudent to discuss weddings in a bit more detail, as many aspects of daily Chinese existence and their psyche are portrayed at these events. If one were doing business in China, it would be an honor for Chinese families to invite their non-Chinese acquaintances, the occasion presenting a perfect opportunity to reciprocate past and future favors.

Weddings are also celebrated banquet style. While Western weddings involve church, followed by a reception, guests at a Chinese wedding are assigned to seats at circular tables where they sit throughout the event. Food is served slowly throughout the event, in between the ceremony, which involves introducing the bride and groom and the parents. There will also be some speeches made (China-Mike, Guanxi).

Wedding guests don't interact much with other guests, but the groom and bride will stop by each table for a toast, and to thank guests for coming. Chinese and Taiwanese people are typically reluctant to introduce themselves to other people, and will wait for a third party to make introductions. Even then, the bride's guests will not typically interact with the groom's guests.

Wedding gifts are another big part of Guanxi. Upon arriving at the wedding, guests would check in by handing a red envelope full of cash to a relative, who would record it. This is done to ensure that everyone is clear on the accumulated amount of Guanxi for future reference.

NEPOTISM & CORRUPTION

Of course, Guanxi is not a perfect system. It has its flaws. Chinese people take pride in the fact that they know powerful people. This leads to nepotism that pervades throughout government and business. People are hired based on connections, rather than on qualifications and merits (China-Mike, Guanxi).

For instance, with the right Guanxi, your child can be accepted into prestigious learning institutions. Such accepted behavior in China brings about chronic corruption and cronyism that becomes increasingly more difficult to eradicate, as back room dealing is a long-established tradition.

A FINAL WORD

As can be seen in Chapters 3, 4 and 5, what really defines the Chinese psyche is the complex interaction between maintaining harmony, managing face and fostering and maintaining relationships. If any of these three areas of inter-existence are stressed, then the other areas of interpersonal relationships are likely to come under pressure too. It is thus so critical to keep these three behaviors in perfect balance with one another, like the forces of good and bad, Yin and Yang, Dragon and Tiger.

In the Western world far less emphasis is placed on balancing these behaviors and deviations from them are easily forgiven and forgotten. The different attitudes between East and West in managing the inter-dependency of these three behavioral sectors is probably the biggest single hurdle in getting natural alignment to occur quickly between these two opposing groups of people. As we have seen, collectivism promotes alignment while individualism does not promote alignment. The psyche make-up and drivers are just so vastly different for these two opposite cultures that it might still require decades to achieve alignment and only if a common behavioral trait can be evolved to, something that will take a lot of discipline and tolerance from both sides.

CHAPTER 6

THE EMPEROR RULES

"The superior man is modest in his speech,
but exceeds in his actions."
—*Confucius*

Since the earliest living memory, the Chinese dynasties created a strong feudal system, created capital cities, and ruled over the lands. The emperor—either a self-appointed warlord or natural heir to the throne—held the dynasty's highest power. Throughout Chinese history, the dynasties fine-tuned its military and political machine through wars, land annexations, and enslaving vast numbers of the populace. Somebody had to go to war, build the cities, but also build the Chinese Walls, erected to keep warring barbarian tribes from the North, in what is today known as Inner and Outer Mongolia, from raiding the fine Chinese civilization.

Many of the emperors inclined towards barbarism them-selves, the next emperor outdoing his predecessor, attacking areas not yet unified into the Chinese state or barbarian lands to the North. The emperors had ultimate power, able to annex and make his subjects, hundreds of thousands of Chinese civilians strong, build monumental public projects, including roads, canals, palace complexes and of course walls. The first defensive walls were built as far back as the third century BC.

While these walls would effectively be earth mounts, constructed from tampered earth until the Ming dynasty built the first mason wall only in the 15th century, nevertheless these projects were of huge scale, requiring tens of thousands of soldiers and civilians to build hundreds of kilometers of walls. And as these earthen walls had a relatively short lifespan, being subjected to the elements, which degenerated these structures relatively quickly, each new dynasty over the centuries built new walls to replace the old crumbling walls and keep the barbarians out as they raided further East or West to bypass existing walls.

The First Emperor of the Qin Dynasty (221 – 206 BC) introduced Legalism, a philosophy which put in place the foundations of subsequent Chinese governments, including a centralized bureaucracy and a uniform legal system. This gave the emperor full reign of power, allowing him ultimate control over the lands and his people. Unlike Confucius who believed that the good subjugated behavior of people could be brought out when engaged with respect and father-like authority, the Legalists worked on the assumption that people were devious by nature and that not even laws would compel them to obey.

This austere control over the Chinese population truly unified the Chinese world for the first time, strictly controlling their lives from paying taxes to reporting on each other if a crime was committed—irrespective of how insignificant. And crimes were harshly punished, often by execution. The Qin Legalist formula was rapidly rolled out throughout the empire, which laid the foundations for the modern, unified, bureaucratic Chinese state of today, which included the standardization of currency, weights, measurements, laws, installing ruthless police controls, and subordinating the peasantry to the government. As recent as the last century, one of the many famous admirers of the First Emperor and his Legalist system was none other than Mao Zedong, probably the most destructive dictator that China has ever had (Lovell, The Great Wall, Page 52,53).

The emperors throughout the centuries had ultimate power, commanding raids on Chinese villages—and barbarians alike—, deciding on construction projects, and having the power over life and death of his court officials, aides, eunuchs, and the greater population at will. The emperor's decision was final.

One emperor would ask his aides to advise him on matters and if he did not agree with the recommendation, would give the aide the option of death by strangulation or suicide right there in front of the emperor. Working for the public service became an unpopular choice however, often individuals were forced to work for the emperor, as the Chinese empire was the only employer, controlling vast swaths of society for the emperor's own gain. Wall building was another matter altogether, with soldiers stationed at these outer frontiers to build them. If they didn't perish in the process, they had to protect the Chinese empire against marauders, often for extended periods and sometimes for life. They would not be given any indication as to when they were allowed to return to their families from active military duty.

Labor was readily available, the work force was aplenty and life was cheap, with hordes of new soldiers and subjects sent to build empire projects and walls at the whim of the emperor. In a single year in 555 AD, the Qi emperor dispatched an astonishing 1.8 million men to build 450 kilometers of wall (Lovell, The Great Wall, Page 121). The loss of life was often astonishing and relentless; fallen workers would be replaced with more workers. In some accounts as many as fifty percent of the workforce died when building a single stretch of wall for the emperor.

MAO ZEDONG

The Western perception of modern China is that the Communist Party ultimately rules over the Chinese nation in a totalitarian political environment, which allows little room for individual brilliance. Larger institutions and companies are certainly government owned, private business ownership having only been allowed since the 1990's. Ultimately, each organization is headed up by a Party loyalist, reporting to a Party appointed board and chairperson. While Chinese empires have long been discontinued, in many ways Mao Zedong's rule of modern China in the 20th century was seen by many Chinese intellectuals as nothing more than a modern version of an autocratic emperor ruling his subjugates at his will. Mao Zedong himself fiercely dissociated himself from such a perceived image, citing his utter distaste for Chinese traditional history, writings, poetry, and mannerisms. He ultimately purged any modern writings of Chinese traditional history and sciences in the now infamous Chinese Cultural Revolution when Mao's Red Guards dished out pummeling and severe beatings to anybody associated with the past literacy and intellectual thinking.

The new Chinese mantra became 'Quotations from Chairman Mao Tse-tung' or the Little Red Book as it became popularly known, containing some 200 quotations from his speeches and writings. It was published for the first time in early 1964 and continued being widely distributed during the Cultural Revolution until Mao's death in 1976. Being seen without it could result in severe punishment, especially during the Cultural Revolution. It was translated into some 20 foreign languages, and sold in some 117 countries, with total global sales estimated to have reached some 6.5 billion by the time Mao died (Wikipedia, Maoism; Wikipedia, Cultural Revolution).

Yet, one has to ask, was Mao's sadistic, one-man-state rule any different to all the Chinese emperors, preceding him? While Communism was just another form of imperialism or empiricism, the outcome had many similarities with ancient Chinese history. The subjects were under the total control of the 'emperor', receiving and executing instruction without questioning. They had no control of their own destiny and committed their working lives to the state machine. They were forced to relocate to execute glorious state conquests without question or beckon.

WESTERN APPROACH

Typically, in Western companies, the modern management style is to empower departmental leaders and functional managers who take on decision responsibilities, working within a matrix team structure. Support services are readily available to supplement functional effort to ensure that the company functions efficiently. Management decisions are generally transparently communicated across the organization using a top down approach. Western business leaders believe that immediate knowledge will ensure a more efficient decision-making process by company departmental teams, ultimately resulting in an ownership and responsibility matrix that starts with the junior workers already aware that their perhaps trivial decision could eventually affect the company performance and direction in which it is headed.

It goes along the theory that a minor weather phenomenon in one part of the world ultimately can cause an El Niño or La Niña on the opposite side of the globe. The individual actions will affect the overall company effectiveness—irrespective of how small such an action might be. The secretary not spell checking a document could ultimately lead to the CEO not securing a deal, which depended on him or her presenting a quality proposal, based on the actions of others.

In the Western concept of managing an organization, the integrated team approach is encouraged, where each individual has a specific function that, when combined, produces a successful outcome that benefits all through incentives and rewards. This approach creates super teams, led by Level 5 leaders (Collins, Good to Great, Pages 17-40), guided by effective policies and procedures, operating ever more effectively in an ever-changing environment.

In essence, Western companies are team run with leaders assigned in a responsibility matrix, to enhance the decision making process in the most effective manner. The Western incentivization principle can however, be rather complicated by having various managers and departments monitored and having their departmental Key Performance Indicators (KPI's) determine their incentives. Those companies that have the ultimate company KPI's or objectives as the only measurement criteria are often more successful than the companies that try to develop individual departmental performance criteria.

CHINESE APPROACH

The Chinese management style takes on a very different role compared to Western management styles. The decision making process in a Chinese enterprise appears to be a rather intricate network of clandestine feedback, parallel reporting structures and single decision makers. These parallel reporting structures are a crucial aspect of Chinese business; it ensures that the leader obtains information from a large variety of sources with many different views and perspectives, which arms the leader with much insight and many options from which to choose. The leader can now make informed decisions taking into account information on those not supporting his decision i.e. his detractors.

Unlike Western companies, people of lower rank in a Chinese company are never functionally empowered to make decisions. The Chinese leader can ill afford junior workers to have the realization that their decision could eventually affect the company performance or direction, as this would then imply that he is not in total charge which will result in him losing face (Mianzi). To this end, the Chinese management system has a favorable approach in that the leader has the 'main company objective' in mind and has no compassion for individual or departmental goals or targets that might not always align with the overall company requirements. Unfortunately, the leader does not communicate this 'main objective' and neither does he harness his team to achieve this. He relies on the information from various sources of parallel reporting to make his own decisions to hopefully take the sole credit in case of success, or—in many cases—to assign blame to sources of information in case of failure.

Having joined the Chinese company, executing a large project in Africa, the project team structure (organogram) was put in place along traditional Western lines, with a head of the team (project director) and multiple area specific managers, reporting directly to the project director. The team consisted of a few Westerners and a large number of Chinese employees. The Chinese co-workers were slotted into the organogram along Western team structuring principles. Oddly, many of the Chinese colleagues had pre-assigned (Chinese company) titles that not necessarily complied with the team structure put in place (according to Western management structures). All appointments had been done by the Chinese senior management, so the senior positions filled by Western persons had been sanctioned by the Chinese senior management team themselves.

It soon became apparent that the Chinese colleagues had a responsibility to report directly to the Chinese senior leaders via a separate, invisible Chinese reporting line that was specifically put in place only for the Chinese team members within our team. These Chinese senior leaders were quickly identifiable, but it was difficult for non-Chinese employees to establish a direct open communication line with them. Clearly, the Chinese team was reporting incessantly on the work progress and performance, writing a myriad of reports in Mandarin that they never discussed or shared with any of the Western team members.

Parallel reporting to their Chinese superiors was the order

of the day, irrespective of team or project commitments and decisions. Effective 'Chinese' reporting was a matter of having an employment opportunity in an exotic location or being in a back office job somewhere in China. The jobs on the project were privileged for a few carefully handpicked Chinese individuals; their command of the English language was a key differentiator. Yet, these reports were written by the dozen and in Mandarin—for a Chinese audience only. This responsibility was never discussed or agreed upon with the (Western) team leaders or work colleagues; it just happened in parallel and was never spoken about or recorded as part of the team's objectives or its deliverables.

While our Chinese colleagues appeared courteous at all times, it was difficult to effectively integrate them into the overall team. Instructions given and requests made to Chinese subordinates were always acknowledged, but not always effectively executed and if completed, they were of inferior quality and the answer often misaligned with the request. In a number of instances, the requests were never executed, but the Chinese colleague would eagerly assure the team that it would be done soonest however, the work output never materialized.

Some Western colleagues assigned this lack of delivery to the language barrier, but it appeared to be rather an act of deference, as their direct reporting lines—while on paper to a Westerner—in actual fact were directly back to an unknown Chinese superior. With time, where harmonious relationships were established, such Chinese individuals would then assist with requests, but taking their time to fit this additional work in with their parallel Chinese work commitments.

Language effectively became the unspoken barrier of effective team cooperation but was never talked about or raised as an issue. On one occasion, the Western team members requested a translator, which was vehemently opposed by our Chinese colleagues and the Chinese leader, as it would cause the Chinese team to lose face. After all, the reason for having been sent abroad was their command of the English language, and a translator would have scuttled their employment effectiveness outside China. A translator would also provide the Westerners with a deeper insight and an immediate means of understanding many unfathomable and poorly understood issues taking place, which probably was not in the best interest of the Chinese team members.

THE PATH OF INSTRUCTION

A large number of our Chinese colleagues always attended meetings, whether they were invited or not. A meeting invite was quickly shared verbally or via email by one invited Chinese colleague with the rest of the team—even at short notice—and a large Chinese contingent would appear at a meeting, might it be a low-key meeting or high profile meeting. Even meetings that officially did not require a single Chinese colleague to attend (no official invite sent to any of the Chinese colleagues), would be mysteriously attended by a number of 'uninvited' Chinese colleagues. How they became aware of the meeting remained a mystery. Requests for them to depart the meeting (as the venue might have been too small or the subject matter was not ready for a greater audience yet) were ignored. This resulted in the uninvited Chinese attendees being ignored and the remainder of the team ultimately proceeding with the meeting as though they were not present.

The Chinese team participants at the meeting would then sit in utter silence, only mustering a response, normally restricted to a short reply, when they were directly addressed. They would not offer an opinion, an idea, or a solution at any point during the meeting, unless specifically asked to respond. And even then, they would be reluctant to provide an opinion or solution, as this would normally have to firstly be vetted by a senior Chinese colleague or in some instances, even by the Chinese leader.

When decisions were taken during meetings, the Chinese colleagues did not object or offer to explore an alternative decision. In the eyes of the Western team members the issue was addressed, a decision had been made, and the issue had been finalized. However, invariably one of the Chinese team members—usually a junior—would directly raise the same issue again after a few days, requesting a changed approach. The Western team member—dismissing the request purely as an enquiry and assuming that the Chinese colleague did not clearly understand the reason for the original decision—, would ignore it.

The junior Chinese colleague would however persist to the point that tension developed. Continued dismissal of this request soon resulted in a subtle call from the most senior Chinese team member, in this case the CEO, for the project team to seriously consider the change request. Certainly, it was now understood that the original change request did not emanate from the junior engineer. Clearly, the meeting decision was communicated upwards via the Chinese invisible reporting line. The senior Chinese manager evaluated it and if found to be unacceptable, he would send a new instruction down via the lowest common denominator to relay back to the Western colleague.

The Western people on the team mistakenly believed they were in a position of authority and were able to make decisions. Soon the reality set in that the Chinese leader directs the team and everyone follows his instructions, received via the Chinese 'grapevine'. Western team member instructions are ignored and the team is compelled to implement the leaders' instructions regardless of whether such instructions are correct or not. Ultimately, even more problems arose because of this incorrect implementation and the Western team members were then requested to provide alternate solutions that were again vetted via the invisible reporting line. If the leader did not agree with the 'Western' solution, he would again provide his own solution, which was being implemented, regardless. And so the perpetual process continues until, eventually, problems are evident everywhere and the project is doomed.

So, it would always appear that the Chinese senior management was never directly involved in the decision making process, especially if unpopular or controversial decisions were made. It became glaringly obvious that the Chinese structure was based on a 'one decision maker' and many 'no decision making' subjects, executing his or her instructions without questioning.

Down the reporting structure, not even the Chinese colleagues were sure of where the instruction came from. Questioning such a request would have not achieved much as it was unclear who gave the instruction in the first instance. Chinese instructions are followed 'blindly' by the Chinese team members, even when it was a questionable instruction or pointless, which would add no value to the effective work outcome of the team.

In a number of instances, our Chinese colleagues generated English reports, tables, and lists, without having been requested to do so by the project team management. They requested assistance from their Western colleagues to generate this work but it was soon realized that this work had no material impact on the greater team effort. These deliverable requests appeared out of nowhere and normally ended in the trash bin. On enquiry, the Chinese colleague would usually be unable to adequately explain why he or she was executing such work. Responses were vague, random, and nonsensical as the individual relied on his or her lack of command of the English language as an excuse. Soon, one would be obliged to give up trying to find out why such work had been generated.

CONFUCIAN HIERARCHY

The Chinese organizational structure operates at distinct horizontal responsibility levels, each level interacting with the level above, receiving instructions, and the level below, who will be given instructions. Each level will seldom actively engage with any of the other organizational levels. Each employee belonging to a specific level will have a specific function and responsibility, normally well described in his designation title. He will execute all work on direct instructions given. Unless he had been asked to do something, he will not use his initiative independently as that could be interpreted as direct disobedience and rogue behavior.

As such, a situation is observed in the Chinese corporate work place where many employees do not ever get into meaningful contact with their senior management. They are unable (and unwilling) to share concerns, new ideas and progress information. Any information is normally requested from the top management down via the Chinese organizational levels to the responsible person; then information is gathered by the responsible person and passed back up via the different levels to the senior manager who has made the request.

It is not uncommon for an intermediate interceptor of the data to take credit for the work done, with the originator of the collated data being completely ignored. Often, the senior manager does not even know the person who did the work and this does not seem to bother Chinese employees in the least. They are there to execute a function—, largely initiated on direct instruction within a vacuum—not clearly understanding the reasoning for such an instruction, nor interested in understanding how his or her actions in preparing the requested information could ultimately steer the path of the organization in one direction or another. This is a major difference when compared to the Western culture where much effort is made to get everyone to understand why things need to be done in specific ways.

Chinese employees work in a box with 'box' responsibilities. They do not comprehend how that box fits into the bigger puzzle, nor are they expected to concern themselves with how their box actions would ultimately integrate with the overall corporate strategy, vision, mission, and performance health. Efficient and obedient box performance could ultimately lead to promotion one level up or—if one is an exceptional performer—perhaps a few levels up, at the whim of his or her ultimate manager who he or she might not even know personally. The Chinese career path and work opportunities are described in more detail in Chapter 10, The Chosen One.

CONFUCIAN WISDOM

In Western corporate setups people are promoted to senior positions, based on superior performance and leadership qualities. Respect is earned, not demanded. In the Chinese business culture, respect exists by default, as leadership positions are allocated based on the right connections (relation-ships or Guanxi), age, and years of work experience. In the Chinese culture, age and grey hair is seen as a sign of maturity and wisdom, which entitles one to assume senior responsibili-ties. Communist party alliances through friends or family or party membership definitely enhances one's chances of appointment into senior positions as well as privileged treatment within the corporate structure.

COMMUNISM IN THE WORKPLACE

In order for the Chinese senior management to have better access to information and understanding of performance of the organization within specific departmental teams, a number of observers are placed within that team. These observers are normally senior employees in the organization, and have a direct reporting line to senior Chinese management. They might well be card-carrying CPC members, and their presence was probably instructed directly by the CPC. They are often referred to as consultants or given obscure Vice President titles that do not really align with the organizational structure. These individuals will not take any instruction from the team leaders and partake only at a high level input within these teams, attending selective meetings and requesting their Chinese colleagues to generate even more progress reports. Such instructions are given directly to the Chinese team members without being cleared by or agreed upon with Western team leaders. This can lead to incoherent and inefficient team performance, but is not seen as a concern by the senior Chinese management. These observers seldom interface with anybody other than the Chinese team members.

Individual team members will never want to be seen as over-achievers, working above their performance expectation, being leaders in their field of expertise, or having intuition and initiative. These attributes would single them out, and cause them to become a threat to co-workers. It might even highlight somebody else's under-performance (a colleague could lose face – see Chapter 4).

The tall tree catches the most wind, and in the Chinese corporate structure, the wind blows hard. Organizational teams are put under constant pressure to perform faster, report on performance, and they are being punished for perceived under-performance (this will be elaborated in more detail in Chapter 9 – The Angry Tiger). But in most cases, they are not pressurized to perform better. They are merely pressurized to work harder. In Western culture, people are motivated to want to work better or smarter, while in Chinese culture people are pressurized to work faster and harder.

Work performance really manifests itself as a problem if the Western management—handpicked and appointed by the Chinese management into key team positions—has an autocratic non-participative, non-communicative management style, which plays right into the hands of the Chinese organizational setup. And such Western managers, feeling comfortable with such managerial behavior, and wanting to please their new masters, are too willing to comply to a management style that has been eradicated in Western corporates at least two to three decades ago. Such mismanagement just exemplifies the poor team performance, creates team misalignment and underperformance, and results in target delays and budget overruns. The general work environment becomes unenjoyable, ineffective, and unprofessional.

THE EMPEROR

As in dynasties of old, there are still strong reporting lines in the Chinese corporate structures with one ultimate decision maker. No intermediate decision makers are encountered, even though Chinese departmental heads are appointed. Departmental managers are not assigned individual area accountability or team performance responsibilities, but rather collectively refer pending decisions upwards to the 'emperor'. Nobody operates above the rest. The team behavior is like one flowing motion of mediocre idiosyncratic subversion, with no starting point or goal driven end—no ownership, no performance responsibilities or ambitious target driven outcomes. The emperor owns you and you shall perform to his instructions, percolated down through a complex reporting structure, which operates in distinct operational structural levels.

A leader within a specific business line, who is directly responsible for the performance of that entity, assumes direct responsibility for everything that happens within that entity. There is no delegation of authority to people within his or her team or entity. While team members will execute work on instruction, they will not be given any responsibilities or exert any authority. Any decision-making is left entirely to their leader. The leader in turn reports to the higher authority, where the same rules apply. Ultimately, instructions in all probability always come from the highest power, namely the Communist Party of China (CPC). In order to have any chance of ever becoming an honorary CPC member, it is imperative that the (party) rules are followed to the tee and that one never applies any independent thought process—or worst, dare to make independent decisions. If such action were identified, it would spell the end of the one's Communist Party career (Wikipedia, Communist Party of China).

In order to curb the power of a business leader, it is typical in a Chinese organization that certain departments in his business fall outside the responsibility of the business leader. As such, it is not uncommon that a representative from the company head office back in China heads key departments in one organization or directly by a CPC representative. Employees within their department only take instruction from this departmental head and not the business leader, e.g. the CEO. It is pertinent to mention here that the business leader is probably still being groomed to become a full CPC representative, although he or she is in all probability a card-carrying member of the Communist Party, so this system provides a good opportunity for the business leader's performance to be monitored at the same time.

Departments that will be administrated independently and report directly to Beijing and probably the CPC are typically IT, Finance, HR, and Health & Safety. New Chinese appointees can replace the departmental heads and their subordinates within these departments at any time without officially notifying the business leader. The business leader merely accepts these changes and continues with his assigned role of responsibilities. It is not his place to interfere with jurisdictions that have not been directly assigned to him.

Very often, decisions to be made in these departments will be referred back directly to China, resulting in lengthy decision-making processes, which can result in much frustration with the organization's Western employees, based in the host country. These management arrangements are never documented or shared with the team and it extenuates one's frustration levels to breaking point.

It takes time by trial and error to figure out how the Chinese business entity actually operates. Once one has discovered the true management structure, one quickly realizes that it is near impossible to influence the decision-making process as typically, the ultimate decision maker is not clearly identified as such in the organogram structure and could well be somebody operating out of the Chinese head office back in Beijing.

The business leader appears to be a committed leader, in charge of all decision making, but in reality, he or she does not have the full authority to make across-the-board decisions for the business entity falling within his or her area of responsibility. The Chinese leader will never admit the status quo as he or she would be losing face—seen as not having full authority. The silent head office and CPC decision-makers—all part of the host country office team—will never entertain an approach by any employee, as the official leader would then lose face.

When working in a Chinese business environment it becomes abundantly clear that the Chinese colleagues are to some extent aware of the Chinese management structure, the decision-makers, the CPC representatives, and those who make which decisions. However, as this is the parallel, silent Chinese-only reporting and management structure, the Chinese work colleagues will never appease a non-Chinese colleague of this. Even when directly questioned, Chinese team members will just not respond or be enticed into an information sharing discussion. It does however become evident at the rare social functions—when the tongue is loosened by the flow of ample alcohol—who their true masters are. It is often astounding to a Westerner once he or she discovers the true reporting and commitment lines within the Chinese fold.

The fact is no doubt that Chinese organizations—even from thousands of miles away in Beijing—are duly influenced by the highest order within government structures. This can be fathomed when one acknowledges that the funds originated directly from government sponsored lending institutions. Chinese businesses are generally government owned, and are thus run as typical parastatal organizations, not unlike those found in Western democracies.

CHAPTER 7

URBAN ANTS

"The demands that good people make are upon themselves;
Those that bad people make are upon others."
—*Confucius*

For millennia of dynasties, subjects were available at will to tend to the Emperor's every need, be it building temples, constructing palaces, tending to the fields to grow crops or farming with livestock or building more walls. If an Emperor wanted to embark on his next grandiose project, a few thousand northern barbarians were rounded up to execute such work.

If the barbarians happened to be able to evade the Emperor's forces, then a Chinese village or two to the South were overrun and the villagers became the newest addition to the migrant labor, forced to work under miserable conditions. Many of these laborers perished in the harsh working environment and those that survived were garrisoned into wall duty, to keep the barbarians out.

The availability of resources was not an issue, as there were always barbarian settlements to the North and Chinese villages—not yet part of the empire—to the South. Simply put, for millennia, people in China were an easily accessible commodity that was expendable and replaceable, available in droves and dispensable at a whim. And people were used on a massive scale, at no or little consideration to their welfare or health. During the Sui Dynasty (581 – 618 AD) the emperor's continuing passion for wall building led him to round up and send some 30,000 people to the Ordos region (today part of Inner Mongolia) to build over 700 li (one li equates to roughly half a kilometer) of wall to prevent barbarian incursions in 585 AD. The following year, 150,000 men were dispatched to construct a broken line of a few dozen garrison posts in the grassy, pebbly desert of Inner Mongolia. In 587 AD, more than 100,000 men were sent on 'wall repair work' for 20 days (Lovell, The Great Wall, Page 126).

During the late Sui Dynasty, for example, the new emperor Yang diverted hordes of corvée labor into the speedy construction of a new capital at Luoyang. Yang's impatience for his new city drove the construction pace so fast that half of the estimated 2 million workers are said to have died (Lovell, The Great Wall, Page 128).

In the contemporary modern age, China's population has ballooned, reaching an estimated 1.4 billion in number by the early 21st Century, a staggering 20% of the world population. Chinese citizens make up the largest single ethnic group of people, governed under one system. After the Mao era, the inflow of peasants to the cities—seeking a better life and fortune for themselves—increased substantially. And survival in the miserable inner city slums required people to get an education as the only hope of bettering one's living standards. The Communist Party launched a mass education drive after the Cultural Revolution. National literacy rates have risen from 67 per cent in 1980 to around 90 per cent today (Chu,

Chinese Whispers, Page 127). The communist state education system introduced Gaokao, a nationwide university entrance exam written every year on the 7th June. In 1998, around 830,000 people graduated from Chinese universities. In 2012, more than 6 million did so (Chu, Chinese Whispers, Page 113).

These large numbers of graduates—often mass educated, but not necessarily quality educated—are starting to pose a serious problem for China. On the monotonous outskirts of most major Chinese cities exist large communities of graduates in their twenties and early thirties, living in overcrowded and crumbling accommodations. These graduates have to travel long distances on public transport into the inner city where they can only find work as shop assistants, data entry clerks, receptionists, and cashiers.

These over-qualified, unlucky youngsters are stuck in dead end jobs, very eager to take on an assignment worthy of their qualifications, no matter where it might take them. These graduates are referred to as the 'ant tribe', a term coined by Professor Lian Si of Peking University. This is not meant to be an insulting reference, but rather a comparison with ant colonies, as the professor explains: *"They share every similarity with ants. They live in colonies in cramped areas. They are intelligent and hardworking, yet anonymous and underpaid."* It is estimated that there are around one million ants across China with a hundred thousand in Beijing alone (Chu, Chinese Whispers, Page 114).

AFRICAN ANTS

My first impression, when I joined the Chinese organization, was that the Chinese organization had brought hundreds of Chinese citizens across the Indian Ocean to work in Africa. The same or better skills were readily available locally, so why the mass incursion of Chinese citizens to the African shores? In the corporate environment, the ratio of non-Chinese to Chinese colleagues was as high as one to six. For one, it was comprehensible that the Chinese organization wanted to ensure control by assigning their entrusted employees to the project. But many of the management positions were filled with Westerners, handpicked by the Chinese senior management team. The answer revealed itself over time, painting a rather interesting but complex picture of how the Chinese business psyche functioned.

As explained earlier, Chinese skilled and qualified resources are plentiful in China, and they are relatively cheap to employ. While Chinese unemployment was only 3.9 percent in 2017, many people are overqualified for the miserable, low paying jobs for which they were employed. They are available to take on any opportunity, even if in Africa, for a relatively low cost of employment (Trading Economics, Unemployment Rate).

A Chinese colleague once mentioned in passing that on Chinese construction sites (in China) the ratio of managers to workers is as high as one to eight, as lowly paid—but highly qualified—managers are readily available in China. Bringing out a horde of degreed engineers to Africa is certainly not a challenge. Secondly, it must be understood that most Chinese corporates are state owned, so by investing in the development of their workforce is beneficial, as the same employee will at some future date in all likelihood work for another state owned enterprise.

Initially, the large number of Chinese co-workers seemed a blessing—something Westerners were not used to—, which would enhance team performance and allow for much faster output of deliverables. But as already elaborated in Chapter 6 (The Emperor Rules), the work performance by our Chinese co-workers was mediocre at best; red tape and invisible directives, presumably coming from the Chinese senior management, constricted output and hampered the meeting of deadlines.

Our Chinese colleagues always appeared busy, like ants, scuttling from one desk to the next, checking lists, generating reports (in Mandarin) and questioning decisions made by Westerners. But they never really contributed to managing the critical workflow, solving problems and issues, and making key decisions. They were happy to repeat the same monotonous workday in and day out, never questioning the instructions coming from their superiors. And they appeared remarkably calm, courteous, and happy most of the time; raised voices and anger outbursts were restricted to a handful of occasions and then only by people in managerial roles.

The ants just carried on working, like robots, without ever complaining or faltering, working at the same pace; deadlines did not faze them in the least. The mediocre output, lack of accountability, and indifference to company drivers conflicted directly with Western business culture, which demands high output, personal accountability, a responsibility towards the corporate goals, and target driven performance.

The work routine was always the same, irrespective of

what deadlines had to be met and whether there was a crisis or not. All Chinese co-workers always arrived promptly at seven thirty A.M., took lunch from twelve A.M. to one thirty P.M., and then left the office at five P.M. However, after close of business, one or two Chinese colleagues always remained at work, until most Western colleagues were making their way home much later that evening. This was clearly a watch system; they were observing the patterns of the Western employees who were working after hours.

There was an expectation from the Chinese superiors that the Chinese co-workers were typically expected to work for another two to three hours at night, reporting regularly on the work progress made. It was a common occurrence to receive emails from the Chinese colleagues, sent at the dead of night or over weekends. Their work and private worlds appeared to be highly regulated, and mass stereotyped behavior was expected twenty-four hours a day. Even their weekend activities were organized for the group as a whole, largely restricted by transportation availability. The majority of Chinese employees were ferried by bus to and from work, and to organized events on the weekends.

Initially, Western colleagues would invite one or two of their direct Chinese colleagues to their private residences, only for the whole Chinese team to arrive over a weekend for a barbecue—collectivism in its raw essence.

KNOWLEDGE IS POWER

The Chinese employee appears to be working in a vacuum; he or she is not officially exposed to the overall company strategy, direction, and performance aspects.

One interesting observation is that any available information or knowledge is readily—albeit clandestinely—distributed between Chinese colleagues, although it is never shared with their Western colleagues. They keep each other informed of what scant information becomes available. It generally is data not meant for their attention—for example, commercial letters—but the commercial representative who had to write or distribute the letter, would send a copy to a small circle of his (Insider) colleagues, with whom he has a trust relationship. Trust is a key ingredient to building a harmonious relationship, and by default, the Chinese co-workers mistrust Westerners.

While the interaction between West and East was always courteous and overly formal, trust was established with difficulty and it was debatable whether true trust levels ever developed in the majority of formed relationships. By nature, Chinese people appear to mistrust each other, probably fearing that shared information or personal views and opinions could be divulged and used against them. A trust relationship must not be confused with the concept of 'face' (see Chapter 4, Mianzi). Giving face, saving face, and showing face when doing business in a Chinese business environment, is a factor of having a harmonious relationship, and fostering inter-relationships (the concept of 'Guanxi') but does not imply that each party trusts each other.

Very pertinent was the observation that knowledge was not readily shared from one management level to the next, or from the top management down to the employees. Clearly, in the Chinese business environment, knowledge equates to power. By minimizing the sharing of knowledge, individuals cannot pre-empt situations or make assertive decisions. It forces individuals to await further instructions before being able to act constructively and proactively in a situation.

This withholding of knowledge manifested itself in the most peculiar way. Chinese co-workers, arriving in Africa would have no idea what their rotation cycle back to China would be. Some individuals stayed in Africa as long as eleven months before being told one sunny morning that they would be on a flight out that same evening back to China.

Most of these people were married and had a child. They were at the mercy of a senior Chinese manager, who alone could decide who would rotate and when. Interestingly, this fate did not befall all. If the individual seemed affiliated with the Communist Party, either by being a card-carrying member or family connected, his or her home rotation cycle was much more regular and frequent.

These individuals also enjoyed other privileges, including the use of a rented car while on assignment in Africa. They were able to bring their families with them and had their own accommodation, whereas the majority of Chinese expatriates came over on single status, stayed in a commune, and were bussed to and from work. It became apparent that privileges are selectively awarded based on a combination of status within the organization, seniority, as well as communist party affiliation.

Some individuals flew back to China, but never returned, although they were clearly under the impression that they would be returning as all their belongings were left behind. Eventually, they would have to make their own arrangements to return their belonging back home. It was surmised that they were perceived to have under-performed or operated outside the expected norm, which prompted the Chinese management to send him or her back home on a one-way ticket. This action was never shared with the Western team leaders nor did they give any reason for the person not coming back. When enquiring about the expected return of the Chinese colleague, the courteous response was always that they were still awaiting the extension of their work permit.

SLEEPING WITH THE ENEMY

One peculiar behavior by a Chinese colleague that would guarantee short-term extradition back to China was if a Chinese colleague started forming a closer relationship with a non-Chinese colleague. It was indelible that these colleagues literally disappeared from one day to the next, the remaining Chinese colleagues citing that the individual had returned to China for his rest and recuperation period. However, they never returned and on enquiry, the Chinese colleagues gave vague explanations that these individuals had been reassigned into new roles back in China, but they were unable to give much more details about where in China, what department, contact details, or more in-depth details of the assignment.

As such, it was rare to have a discussion with a Chinese colleague on a one-to-one basis. Within minutes of engaging a Chinese colleague in discussion, another Chinese colleague would join the discussion circle, without necessarily participating in the discussion. This appeared to be a clear protection mechanism so that the Chinese individual would (1) not share confidential or controversial information for 'Chinese ears only', or (2) discuss taboo topics such as politics, or (3) most importantly, be singled out and accused by fellow Chinese colleagues of having infringed on items one or two.

On very rare occasions, I obtained a true opinion from one of my Chinese colleagues. This only happened when we found ourselves in a very isolated environment, for example being the only two company representatives on the same flight. And whatever opinions my Chinese colleague might have shared then, these were never to be repeated or acknowledged when we found ourselves back in the Chinese work spider web, where every wall appeared to be listening in and every Chinese colleague appeared to be observing the team interaction and workings.

PERFORMANCE

Performance, deemed unsatisfactory in the eyes of the Chinese management, is not acceptable in any form. While the general performance of the Chinese colleagues was viewed as bland by the Western colleagues most of the time, there was no doubt that they poured out the requisite data and reports satisfactorily for their Chinese superiors, as quarrels and reprimands were far and few between.

On one occasion, a Chinese junior engineer did err, a mistake that became known to the whole team and had some repercussions. The individual involved, was promptly sent back to China within days of the incident. He only returned some three months later, the Western colleagues by now having assumed that he had been sent to the Chinese back office permanently as punishment.

His arrival back in the office came as unannounced as his sudden departure. The usual 'work permit delay' excuse was given when one enquired about his movements. This incident highlighted the low tolerance for incorrect performance; another ant can easily replace an under-performing ant at any time.

In a few instances, some individuals never returned, and their work was allocated to another ant. This explains the low willingness by the Chinese employee to be bold, audacious, individualistic, intuitive, and accountable. Uniqueness is cut down like a long blade of grass protruding from a perfectly level lawn.

This was highlighted on a number of occasions when the Chinese persons, responsible for a certain area of work—in this case, an area manager—were asked whether they were dealing with any problems. The response was mind blowing as the individual said something along the lines of, *"I am waiting for my boss to tell me if there are any problems"*. The general lack of ownership was crystallized in one short response, a phenomenon germane to the Chinese work culture as a whole.

MASTER AND SERVANT

The lack of perceived enthusiasm and proactiveness to effectively and efficiently manage the job very quickly resulted in frustration by the non-Chinese colleagues, who were generally left to deal with any work issues without the assistance of their Chinese colleagues. Any requests for Chinese colleagues to assist were flatly ignored.

Raising this concern with the Western manager bore little fruit, as his or her continuous pleas for assistance by the Chinese team members also generally were ignored. The only option was to raise the concern to the senior Chinese management level and ultimately to the CEO. The CEO's rhetoric response curtailed any further ambition to try to manage the bigger Sino-Anglo team. The CEO courteously advised the Western team members that all the Chinese colleagues were being assigned to this expatriate work team, not to work, but to learn. It was not clarified whether they were to learn the ropes on their own or if they were to be coached and mentored by their non-Chinese work colleagues. The work environment very quickly disseminated into a Chinese work camp and a non-Chinese (or Western) work camp, going about their separate business.

While initially non-Chinese team members were under the clear impression that they had to fulfill a management responsibility, the work environment subjugated itself into a scenario where their decisions, opinions, and management instructions were largely ignored by the Chinese colleagues. However, these non-Chinese managers were still held accountable for the outcome of the team performance and in most cases, team non-performance. The Chinese leader would freely express his dissatisfaction with the lack of progress and achievement but would not entertain any criticism of the non-performance of the Chinese colleagues, which clearly formed part of the problem.

Continued under-performance of the team as a whole prompted the Chinese leader to appoint Chinese deputies for each non-Chinese manager. In most cases, these Chinese deputies did not have the experience to take on the responsibilities of such a role; however, the Chinese leader frowned upon any concern raised by the non-Chinese manager with regard to this appointment. Non-Chinese managers were thus reluctantly obliged to accept their deputies.

Often, one of the younger Chinese team members, who had been working directly under a Western manager, was appointed as his or her deputy. These deputies rarely cooperated with their Western superiors, did not take instruction, would not manage any delegated work, nor pass on instructions to the Chinese colleagues if such instructions indeed came from the non-Chinese manager. This was in part because the newly appointed deputies were way out of their depth contemplating how to deal with this new role, but also appeased any instruction coming down the unofficial Chinese management ladder, which allowed them little time to effectively manage the official deputy role in parallel. Also, they would not—or were incapable of—acting on behalf of their superior when the manager was absent.

The Western manager was often forced to ask another Western colleague on the team to execute his fiduciary duties while out of the office. This had to be done unofficially, as any official notification of such an approach would have irritated the Chinese senior management. With time, it became blatantly evident that the deputy role comprised an 'observe and report back' role. To put this into more stark words, the deputy was there to spy on the Western manager and report all behavior and managerial decisions back to the Chinese leader. It was not uncommon for the Western manager to be quizzed by the Chinese leader in a management meeting on numerous issues that had just occurred or were still in the process of being addressed and resolved.

More bizarrely, Chinese team members were swapped out intermittently into other areas of responsibility and other departments, without notifying their Western superior. This caused much consternation and upheaval, as managers were unable to achieve effective team alignment and teamwork.

PATRIOTISM

Chinese patriotism comes in many forms. It is all around one, ranging from interpersonal relationships, work practices, management style, appointment of the leaders, interaction with other Chinese strangers, and making use of their own creed. As discussed previously, Chinese citizens are entering Africa en masse. They come from all walks of life, representing the different echelons of Chinese society; from the street hawker competing with locals on every street corner, to prostitutes to entertain lonely men—not sure when they will be returning back to China—, right through to engineers, doctors, and scientists.

It is rumored in many African countries that China has brought Chinese convicts and prisoners to do blue-collar work. Presumably, it comes with a prequalification to behave and work hard in a foreign land and—if done properly for an allotted period—will secure freedom in this new economic colony. This can only be speculated, as it is notoriously difficult for Chinese compatriots to share the inner workings of the Chinese engine. Talking about such things is not even up for consideration as being found out could mean an immediate trip back to China.

Many Chinese companies have also established themselves on this new continent. And all these people need to be kept busy. During my dealings with my Chinese employer, it became evident that every Chinese citizen as well as every

Chinese company has an obligatory duty to look after his fellow 'countrymen'. This emulated itself in the most interesting way, as allotment of work and services had to be gently coached in the right direction.

Elaborate Western procurement processes, which could take weeks to finalize, were clandestinely redirected to facilitate it being awarded to a Chinese bidder. Where Chinese bidders were competing for the same opportunity, one bidder could easily disqualify itself with a new unsolicited tender submission, which now made this bidder more costly. Against normal Western work practices, this unsolicited submission had to be considered, as per instruction from the Chinese management. Clearly, the work was being directed to a specific Chinese contractor.

No doubt, the Chinese machine that has its cogs in remote Africa was geared to disseminate work evenly among the available Chinese contractors operating in the local environment. This will ensure longevity and sustainability of every Chinese contractor, and more importantly, secure the work place of every employed Chinese expatriate. It would be rather foolhardy for the expatriate Chinese contractors to be exposed to famine and feast, which would result in a fluctuating workforce, some of whom might have to be sent back temporarily to China at a great cost. This new Chinese anthill in Africa has quickly become self-sufficient and sustainable, ensuring the survival of the new African ant colony against all odds.

In many African countries—as in other countries around the world—Chinese population groups are establishing and expanding, starting to form considerable communities within their local areas of establishment. Many anthill colonies are springing up, and it is only a matter of time before super anthill communities will be established. There is no doubt that China is here to stay in Africa, securing access to commodities to feed its ants in its new territories as well as support the belly of the Tiger, lambasting in the Far East. Like ants expand their territories across hostile and unknown new real estate, so China is establishing themselves globally as a world order and colonizing new land with its people.

China's success can be based on foresight, tenacity, and courage. Many people make light work. Masses of people can ultimately achieve brilliance, even if it takes relentless effort. There are many worker ants, each one with no particular outstanding individual brilliance, but together they can move mountains, create new colonies, and change the landscape forever. They are highly motivated, forming a committed sea of yellow working in the interest of China, anywhere in the world where they are sent to. And they do it without demur, understanding the once in a lifetime opportunity that they have been given; back in China, they are just another urban ant, without much hope and aspiration.

CHAPTER 8

EDUCATION

*"Shall I teach you what knowledge? When you know a
thing, say that you know it; when you do not know a thing,
admit that you do not know it. That is knowledge"*

—Confucius

China has always been viewed from a distance by the West;
that far away mysterious land of hard working and productive
people, about whom we know very little. A country with
phenomenal GDP growth, generating every conceivable
product to be acquired in the West at nominal prices, surely
has to generate top end academics who can conceive better and
cheaper innovations to wow the non-Chinese markets in
acquiring Chinese products in preference to proven Western
products around the rest of the globe.

HISTORY EDUCATES

To understand the Chinese educational system, one must firstly
understand the Chinese educational history and modern
China's educational programs and institutions.

From the birth of China's history to the modern day, China as a people has always educated their kin. China is—after
all—one of the earliest collections of people who had aligned
cultural values; who developed the ability to record their lives

with the written word more than three thousand years ago. Even the earliest Chinese empires placed great value in educating their brethren to a desired state of knowledge so that they could add value to the task assigned to them. While people were still educated selectively, such skills development was not limited to the emperor's clan or to a fortunate few.

As we have already seen, one of the most well known Chinese philosophers was Confucius, who lived in the sixth and fifth century BC (551 – 479 BC). Confucian teachings continue to be ingrained in Chinese culture from an early age. Confucian education has been entrenched in the Chinese psyche to such a degree that it has taken on religious overtures, comprising one of the three major religions being practiced (again) in mainland China. The Eastern Zhou (771 – 256 BC) dynasty were the first to enshrine the Confucian teachings and values into their political and social codes (Lovell, The Great Wall, Page 48). While the moral values of Confucianism have shaped the Chinese nation in many ways, Confucian education has also always comprised a complex level of Chinese ancient teachings, including poetry, verse, and rhyme. Candidates had to learn realms of such poesy off by heart just to be able to enter into a civil service role. While the actual learning material had little relevance for the post to be fulfilled, high emphasis was placed on being able to regurgitate such teachings. This educational ideology entrenched itself into the Chinese scholarly system and structure to the present day.

All Chinese scholars are compelled to write the Gaokao higher education exam, a grueling nine-hour paper under strict surveillance over two days. This single exam determines the future of every individual in China. Without this achievement, all tertiary education options are effectively unavailable for future education. So the schooling system already entrenches a culture of parrot fashion learning, rather than an intuitive and enquiring mindset.

When first exposed to the Chinese company that employed me, I was introduced to a plethora of highly educated Chinese colleagues. Everyone had a master's degree and quite a few had doctorates. The work teams were made up of large numbers of Chinese staff, which at first gave the impression that the work output was more valued over cost drivers (Chinese remunerations are low when compared to those of the West). I anticipated an interactive, highly skilled team environment at the onset.

In reality, the Chinese work environment panned out to be rather different (also see Chapter 6: The Emperor Rules, and Chapter 7: Urban Ants); it all related back to an educational system that shaped a nation with a business culture quite foreign to Western business values and expectations. While they all had impressive qualifications, they were not armed with the ability to think and solve problems on their own. They would rather discuss problems internally and wait for the leader to provide a solution. Highly qualified people would then implement this solution without question, even if it was evident that the solution would fail. Companies did not benefit from their highly qualified employees for two reasons; (1) due to the qualification being obtained by learning the study material in parrot fashion; and (2) due to the cultural aspect of the leadership solution always trumping all other inputs.

I AM ALWAYS RIGHT

Many of our Chinese team members had a university Master's degree. While a Master's degree comes with certain attained qualities in Western countries, it quickly became apparent that the ability of a Chinese graduate couldn't be directly compared to a Western education. While individuals had a good knowledge of the theory, they struggled to apply it pragmatically in the work environment.

The single most important aspect lacking in educated Chinese persons is that they tend to lack intuition. While they were able to recognize problems, many Chinese colleagues were unable to resolve the problem or indeed find a suitable solution. They could not resolve highly complex problems; instead, they tackled issues in bits and pieces. Their approach involved trying to achieve an outcome by implementing a number of potential solutions in series. Each sub-solution failed to take cognizance of the desired outcome, which often resulted in the solution approach going off target. Once they realized this, they would tackle the problem afresh.

Western opinion was largely ignored as the Chinese colleagues held their own clandestine meetings to try to resolve the issue. They again actioned their determined solution without notifying their Western superior or Western team members. In parallel and unknowingly, the Western team colleagues also implemented their determined solutions. Once the two separate solutions crossed paths, the issue typically came to a head, and the conflict situation was then immediately elevated to the most senior Chinese leader who would immediately interject and instruct his recommended solution. Of course, solutions would be skewed in favor of the proposed

Chinese solution. After all, it was not optional for the Chinese team to 'lose face'—even if their solution turned out to be less effective.

In Chinese culture, the leader has to be seen as knowing everything at all levels of detail. Thus, senior Chinese managers would concoct a preferred solution, often with some input from a Chinese advisor. This solution is never up for debate, even if the recommended solution is not ideal.

As already discussed in Chapter 4 – Mianzi, it is not advisable to challenge the Chinese leader, as he (and subsequently you) would then invariably lose face. Certainly, the Chinese team members will never consider challenging the recommendations made by their leader. They would rather follow the instruction blindly, even if that would lead to further delay and cost. Chinese leaders take any formal challenges very personally, especially with others present. If such challenges are deemed necessary, this should be done very carefully and with utmost diplomacy. Ideally, one should have a one-on-one discussion with a Chinese leader before he is obliged to propose his solution (once elevated to this level). In this environment he might consider an alternative approach, but only if he will not be exposed.

Unfortunately, the Chinese management team will often consider their solution in parallel and in isolation and propose a way forward while the team back in the office is still fine-tuning their solution. It takes much foresight and careful planning to pre-empt the actions by the Chinese management and try to timeously interject in order to keep the work progress on the right path. If the Chinese management has lost faith in the ability of non-Chinese team members to resolve the issues in the best interest of the Chinese façade (rather than in the best interest of the work progress), then it becomes a rather futile exercise to try to sway the opinion of the Chinese management. It is expected that any Chinese solution is not only actioned, but will be successful in resolving the issue.

ANALYSIS VERSUS INTERPRETATION

Chinese colleagues have the inept ability to sift through tons of data and find the relevant key information. When trying to identify an issue, one needs to clearly specify what data needs to be assimilated or summarized. It doesn't help to only advise a Chinese colleague of the problem, and expect him to find the right data in support. Instructions need to be clear.

Also, don't inform him or her of the reason he needs to analyze the data, as this will sidetrack him. In Western culture, we believe in informing someone as to the reason for doing the work. This is somewhat counterproductive with Chinese colleagues.

The Chinese colleague should then be able to rather efficiently extract the data from many sources and compile it in the requested format. They will be able to compare data from one source to the next, quickly identifying any discrepancies. However, they cannot interpret the impact of the wrong data, or indeed deduce a pattern or trend of collated data anomalies. Data differences, e.g. decimal commas out by a factor, when compared to another source, can be identified quickly, but they cannot identify the compounded impact on other work easily.

CENTRAL DATABASE

Interacting with Chinese colleagues on a day-to-day basis, it became ostensive that Chinese compatriots want to observe as much from the Western environment in which they find themselves, as possible.

Individuals vigorously gathered information, regardless of whether they are aware of the meaning and proper application of such information. They would even gather information that did not directly involve their field of expertise.

Chinese colleagues always volunteered to visit service providers, fabrication shops, and consultants. Remarkably, they would photograph everything, including arbitrary layouts, and safety signs on factory walls and general work areas.

To an outside observer, it appears that Chinese workers are expected to collate data of everything in which they are involved. To substantiate this behavior, one might notice that the Chinese colleagues will want a copy of everything and anything that is produced by their Western counterparts in the workplace. However, Chinese colleagues are not prepared to share the simplest Chinese generated flowchart or document, which they consider intellectual property in their mind. This could become rather frustrating as a Chinese colleague would present a concept in a meeting, but then he or she would be rather unwilling to share a copy of such information with the rest of the team, especially with their Western colleagues.

Although it is not possible to provide direct evidence (and Chinese colleagues were unwilling to even discuss the possibility of this behavior), it is thought that the collected data is possibly sent to a central information database. Once they had collected enough data on a specific topic, the Chinese industrial engine can very quickly get a feel of the best practices employed in the West, and implement such practices in their own factories and businesses across China and around the world.

It is no secret that China is good at producing consumer goods, based on technology already available around the world. China reverse engineers technology and once successful, will mass produce it for the export market outside China, where the technology in all probability originated, but now will be available to those countries at a much more affordable price.

Over the years, I have come across a number of Chinese citizens now residing in the West. In particular, one such person who I worked with has an interesting tale to share about his journey to the West.

In the early nineties, the first South African Trade Mission visited many Chinese cities and factories. As many Chinese people do not command the English language, it is emblematic for the Chinese host to provide a translator who is proficient in both Mandarin and English. One of the South African Chairpersons of a rather large, well-established South African Engineering company was rather impressed with one of the translators at one of the Chinese companies. He emphatically joked with the translator that he is always welcome in South Africa and should he ever decide to immigrate to South Africa, he could have a job at his company.

The South African Trade Mission came to an end and the South African delegation returned home. Some two weeks later, the chairperson received a frantic call from reception at his company, cautioning him of an unknown visitor insisting on seeing him. Intrigued, the chairperson awaited the arrival of the visitor who turned out to be none other than the Chinese translator with whom he had crossed paths some two weeks earlier in China.

The translator exhorted that he had come to South Africa for the promised employment. Perplexed, the chairperson had little choice but to employ him. Some twenty-five years later, the translator, who now works as a qualified engineer, is still in the employ of the same company.

Another interesting Chinese character has resided in North America for the last twenty-five years. He lives a Western lifestyle, has three children, and works for Western companies. What is rather intriguing about this character—as well as the translator and other Chinese citizens now living as expatriates in Western countries—is that they are still as Chinese as their countrymen living in downtown Beijing. Even after a quarter-century of living outside of China, their command of the English language is challenged and they still have a very strong accent. Their mannerisms are typically Chinese and the entrenched Chinese psyche is vividly noticeable.

One would think that they would have adapted to a Western business culture, but typically they are still well entrenched in the Chinese business culture. Astonishingly, they adhered to all the Chinese business practices when engaging with Chinese companies and Chinese business people. Requests for them to challenge the Chinese client or ask sensitive questions in Mandarin were ignored. They are unwilling to challenge counterparts on the opposite team due to the deep-set line of respect and Communist hierarchy that is invisible to a Westerner.

Typically, Western based Chinese expatriates still have

family ties back in China and they clearly understand their place within the bigger Chinese picture. Therefore, it is in their interest to ensure that they avoid a potential backlash by the Chinese authorities against their families back in China.

While it is near impossible to provide direct evidence of such interactions (unless you work for the Chinese authorities or do some risky investigative journalism), it can be deduced from daily news reels that Chinese authorities are not very tolerant of people behaving counter-intuitively of Chinese ideology. In 2017, the CIA announced that some thirty odd Chinese CIA operatives in China had either been eliminated or incarcerated by Chinese authorities over a period of two years (effectively stifling their intelligence-gathering ability in China). Many more examples exist of senior Chinese officials being put on trial for alleged corruption and bribery charges. They are taken out of the system if they are seen to no longer be aligned with the Chinese mantra. China does not engage in press freedom and so it is notoriously difficult to get anybody to admit this authoritarian behavior, as it may not be spoken about to any Outsiders.

One prominent case did however make the international news spectacularly in 2013. Bo Xilai, a high ranking CPC member and once a rising political star who was once considered a potentially suitable candidate for China's most senior political body, was put on trial on charges of corruption, bribery, abuse of power, and embezzlement. His wife, Gu Kailai, was also put on trial for allegedly having killed a British businessman. Bo was the "princeling" son of a famous Communist veteran. He was also the leader of Chongqing, a group that made waves leading high-profile populist campaigns. Their one focus was the drive against organized crime (Rediff).

It was alleged that Bo's most serious crime had been his ruthless anti-gang campaign, which was not mentioned at all during his trial. While Bo Xilai denied all charges against him, he received a life sentence, and his wife Gu received a suspended death sentence for the murder of Neil Heywood. Some associates and people, seen as close to or critical of Bo's trial were also arrested and put on trial while others suddenly resigned from their positions (Rediff).

President Xi Jinping continues his steady efforts to consolidate control, clean up the party, and sideline opponents with a series of detentions and arrests. Xi Jinping has sought to restore the party's credibility by attacking "flies and tigers"—corrupt junior and senior officials at all levels. Joseph Cheng, professor of political science at the City University of Hong Kong, is of the view that cases such as Bo's seemed to have more to do with political maneuvering and their outcomes appeared to have been agreed before charges were laid. According to The Guardian, he said, *"If you look at these trials, the defendants all admit their guilt quietly; they don't claim to offer important revelations about other networks and supporters; and they get very lenient sentences"*. Often, the life sentences are commuted after a few years, or the accused is given medical parole early during the jail term.

So getting back to Chinese people working in the West— as much as these individuals behave in a Western way in a Western environment when engaging with Western people, they immediately re-characterize themselves when dealing with Chinese citizens, even when operating outside China.

Many Chinese citizens emigrated to the West as from the early 90s, as soon as Deng Xiaoping opened China up for trade with the West. Their sole purpose was to learn from the West, share collected knowledge with mainland China, and probably report on fellow Chinese expatriates who step out of line. Again, it is hard to prove that the Chinese authorities enforce this behavior, but it is a well-known fact that in Communist countries, citizens are expected to spy on each other and they are expected to work in the best interest of their home country and not that of the host country.

A former work colleague, having come from one of the former European East bloc countries, elaborated this behavior. In exchange for a Western job being paid in hard currency, he was expected to tell on expatriate colleagues and otherwise share his observations and work knowledge gathered with authorities back home. Importantly, if a colleague spoke badly of the Communist Party or of its dealings, he was expected to report on that person. And traps were set, where one colleague would purposely scathe the political system, only to see if his other colleagues would report him. Not reporting somebody would result in immediate political harassment, possibly trials, and potential prison sentences. The communist network of surveillance and intelligentsia is all encompassing on a global level.

These Chinese expatriates still regularly visit the Chinese mainland and some have now even started working for Chinese enterprises again, operating outside China.

I AM CHINA

Western people see the poor command of a Western language as a barrier for Chinese to succeed in an alien Western working environment. While the spoken English language challenges many Chinese, the true barrier is their inability to intuitively apply their learning in a fast moving and dynamic world. Chinese expatriates are obliged to behave in a certain way that complies with the mantra of the Communist Party of China (CPC). They are allowed very little room to adapt their behavior and work practices to suit the local environment (outside China) in which they operate. Rather, they try to enforce Chinese behavior and business practices onto the local population. They make no real effort to understand local culture, interpersonal behavior, business practices, or indeed the local psyche. Chinese management shuns any efforts made to align these very different cultures in order to create team spirit. Consequently, the work environment becomes stressed with no trust between team members being fostered, a fundamental requirement if team alignment and team effectiveness is to be achieved. The ongoing mistrust ultimately creates a toxic work environment, where work productivity by team members on all sides is impaired.

Chinese people see themselves as superior to other nationalities. They believe that they have a superior education, culture, and social structure—something other races will never achieve. While courteous when engaging, Chinese people will always appear to be speaking to non-Chinese people with an air of aloofness. A definite level of indifference and disrespect for other nationalities gives one the distinct feeling that Chinese nationals are intolerant towards other races.

As a race and culture, China does not trust in the capability and capacity of non-Chinese citizens. This ingrained belief does not bode well for cultural tolerance and intercultural relationship building. They do however tolerate other cultures if this has a distinct benefit for them – look at their relationship with African governments and the resultant access to mineral wealth as an example.

THE DEVIL IS IN THE DETAIL

Command of knowledge is highly revered in Chinese culture. Any competent person must be able to regurgitate the most intricate details of a subject or otherwise he or she is not viewed as a wise person who is worthy of the task. This appears to go hand-in-hand with the Chinese educational standard, starting with the Gaokao in modern times and going back millennia; having become entrenched in the Chinese culture where learning and reciting arbitrary information—from poems to administrative processes—is more highly sought after than resolving issues with logic and intuition. The order of the day is to first demonstrate the details of an assignment before executing the assignment. One must demonstrate the in-depth knowledge of a subject to be worthy of being able to execute the work.

This is counterintuitive to Western business culture where a strategy is first developed around how to deal with a task or issue, the strategy is debated, and once accepted by management, the framework is developed before the detail is collated. The approach to problem solving is worlds apart in the Chinese and Western educational practices, thus creating direct conflict in the way business is accomplished. In many cases where a problem was pointed out to the Chinese leader, he would immediately start posing detailed questions on the issue and if one was unable to answer these questions in accurate detail, he would dismiss one's approach to solving the problem or even dismiss the fact that there was a problem.

This expectation exemplified itself repeatedly in the workplace. The Chinese leader would target and question a Western subordinate incessantly to reveal more detail about a specific subject until he or she failed to answer satisfactorily, only to be lambasted, and ridiculed in front of all about his or her inability to do his or her work to the expectation of the Chinese organization. This approach served several purposes; (1) to abase the subordinate by sheer brunt into his or her rank category; (2) it served to create a potential reason for future dismissal; (3) to demonstrate to all present who the person with all the power was; and (4) to show everyone that the leader was indeed deeply knowledgeable about the most infinitesimal details of the business or project. It is assumed that the person asking all the elaborate and detailed questions already knows the answers and only wants to understand whether his or her subordinates have the same level of ingrained understanding.

CHAPTER 9

THE ANGRY TIGER

"You will never know how sharp a sword is
unless it's drawn from its sheath."
—*Confucius*

If Confucius left the Chinese people with one indelible thought, then it was the art of practicing harmony in a tumultuous and chaotic environment. While Chinese people sometimes let their guard down and may be observed in an annoyed and angry state, they can do even that with an air of patient virtue.

Three thousand years of Chinese history quickly revealed a people not driven by short-term material objectives, but rather by ethereal virtues of eternal achievement. Personal achievements are never recognized, acknowledged, or rewarded. One's contribution is for the greater good of a nation, of a people and of its place in the universe.

Expressions of anger are used rather as a negotiating tool than as a display of genuine emotional frustration. As quickly as a situation turns into an explosive turmoil, it can diffuse into instant harmony. People will be at each other's throats the one minute and then share a laugh the next.

Frustration and anger is usually seen in people dealing with their Chinese counterparts. Non-Chinese people—but especially Western people—like to deal with issues at the moment and resolve the best way forward now. Western discussions will be to the point, factual, and focused. The Chinese approach any issues requiring resolution in a circum-vented and convoluted strategy that leaves most Western people confused, distrusting, and impatient; and often feeling that the issue is not resolved but rather ignored or side-stepped. This leaves Westerners to believe that the issue is still there and still needs to be addressed, while the Chinese team acts as if the issue has been dealt with.

By nature, Chinese people do not like dealing with conflict in a direct and transparent manner. After all, their predecessors have preached and practiced Confucian philosophy of harmonious co-existence for millennia. Direct conflict is outright avoided at best, with only the odd Chinese team member adopting a Western approach to conflict resolution. This mostly leads to a dismal situation that inflames rather than resolves a conflict situation. Chinese people are poor at conflict resolution in the context of a Western work ethic.

ENTROPY

Ironically, Chinese managers appear to be masters at creating conflict situations. One gets the distinct impression that a harmonious work environment is discouraged; that a high conflict and high entropy work situation thrives in a Chinese work environment. So how can these two situations co-exist—one where conflict between people is avoided in the work environment and where the state of efficient operation and co-existence is constantly challenged to create highly stressed and charged tension at the best of times?

Chinese people are essentially driven by two simple rules: (1) Harmonious relationships are paramount to one's existence. (2) One has to challenge the status quo continuously to achieve the best outcome. While this is not that different in other cultures, the method of achieving it does differ greatly.

Harmony is a state of mind, rather than a state of situation. While Western people will judge a situation by the external factors that cause it, Chinese people will exist in a mental state of harmony with their immediate relational fellow citizens, even if the external environment is in a state of chaos. As long as the mental harmony is maintained, there is actually no perceived conflict. In the Chinese mind, conflict is created mentally; in the Western world, conflict between people is created by external factors. This opens the further debate around how one can possibly not be affected by external factors.

After all, disparity, inequality, and war can only lead to one party resenting the other. Again, this results from cultural values that have been nurtured in a nation driven by Confucian values and the belief that one's existence on earth is foreordained. Additionally, Chinese belief prescribes that relationships are determined at birth and destined for a lifetime, and not as a result of interacting with strangers who then start relating to your life (either in a good or bad way). Harmonious relationships are thus created by fate and destiny and not by interaction and co-existence in the same space. Harmony also starts in the smallest circle of relationships, which is the family entity. Harmony will emanate within the family, and spread to wider family circles, which in turn, will create a harmonious nation.

Thus, Chinese work teams are often made up of family members and long term family acquaintances that have worked together for most of their lives. And these 'family' work groups will move together through their lives in both the work and social environment, as fate has brought them together on the journey of life.

It is rather common for Chinese work teams to consist of both capable and incapable team members. The fact that incapable Chinese team members have a permanent and protected space within the Chinese team is inexplicable to the Western mind. One fails to understand why such team members are not challenged for poor performance; let alone challenged in front of any non-Chinese colleagues. This can create frustration and ultimately angers Western people.

The Tiger is not angry; however, anger has been induced by the Tiger into the immediate environment. High entropy is continuously achieved by putting organizational teams under continuous pressure to perform better, having to report on performance (on issues not yet closed out effectively), and being reprimanded for perceived under-performance. The Chinese leader thrives on acquiring reports from various sources, which he uses to create entropy as the reports inevitably differ.

Chinese co-workers rarely show anger towards each other or towards their non-Chinese colleagues. At the outset it appears that nothing can shake them into reactive anger. Even when showing visible frustration towards a Chinese colleague, he or she typically maintains a calm composure. The more one tries to extract a reaction and response out of them, the less they appear to revert to such requests. Non-Chinese people become visibly angry and frustrated in such situations, seemingly unable to entice an expected reaction.

While Chinese colleagues do not openly and directly tempt a confrontation, their mannerisms can induce heated reactions from their Western counterparts. Chinese colleagues will typically nag for the same information, even if they are told explicitly that such information is not yet available or ready for sharing. They will stubbornly bug the Western colleagues. Frustratingly, they will insist upon a commitment, when such a commitment is premature.

Typically, Westerners will willingly give an approximate assignment completion date. When that deadline is missed for whatever internal or external reason, the Chinese colleague will insist on the deliverable and no explanation or counter argument will suffice. No doubt, the Chinese colleague has made a commitment on the deliverable up his or her Chinese command chain, and he or she will be in trouble if the deliverable cannot be produced on time as promised. Failure to deliver in a Chinese environment is paramount to treason, and is not taken lightly. A Chinese colleague and the Chinese leadership will lose respect and face and will view you as being incapable of doing your job if you continue missing promised deadlines—even if it is not your fault. Chinese business takes agreed deadlines very seriously.

They insist on optimistic target dates—often agreed with the Chinese leader under duress—and failure to achieve these target dates puts one into a serious negative light. The alternative—to not be bullied into accepting an unrealistic target date or assignment—is also viewed with disdain and mistrust. Either way, you will find yourself caught in a difficult situation, having little room to maneuver out of a precarious situation forced upon you by the Chinese expectations in the first place. When you are forced to take a certain 'fatal flaw' direction, it is always wise to document it in writing, with utmost care and tact.

It is in the nature of the beast for the Tiger to corner you into a tight spot and to challenge your ingenuity and ability. While harmony between people is of paramount importance, the Tiger must always challenge what others are doing, and in doing so, will challenge himself to perform at his optimum.

The Chinese management team always creates more and new unrealistic deadlines in order to make you feel as though you are constantly failing. This forces you to eventually go on the defensive. It takes your eye off the ball of actually doing your job and you will spend vast amounts of time and energy explaining why you missed a deadline. Even this explanation will not be accepted, as the leader believes you should have managed the situation better—regardless of the fact that he disempowered you.

INFORMERS

Chinese management makes use of informers—strategically placed throughout the organization—to gather information about everyone and everything. Nobody really knows who the informers are, although—with time—it does become blatantly apparent who is asking the questions and who is aware of situational details. Not cooperating with the informers—usually people who don't work directly with you—is as detrimental as providing only vague information or being totally transparent. One of the most blatant methods by which Chinese informers inform their leader is to provide him with feedback on meetings. It starts with somebody taking pictures of the meeting attendees, which is then immediately sent to the Chinese leaders. Further, the meeting progress is reported back to the Chinese leader while the meeting is still in progress. From the photos taken at the start of the meetings, the leader will then be able to criticize over-attendance or lack of attendance. The meeting chairperson can expect a call from the Chinese leader as soon as the meeting has been called to an end. Any unresolved issues—or issues not addressed to the satisfaction of the Chinese leader—are immediately queried, providing little chance for the meeting chairperson to explain or first rectify issues immediately after the meeting. One is always on the proverbial back foot, without sufficient time to deal with issues that have just been raised.

Western style meetings are often about management getting information from the team on the work and discussing issues and either resolving them in the meeting, or if this is not possible, then setting up a session outside of the meeting to reach a resolution. Chinese see this as weak, because in their culture a meeting is not about management getting feedback. After all, the Chinese leader already knows the status from his parallel reporting line.

Meetings are also not about discussing issues, as the leader will tell you what to do, rather than discussing what should be done. Chinese meetings are about the leader doing the talking and everyone else listening. If the leader asks you a question, be aware. This is normally a sign that he will pull your answer apart or ask more and more detail in order to target you.

The Chinese leader will puzzle together the facts on the

ground by triangulating information from multiple informers, as well as occasionally requesting status updates directly from team members. Once concerns are identified, the Chinese leader will call random meetings at short notice to challenge team members.

Information provided by informers is often skewed, as the informant may be reluctant to tell the truth that no longer aligns with his previous version of events.

Internal communication between Chinese colleagues is much better as it prepares them for such meetings. Western team members are often summoned to a meeting with Chinese management at short notice. In what appears to be a conspiracy, the Chinese leader will gladly accept the version of a Chinese colleague, while failing to accept the version of a Western colleague.

Allegiance across Chinese reporting lines is clear. That is where the family ties and relationships have been nurtured for decades. A Chinese leader will not allow any of his compatriots to lose face, especially not in front of an Outsider. The Chinese management uses such meetings to target one or two Western team members and give them a good scolding in front of all. As already highlighted in the previous Chapter, the targeted individual is typically quizzed at great length until he finally cannot answer anymore. This is then seen as a failure of competency, and the individual receives a few verbal lashings.

CHINESE WORK CULTURE

This Chinese management approach is interpreted as precipitating frustration and anger, but it is really just a management methodology. Chinese business culture pushes individuals beyond their comfort levels and exposes them to situations for which they are ill prepared. In this way, everybody is always expecting to be challenged, and this keeps him or her constantly engrossed in the detail, which provides a level of comfort to the Chinese management. If you understand the detail, then you must be able to execute the work effectively.

The job of each team member is to execute specific work tasks. These tasks must be delivered blindly, without worrying too much about external issues that might affect these individual tasks. Further, one's individual work must not attempt to consider how it would fit in with other areas of work. The work should be carried out exactly as per instructions received—no more and no less.

In short, lateral and strategic thinking by individual team members is not at all encouraged. This is left to the leaders who will mull over new tactics. Once such new strategized tactics are agreed, the individual who will have to execute the task will be notified of the new work output requirements; however, the overall new strategic approach will not be shared with the wider team.

In fact, communication is one of the biggest hazards in Chinese-run enterprises. Communication is on a need-to-know basis only. Different work team echelons do not communicate vertically up and down with one another in a transparent manner. Chinese colleagues often fail to share—and purposely ignore—requested information, resulting in the Western team members eventually giving up after numerous requests. It all comes down to 'knowledge is power', a management style that was disused in Western companies back in the eighties.

Sometimes, a Chinese leader will give an instruction directly to a lower level employee, bypassing his superior entirely, especially if the immediate manager is not Chinese. Written communication is shunned, as it establishes a record. Decisions are seldom recorded in writing, as they can otherwise be traced back to the original decision maker. Instead, information is passed on orally along unofficial communication hierarchies.

In many instances, Westerners only find out about decisions made once the decision is being implemented. This poor communication often leads to frustration and ultimately Western team members start distrusting the Chinese management.

Trust is ultimately the cornerstone of any successful undertaking. Sound management can influence team alignment and transparency. However, trust is earned and teamwork will develop over time, as trust is established between team members and with an effective management culture. If trust and transparency cannot be achieved, then the team is unlikely to achieve their objectives.

If Chinese people feel that their trust has been breached, then they will try to expose the 'guilty party' in open forums. And to breach that trust is as easy as not agreeing with a Chinese colleague on his or her viewpoint, or challenging their work output. Exposing Western colleagues is attempted by questioning issues that have already been resolved or bringing issues to light where one has not reached consensus with the Chinese colleague yet. It is clearly another subtle form of intimidation used to try to show the Western person up as being incapable of doing his or her job to the expectation of the Chinese employer. And as the Western colleague is an

Outsider, Confucian Harmony, Mianzi, and Guanxi are waived in these conflict situations.

Western business culture encourages individualism, as well as rewarding and recognizing initiative and intuition. One is encouraged to identify and highlight any issues and concerns, which can be addressed and debated in a collective meeting forum. The person, department, or entity directly responsible for the area of concern is given the opportunity to rectify the situation with adequate support from other parties and management, as required. The issue at hand is dealt with in a transparent manner, to facilitate quick resolve.

In a Chinese work environment, problem solving is handled in the most peculiar manner, rather different to a Western norm.

Remarkably, senior Chinese management does not at all encourage workers to bring problems and issues to the surface. There is also no purpose or conviction by the team to identify any concerns for a greater audience. Any identified problems are dealt with quietly on the side. In fact, problems highlight a disunity and dysfunction of the team and therefore team members rarely raise any issues in a formal environment, such as meetings.

Meetings become a mundane act, mostly used to communicate the views and instructions from the Chinese leaders down to the team. It is not uncommon for a senior Chinese leader at the highest position within the organization to randomly join meetings and take over the chairperson role, irrespective of who has called the meeting. This in itself discourages team members from bringing bad news into a formal discussion environment. Problems are generally the result of a string of issues that have compounded, such as the result of human error—not just one person but the multiple inputs or lack thereof of a group of people closely associated around a task driven deliverable. Thus, identifying a problem area would immediately implicate multiple people, who would in essence all lose face in front of each other as well as with their management. Practicing the principles of Mianzi and Guangxi, this would seriously test the devoir of Confucian principles of harmony.

In the interest of maintaining long-lasting relationships, it is not favorable to implicate any of your Chinese colleagues in any matters of controversy. The same cannot be said when the issue at hand can be blamed on a non-Chinese colleague. After all, they do not prescribe to Confucian principles, something that one is only entitled to by birthright. As such, pointing out a problem to the Chinese leader that squarely falls in the lap of a non-Chinese colleague would not upset the principles of Yin and Yang energy. Many a Western colleague are rather perplexed when a perceived issue—not fully understood by his or her Chinese colleague—is raised at a critical forum, usually when the Chinese leader is in attendance. Such information may also be divulged to the Chinese leader before engaging in a meeting environment, without sharing the Chinese colleague's concern with the Western colleague beforehand. It typically comes as a great surprise when a problem is raised directly by the Chinese leader about an issue that is not actually a problem.

When the Western colleague defends or justifies the issue, the Chinese leader will become louder and verbally aggressive. Ultimately, it is wise to avoid agitating the situation further, even if you are right. Simply continue to absorb the accusations and readily accept the solutions offered by the Chinese leader, even if such a solution is not required or nor beneficial. As one has no idea who informed the leader of the perceived issue, it bears little use to try to extract such information during the forum discussion. One is unlikely to ever get to the bottom of where the highlighting of the 'problem' originated. One has to accept the status quo and move on, or else one ends in a state of annoyance and resentment.

Western team members—new to the team and not understanding the principles of Mianzi, Guangxi, and Confucian Harmony—will eagerly trouble shoot, identify problems, and deal with them directly with the responsible person. The responsible person, often a Chinese colleague, will typically not acknowledge or indeed agree to action the problem or issue; after all, he or she will lose face. Frustratingly, the Western colleague is then compelled to raise the issue to management, typically in a meeting environment—where one normally raises issues, deals with conflict, proposes plausible solutions, and makes corrective decisions for actioning. Of course, this typical Western approach results in consternation. And the Chinese leader, rather than trying to understand the source of the problem, will start questioning the Western informant on the problem, expecting him or her to understand the full details of the problem and to resolve it.

If you identify a problem, you by default become accountable for the problem, even if the problem falls outside your sphere of expertise. This approach quickly encourages Western team members to abstain from raising any issues in a formal environment. Rather, they will attempt to resolve the issue themselves with any willing assistance, normally from other Western team members. Being unable to communicate any issues vertically upwards and directly with Chinese colleagues introduces a huge inefficiency factor that very quickly affects the performance of the team and the quality of the outcome.

By fate and conviction, a Chinese leader is compelled to believe what he is being told by his Chinese subordinates. The relationship is based on long-standing trust, after all. The same principle does not apply when Chinese people engage with a non-Chinese person.

Chinese believe that people are always out to optimize their own positions. They view Non-Chinese people (Outsiders) as willing to manipulate a situation to their own benefit. As fate has not determined there to be an umbilical relationship connection, by default, any interaction must be carefully interpreted, as there is no need to preserve face or maintain a relationship with Outsiders, especially Westerners. Interaction with other people, who are not part of your fated inner circle, must therefore always be interpreted with caution. Any interaction comes down to some form of negotiation; the Chinese party careful not to be outdone and outsmarted by his or her Western counterpart. This explains why interactions with Chinese colleagues are generally unrewarding; Chinese colleagues rarely tend to open up. Discussions are kept at a superficial level and if the discussion issue becomes too complex or too involved, a Chinese counterpart will typically start withdrawing from the conversation. Sharing too much knowledge could give the non-Chinese discussion partner an edge in future negotiations. In the true sense, Chinese communication behavior can be interpreted as a 'closed door' approach, and in light of interactions being limited, Chinese people come across as being mistrusting, cagey, and sly.

It is near impossible to build meaningful relationships—which are the key to more open and constructive communication—with Chinese people. After all, relationships are something that one is born into in the eye of Chinese culture. Any Outsider relationships that one builds during one's lifetime are there purely to achieve certain objectives, and will only be maintained for as long as the relationship is of benefit. As soon as the objective has been achieved—or your usefulness has expired—, the relationship will revert to that of a superficial and courteous acquaintance. Seldom will a friendship develop that will be maintained outside the work environment or indeed after each party moves onto other challenges in other parts of the world. As observed previously, it might indeed be detrimental for Chinese people to stay in touch or maintain a relationship with people who are not a part of their inner circle, as this could be interpreted as breach of trust with all his or her inner circle relations. Also, maintaining a relationship with non-Chinese people over extended periods might be seen as treason against the values of Chinese culture as well as the party values of the CPC.

CONFLICT MANAGEMENT

It is a known fact that Chinese culture does not encourage direct conflict. Chinese conflict is therefore dealt with in a most peculiar way. Conflict in a professional environment needs to be dealt with swiftly and effectively. In a Western business environment, conflict management in an open forum is encouraged. Of course, there might be situations where conflict needs to be dealt with on a one-to-one basis, but if the issue involves multiple parties, meetings provide a typical environment in which to address conflict.

When raising a conflict issue in the Chinese business environment, it is unlikely to receive an initial response from any of the meeting participants. In fact the issue raised is flatly ignored and only minuted if insisted upon—and then with great reluctance. It all comes back to the same thing; conflict is created by people and by raising a conflict issue, you will cause somebody to lose face. As such, conflict discussions are avoided altogether—to the uninitiated Western colleague, this may all seem rather perplexing.

The best way to deal with conflict in a Chinese work environment is to raise the perceived conflict directly to the highest level of the Chinese leadership team that can be accessed in a one-on-one discussion. One must enter the conversation well prepared, present the problem in all its detail, and at the same time embed the solution tactfully into the discussion, for the Chinese leader to be able to interpret. The Chinese leader will then embrace the solution as his own—if he is in agreement with it—and pass it down the silent Chinese management structure to the affected Chinese colleague, who will then be obliged to accept and implement the solution. And viola, the conflict is resolved. Alternatively, the Chinese leader may suggest his or her solution and instruct that it be implemented. This is still a better scenario than the unresolved conflict situation.

One must realize that conflict often arises as a result of a difference in opinion. Westerners should take care and understand that the Chinese opinion on an issue will always be favored. You need to employ a strategy to get your opinion heard and accepted. This strategy is through the Chinese leader as he is the only one who has the power to override a Chinese colleague. You must however, ensure that the leader takes on your opinion as his own, and this is achieved in one-on-one discussions where you present your opinion in such a way to entice the leader to agree with it. Don't expect any credit as this will expose him; just be thankful that your opinion was heard and may be implemented.

THE VIRTUE OF PATIENCE

When negotiating a solution, an outcome, or a contract, it is typically dealt with head on and as efficiently as possible in a Western environment. After all 'time is money'. Interestingly, Chinese business culture approaches the same topic in a very different manner. We have heard many stories of negotiations going nowhere, the Western negotiators having a deadline and a plane to catch, while the Chinese negotiators are protracting the discussions by all means possible, e.g. communication barriers, key people suddenly not being available, key documentation gone missing, printer stopped working, and so forth. This all culminates in a calculated accession to achieve the upper hand in the negotiations.

Likewise, a similar pattern can be observed when dealing with Chinese colleagues in a work environment. While a Western colleague is desperately scrambling to table information or data, the Chinese colleague will take all the time in the world to provide the requested information. Often, deadlines are missed due to unavailable information.

Contract negotiations can be drawn out over long periods,

forcing a non-Chinese negotiator to compromise on issues in order to achieve a targeted deadline to bring in the work. The same principle is applied when trying to resolve issues in the workplace. Initially, the issue is all but ignored, to the utter frustration of Western team members.

In desperation, Western team members might attempt to resolve the issues themselves. This plays directly into the hands of the Chinese colleagues, who may now not be held accountable for the actions taken. It all comes down to one simple virtue, the art of having patience to achieve one's ultimate objective. It culminates in a 'wait and see' approach—not unique to the Chinese culture, but certainly not a quality at which Western people excel—often compromising their negotiating positions at the expense of time and money.

This approach often results in virtually no options remaining as time runs out. No proactive approach is followed and options disappear over time, leaving only one—or sometimes no options—to resolve the issue.

A Westerner will feel as if he is disempowered to resolve an issue. Once the time has lapsed, the leader can now blame someone else for the issue not being resolved. The leader now also has an opportunity to come in and save the day by offering a solution that may have been obvious to others from the start, but no one had the authority to make the decision except the Chinese leader.

ANGER MANAGEMENT

Anger is a strong feeling of annoyance, displeasure, or hostility, caused by the failure to achieve alignment around a perceived concern or issue. Anger can manifest itself internally or it may be expressed outwardly through facial expressions, body language, and verbal interaction. In the Western world, anger expression is encouraged as it relieves tension and allows one to better focus on finding a solution.

Of course, there are certain behavioral norms around anger management, but in essence, it is acceptable to deal with conflict in an open environment, before serious anger issues might surface. It's all about letting it out and not bottling up issues.

It is not very simple to understand how Chinese people deal with anger, but clearly, anger is managed in a much more harmonious way. One seldom comes across a Chinese colleague who expresses anger either through body language, behavior, or verbally. They always come across as friendly, happy, and in accord with their surroundings and their colleagues. While they might be bottling up their anger issues, this cannot be surmised from their external behavior. Chinese colleagues rarely come across as aggressive or frustrated, even when circumstances lend themselves to such outbursts.

However, they do seem somewhat aggressive when communicating with one another in Mandarin but this is merely the Westerner's lack of understanding of the language and pronunciations. They tend to talk simultaneously and therefore become louder, and Westerners mistakenly perceive this as aggressiveness. Frankly, it is rather difficult to enrage a Chinese colleague, no matter how hard one pushes the boundaries. Of course, not the same can be said when engaging with a Chinese leader, as mentioned earlier. In the office environment, one seldom sees Chinese colleagues having anger outbursts, but it can happen.

Chinese colleagues can lay into each other unexpectedly. Encounters are generally brief and the exchange is always in Mandarin (understandable). As quickly as it started, it will end, and both parties will continue working as though nothing has happened just minutes earlier.

Rarely has a confrontation required the intervention of a more senior Chinese colleague, but if needed, he will quickly subdue both parties. On enquiry, the reason for the conflict and aggression cannot be drawn out of either party, and therefore one is never sure if it was a personal spat or a work-related issue.

Even rarer is a physical confrontation, but can happen, with a fist or two flying. Never have I seen a physical confrontation ending with disciplinary action, something we take for granted in a Western working environment where physical confrontation is treated with zero tolerance. Without doubt, different rules apply to the Chinese working environment for Chinese employees.

While Chinese colleagues will not physically harm one, during a heated discussion they tend to get into your space, and start touching and pushing you. This is of course not 'aggressive' behavior per se, but it is also not acceptable behavior by Western standards. It can, at best, be interpreted as a gentle form of subdued intimation calisthenics. A firm reminder to them that such behavior is not tolerated in a Western work environment quickly brings the Chinese colleague to his senses. Female Chinese colleagues seem to be more subdued in the workplace, as I have never witnessed any conflict by or among them.

CHINESE PROBLEM SOLVING

Chinese problem solving works in series. The current issue at hand is perceived as the problem and the complexity of interdependent issues is not considered when resolving the primary problem at hand. Simple solutions are often proposed and implemented. By default, the next closest critical issue will then appear at the surface, exposing itself as a problem. Again, the next simple remedial action is implemented to curb the problem. This perceived lack of insight into complex problem solving induces much frustration and concern with Western colleagues, but to no avail. This approach to problem solving often does not end with the desired outcome, as the interim temporary solutions tend to go off track. This happens because the intended outcome is never really understood, and therefore it is not correctly targeted from the start.

Chinese colleagues are masters at trying to get non-Chinese team members to execute all the tasks by asking the same questions repeatedly and making the same requests on multiple occasions, until recipients feel pressurized to do something to assist his/her Chinese colleague with such requested information.

WE DON'T NEED YOU ANYMORE

Another striking Chinese business practice is to terminate a Western employee before his work assignment has been completed. To guard against this early termination it is suggested that a carefully worded termination clause be inserted into contracts. Chinese do honor contracts and one should use this to one's advantage. A termination clause that links a monetary payout to early termination is an example of a clause that can safeguard you.

It appears that residual memory is not welcomed; such information could be counterintuitive, when present failures are blamed on prior decisions often made by the Chinese management. Should such an issue surface while the Western colleague who was present at the time of the decision being made, is still in the employ of the Chinese organization, then it is often implied that the Western expert who was employed specifically for their local knowledge and expertise was responsible for the decision. If the Western colleague has already been terminated from the company's employ, then he or she is likely to be blamed for the 'bad' decision made.

This practice becomes apparent throughout the lifecycle of employment, as other colleagues are dismissed prematurely. It does create a level of angst within the team. In the same light, Chinese colleagues are constantly expecting to be sent back to China at short notice. The reason for premature termination is never discussed with either Western or Chinese employees. It just happens. And upon enquiry, one runs up against many Chinese Walls that will not give way to reason and justification.

CHINESE SUPERIORITY

Other triggers bringing out frustration, anger, and resentment culminate themselves in selected Chinese colleagues considering themselves superior within the team hierarchy, due to having direct links to the Chinese senior management. These Chinese colleagues treat not only some of their Chinese colleagues, but also certainly many of the Westerners, with aloofness and subtle disrespect and condescension, portraying tendencies of racism towards their non-Chinese team members.

Staying out of the Tiger's claws would be a rather futile attempt. Every subject under the control of the Tiger will feel his wrath. It is a matter of time before you start sensing the hot breath coming down on you like a typhoon. It is in the Tiger's nature to tame every one of his subjects to do as he pleases and as he demands.

Because the Tiger has the power, you cannot question or reason with his demands. Any resistance to the Tiger's advances shall be met with callous retribution and if one does not fall in line, the end can be nigh. Being under the Tiger's domination requires clever political maneuvering, subtle diplomacy, and astute interpersonal skills in order to avoid his indignation and subsequent desecration.

CHAPTER 10

THE CHOSEN ONE

*"By nature, men are nearly alike; by practice,
they get to be wide apart."*

—*Confucius*

Throughout China's millennia of history, privilege and preference has always been handed out to the select few. The next emperor was chosen either by decree of the previous emperor or along family lines. The masses were not entitled to benefit from the riches of the empire. Even the royal courtship was made up of people associated with the ruling of the empire over many generations. Chinese civilization was considered a prestige, available only to the elite.

When the Communist Party came into power in 1949, Mao Zedong devised a Communist Party rating system, which entitled one to certain levels of privileges based on one's loyalty, commitment, and sacrifice for the Communist Party. In essence, the masses did not enjoy the fruits of liberation from Nationalist rule or indeed dynastic rule.

One's privileges were not guaranteed. If for whatever reason one fell out of a favor with the communist leadership, rank and privileges dissolved into thin air in an instant with banishment into a labor camp or at best, renewed peasant duties.

In 1957, one year after Chinese party members and civilians were asked to openly criticize the Communist government, in order that the Communist government could then better itself, Mao Zedong hunted down and imprisoned over half a million people, mostly card carrying party members, for speaking out against the Party.

The Mao era rule left a populace devoid of free thought, terrified of doing wrong and adhering to the Communist Party's every doctrine, whim, and demand. Showing any resistance, lack of enthusiasm, or party allegiance could mean the difference between having some reasonable existence and a life of suffering.

THE COMMUNIST PARTY OF CHINA

Anybody can become a card-carrying member of the Communist Party of China (CPC) once they reach eighteen years of age. Rather than conforming to ideological criteria, emphasis was placed on intellect and education. Bright young candidates are sought out to be groomed for a long-term affiliation with the CPC. The other criteria to become a successful CPC member includes following the Communist mantra religiously. A member must at all times follow orders, be disciplined, uphold unity, serve the Party, the people, and the country, and promote the socialist way of life (Military Wikia). Any deviation from these simple principles could spell the end to one's career in the Communist Party. The Communist Party admission oath sums the requirements up perfectly:

"It is my will to join the Communist Party of China, uphold the Party's program, observe the provisions of the Party constitution, fulfill a Party member's duties, carry out the Party's decisions, strictly observe Party discipline, guard Party secrets, be loyal to the Party, work hard, fight for communism throughout my life, be ready at all times to sacrifice my all for the Party and the people, and never betray the Party." (Stalin's Moustache, Oath of Admission)

By mid 2016, the CPC has been estimated to have 89 million card-carrying members. The Communist Youth League (CYL) can boast a similar number of members. One in seven Chinese nationals is affiliated with the Communist Party (Wikipedia, Communist Party of China).

In parallel to one's working career, one can also make progress in the CPC. It is a life-long commitment that takes one through a number of gates, ultimately culminating in becoming a party member for life. These gates roughly track your progress in effectively fulfilling your party role in business. It measures your ability to take on bigger responsibility in the business environment, such as being in charge of a parastatal company, giving back to young cadres by lecturing for some years at a university at the end of a successful business career; and finally, becoming an honorary life member and official party representative of the CPC.

It was generally rumored that the CPC career path required one to master five career phases of development, but it was impossible to prove or extract such information from literature or any of our Chinese colleagues (talking Chinese politics to Chinese citizens is, of course, totally taboo). A typical career path would probably look something like this:

qualified professional, manager, business leader, lecturer, permanent party representative. It could be observed in the work environment that a (normally older) Chinese expert in his field would be appointed into a senior management or even executive position, regardless of whether he had the management skills and business sense for the position. It was a necessary stepping-stone for the collective and probable CPC career path.

People were not recruited into the roles that suited their personality and character, but rather inserted into stereotyped roles within their field of expertise that the system deemed necessary for the greater good of the Tiger's belly. The last thing that would be tolerated is for such individuals to question these decisions taken about them and their lives by a higher order of Chinese compatriots who were in all probability also CPC patriots.

Committing any acts considered treason within the CPC e.g. having been involved in bribery or corruption, will seriously impair one's CPC career. This does not imply an instant dismissal from the Party, but one has to go a step back and prove to the Party that one has conformed to the Party's rules and that one has reformed one's own behavior. In terms of the CPC career, this would constitute a serious setback, which will ultimately affect one's position and benefits within the Party. Such misdemeanors are rarely shared with the outside world, but in one specific case, a Chinese company CEO was sent on a long term Africa assignment to prove his worth and commitment to the CPC, because he had been caught red handed in a bribery scandal while working his way up the Communist Party career ladder back in China. Being sent on assignments to a third world country in a remote earthly corner could therefore be construed as a form of punishment, repentance, and career revival move all in one. The fate is in the hands of the CPC leadership and not the individual, who shall be obliged to follow the orders bestowed on him or her.

Chinese citizens who are not members of the CPC do not qualify for the same lustrous career opportunities as Party members. Card-carrying members receive preferential treatment, not only when in the folds of the Communist Party, but certainly during their lifetime of work.

EXPLORING THE WORLD

In China, it is considered a privilege to be sent abroad. This does not happen by one's own choice alone. While one can apply for an offshore position, one's superior makes the final call, and no doubt, your work performance as well as your party credentials are considered.

One advantage that supersedes all other qualifications by far is if the applicant commands the English language. That constitutes the passport to traveling abroad and greater prosperity. One does not so much plan one's own career, as the Communist Party as well as the company that you work for decide what is best—not for you, but for the better good of the company, the Communist Party, and the nation as whole. In other words, individuals are allocated to a particular job, assignment, project, or other work task without much say in the matter. They will find themselves being transferred to a different location within China or indeed halfway across the planet to a remote setting. They will not question the reassignment, but dutifully follow the instruction.

Depending on your stature in the company and within the Communist Party, you will be relocated on single status or married status. The relocation period is unspecified when individuals leave the shores of China for an indefinite period. Wives and children are left behind in China, but the father may visit occasionally. If you have a preferred standing within the organization, your rest and recuperation trips back to China might be more frequent than that of a colleague.

I AM BETTER THAN YOU

It is blatantly obvious that some people receive preferential treatment over others. As mentioned in previous chapters, being a family member of a Chinese leader brings many benefits. Apart from being assigned into a comfortable job with a fancy title, irrespective of your capabilities, your corporate benefits would also be better.

A similar rule of thumb applies to prominent and revered CPC members who have the necessary influence back in China. Preferential benefits include access to a luxury rental car (seeing luxury German sedans in the parking area outside the offices was not uncommon), a private apartment, bringing family members along (depending on your status, this could even include some extended family) and more frequent return trips to China (including your family if they have joined the expatriate lifestyle). These individuals also crack the nod for invites to dinner parties (banquets) with guests of importance, as well as visits by high profile delegates from China (both corporate and political, which in the Chinese environment are sometimes difficult to differentiate), or high powered government delegations from the host country or regional countries.

The difference in return trips to China can range from two months for one person to 12 months for another. And such return trips are not guaranteed, nor scheduled ahead of time. One will submit a travel request to the HR department, whose manager will then decide when you can go. The individual is often not notified of the travel arrangements until a few days before the time. In some instances, Chinese colleagues would only be notified on the morning of the return flight. The same rule applied to transfers. Many a Chinese colleague would be given short notice for a permanent transfer to another location, giving him or her little time to prepare and pack their belongings. They would then ask other Chinese and non-Chinese team members alike to bring bits and pieces of their belongings with to the new location, every time an opportunity arose. It sometimes took weeks, even months, for them to be reunited with all their belongings. Relocation logistics were left to the individual, the company unconcerned with such trivia.

AM I TRULY FREE?

Chinese passport management takes on an interesting angle, unlike anything seen in the West. A Chinese citizen, if privileged enough to travel, will typically have two passports, (1) a business passport and (2) a personal travel passport. Both passports will be in the possession of the Chinese authorities, whether one is in China or located offshore. When traveling abroad, the business passport will grant only access to the country or countries where the work is to be executed. This will prevent individuals from traveling to unspecified destinations whilst outside China. This is a control mechanism to prevent Chinese citizens from 'emigrating' at their own free will. While traveling on business or working in a foreign country, Chinese citizens are not issued with their personal travel passports, which are locked up in China. Should a Chinese person wish to take a holiday or visit a family member in another country, he or she would first have to travel back to China, hand in their business passport, collect their personal travel passport, and then be off to their holiday destination of choice. No doubt, the personal travel passport will also be restricted to the country or countries to be visited during the holiday, to prevent the embarrassment of an unplanned side trip to an unknown destination. As in China, once a person has arrived at their destination, he or she is compelled to hand in his or her passport for the duration of the stay, normally to a card carrying party member. So while travel for Chinese citizens has become far easier than some 25 years ago, individual movement is still very much controlled within the framework of the Communist Party rules and regulations.

FATE IS MY COMPANION

In the work environment, certain Chinese colleagues are clearly singled out to be groomed for bigger things, be it in business or in the Communist Party. The primary pre-requisite is intelligence. While it is sometimes challenging to judge other people's true intelligence, it is rather difficult when engaging with Chinese colleagues. Apart from the language barrier, Chinese people behave in a most stereotyped manner. Intelligence and intellect are observed and accessed by engaging directly with a person in detailed discussions—debating complex topics, and stimulating lateral thought processes. Since Chinese citizens are not compelled or indeed allowed to enter into vigorous debates, nor share their personal opinions with others, it becomes more difficult to gage one's dialogue opponent. However, in one aspect individuals can shine, silently radiating out their intellectual capabilities and this is when they are given a task or assignment to complete. It very quickly becomes apparent who can and who cannot resolve complex task problems. Also, the speed of resolution directly portrays a person's capabilities and capacity to deal with issues beyond their experience and educational achievements. It was enlightening to see that young Chinese graduates clearly had an edge over their older colleagues, dealing with problem solving in a more Western attuned manner. This in itself might highlight, that the Chinese educational system is progressing their teaching methods to adapt to a more global format.

These singled out, typically young Chinese colleagues would be assigned to different departments every couple of months. They were there not only to 'learn the ropes' but to start playing the 'informant' role for the Chinese management. Being an informant, who informs on either his or her own Chinese colleagues or Western colleagues, is a pre-requisite to becoming a good Party member. After all, loyalty to the Party is far more important than loyalty to family and friends, if one wants to progress in the CPC. These young informants observed behavior and output, often understanding little of the issue and topic at hand, however keenly recording the visible outcomes and issues. Issues observed were not queried, but rather reported to the Chinese leadership, as they were observed. With limited work experience, these young informers did not have the capability to interpret situations or interpret the complex mechanisms behind operational progress. Reason was not applied to interpret an observation or output, but reported as it appeared. If a task appeared to be delayed, the reasons for such a delay were not investigated or even identified, but reported as a 'simple' problem.

While some Western colleagues viewed this act of spying as a machination to ultimately curtail one's newly found Chinese career ambitions, this did not appear to be the case. It was simply a mechanism of keeping the leader informed of all aspects of the business. Yes, of course reporting on ongoing delays and recurring problems would ultimately swing the Chinese leader's opinion of an employee, which in the long term could influence the leader's decision to terminate one's service prematurely. The use of 'spies' to inform the leader on detailed day-to-day operational issues in itself is a foreign concept in modern Western business practices, where senior management deals with strategic issues, delegating authority to departmental heads to deal with the issues on the ground.

An interesting aspect of these career informants was that some Chinese colleagues also despised them, as the spying activities did not consider loyalty, color, or creed. It was a career stepping stone both within the business organization as well as for their Communist Party ambitions.

The choice, to be singled out for greatness and growth, is not given to the individual. Once a CPC member on the team identified an individual for greater things, it would be fool-hardy to refuse the offer. It is not a choice, but rather a predisposed career destination, determined by other unknown forces. Questioning the career path determined by others, would be detrimental. In the Chinese business as well as political environment, one shall do as one is told, without resolve or issue. In one such example, a young, promising Chinese engineer in our company was handpicked to be groomed for bigger things. He was suddenly taken out of the team and sent to the company's head office to fulfill the role of CEO assistant. When we queried this with the CEO and requested him to be sent back to the team, the CEO agreed but then never sent him back to the design office.

FAMILY TIES

One's career is initiated from an early age by one's parents' circumstances. If they are loyal Party members or indeed highly regarded Party members, then one would benefit from an early age. It starts with the choice of school, Communist Youth League membership, introduction to influential people, the right tertiary education (which could mean being sent to study abroad at one of the prized Western universities) and ultimately being allotted to the right people—often family members or acquaintances—throughout your working career who will ensure your success.

In many ways, your work and political careers are pre-determined by fate and circumstance at the time you enter the world. The children of prominent and influential senior communist officials in the People's Republic of China are known as the Princelings, also translated as the Party's Crown Princes. It is an informal—and often derogatory categorization—to describe children who benefit directly from nepotism and cronyism because of the positions their parents hold.

THE END

In the same light, one's pre-determined career path can be cut short, should one have strayed out of expected doctrine of behavior and performance. If the party rules are disobeyed, one can find oneself being isolated very quickly. While the Chinese management can often overlook bad work performance of Chinese employees, some individuals can be singled out when they consistently underachieve. Typically, these individuals are not closely associated with anybody in the organizational management nor are they prominent party members. Once a person has been earmarked, they are expediently sent back to China to take up a back office job with no further career growth opportunities.

Being well connected through the family and the CPC no doubt protects individuals, being forgiven more easily for straying away from the Communist Party mantra, underperforming or indeed not performing at all, or even having engaged in some self-enrichment practices through bribery and corruption. The authorities may ignore a bit of corruption but there is a fine line between overindulgence and acceptance of these practices. In recent years, the CPC has cracked down noticeably on individuals seen to enrich themselves at the expense of the system.

Until 2015, China adhered to a strict one-child policy (except for minority ethnic groups, and cases where twins were born). If this strict requirement were not adhered to, then a typical punishment would be banishment to a mundane job in some back office with minimal pay and no future growth prospects.

While missing deadlines for some preferred Chinese colleagues was casually dismissed to be of no impact or importance, other Chinese team members had to deliver. If an agreed deadline was missed, it could spell immediate retribution in the form of not receiving one's salary until the deliverable was achieved. This often resulted in tasks being vehemently signed off for implementation even if the work was not completed yet. It was easier to pretend that a deadline had been met and then deal with the aftermath of a half implemented project, than face the wrath of the Tiger (and no income), as missing deadlines causes many prominent people to lose face.

CHAPTER 11

CORPORATE ANTICS

"The will to win, the desire to succeed, the urge to reach your full potential… these are the keys that will unlock the door to personal excellence."

—*Confucius*

The understanding of how Chinese business works is as abstract to Western companies as is the dark side of the Moon to humankind. Apart from being shrouded in a vague cloud of communistic management and influence, the Chinese business structures, service infrastructure, and corporate culture are poorly understood by Western people. Chinese companies seem to have an endless list of presidents and vice presidents, managers and assistant managers, as well as people with some authority or another. Yet, few of the people have the power of management, as described adequately in earlier chapters.

Chinese organization structures are complex and confusing at best. It is difficult to understand who reports to whom and who the decision-makers are. The official organogram, resembling typical corporate layouts, does not reflect the actual intricate organizational arrangement put in place specifically for the Chinese 'silent' reporting hierarchy. In fact, official organograms are a key aspect of Chinese corporates, creating a sense of comfort among Chinese colleagues when being prepared and presented. However, on the ground the team operational interactions seldom adhere to the official organogram structure.

While Chinese corporations enthusiastically apply Western management principles and processes, they do not change their management behavior. As such, they never truly adapt to an expatriate environment and a more international work culture. Non-Chinese (and often Western-trained and Western thinking) senior managers are appointed in key roles at these expatriate Chinese companies, and the Chinese leadership assume that their company is now being operated on more international principles. However, as the corporation is not run along Western management lines—nor are the Western managers truly empowered to manage the company or make key decisions—this often results in a company that stresses and strains in a hostile host country environment. It tries to execute work along Chinese corporate principles with a Chinese stereotyped management style that does not bode itself well outside the mainland Chinese environment.

The focus of this chapter will be to delve into the corporate setup and operation of a Chinese company in an expatriate environment, which has required the Chinese management to incorporate the locally hired staff, regional HR (Human Resources) practices as well as to adhere to the in-country legislation and best business practices.

RELATIONSHIP WITH THE HOST COUNTRY GOVERNMENT

Chinese companies operating outside China are mostly parastatals. Before even setting themselves up in an offshore country, contact is made at government level and key political relationships are established early. The ground rules of investment and operation in the host country are established at government level. While Chinese companies are typically setting themselves up to develop and export commodities to China, the investment portfolio will include a broader spectrum of deliverables including infrastructure upgrades, social responsibility programs, as well as direct investment and debt financing programs with the host country government. Typically, the host country government could become a direct stakeholder in the Chinese investment, with the intent that they would receive a percentage of the profits generated from the investment.

The Chinese parastatal organization, through financing received from Chinese government supported banking facilities, will finance the entire investment, which includes buying the concession rights, building of the facilities, upgrading of regional infrastructure, making use of local construction labor, and then employing locals to operate the facility. In return, the Chinese parastatal requires the full commodity production to be exported to a Chinese destination of choice and further, the Chinese company wants access to other commodity targets in the host country.

The host country government is seen as creating more jobs for its citizens by upgrading dated and dilapidating infrastructure. This bodes well for the host country Government to stay in favor with its populace. Typically, the Chinese investment will focus on specific infrastructure that will facilitate the more efficient transportation of host country imports as well as exports from its newly acquired and developed operational sites.

The relationship between the Chinese organization and the host country government can be considered symbiotic with both parties benefiting from the deal. The arrangement does come with strings attached from both sides. The host country government expects some of the key management positions at the new Chinese operation to be filled by politically affiliated local (host country) citizens. As mentioned earlier, the government also wants a stake in the business, typically somewhere between 10 and 25%.

Further, one of the Chinese parastatal banks might grant interest free loans to the host country government. The Chinese company expects reduced or no import duties for imported Chinese equipment, no export restrictions, or royalty taxes, and that the investment would qualify for corporate tax exclusions (by the production site being granted tax-free trading zone status) in return. Further, the visa and work permit restrictions should not be applied to Chinese citizens working on the projects. Finally, lenient immigration laws for Chinese citizens would allow a considerable portion of the 'imported' workforce to remain in the host country for an indefinite period—if not permanently—enabling them to work on the other investment projects or to start up local Chinese businesses.

In many African countries, the Chinese population has grown exponentially over the last decade or so, now quantifying in the top three or four by ethnicity ranking. And many Chinese remain behind in the host country to start a new life outside China. China has certainly appeared to engage into a human resettlement program in their host countries, bringing in a Chinese populace cross section ranging from the lower ranks of society like hawkers and prostitutes right through to engineers, doctors, and scientists.

While many African countries achieved their independence in the late 1950s and early 1960s, some Southern African countries remained in the grip of Europeans whose ancestors had colonized these African expanses in the 17th to the 19th centuries. These countries encompassed Zimbabwe (Rhodesia before independence in 1980), Namibia (South West Africa before 1990), and South Africa (controlled by the white Apartheid regime up to 1994). Segregation was practiced in these countries, severely affecting the economic wellbeing of its non-White citizens.

This also affected Chinese citizens who were classified as non-Whites, and as such prohibited them from engaging in mainstream economic activities of these countries. After independence, the new black led governments introduced legislation to balance the country's wealth across all demographics. This was generally referred to as Black Economic Empowerment (BBE) legislation, which forced white owned companies to sell part of their businesses to previously disadvantaged non-White business people and BEE companies. Further, the company management structure had to start introducing non-White executives, guided by strict legislation. Non-compliance would result in fines to be paid. Of course, this legislation only applied to white businesses or majority white owned businesses but not to BEE or non-White businesses. This included Chinese companies that were set up in these countries. Chinese businesses are thus able to bypass BEE requirements, allowing them to fill positions with

Chinese citizens and not necessarily indigenous host country people, which was the original intent of BEE. Indigenous people are usually only employed in low-level unskilled labor jobs with poor pay, while a few senior management positions are filled with politically connected indigenous people, normally associated with the host country government cronies of the day.

COMPANY TEAM COMPOSITION

A number of non-Chinese and specifically Westerners are brought into the Chinese team at the start of the investment project or company setup, being appointed in key management positions. Titles and responsibilities are carefully compiled and broadly advertized within the organization. From a Western perspective, this is considered normal and the individuals will immediately assume responsibility and ownership of his or her division, department, or area of work responsibility assigned.

Although organization organograms and titles seem to be very important to Chinese, the fact that someone is put into a position but is not actually fulfilling that role or doing the specific job is seemingly not a problem, as long as the company is fully staffed and everyone is following the Chinese leader's instructions. Westerners are placed in key operational roles but not in key administrative roles that control the company such as CEO, Finance, HR and IT. Chinese are placed in operational roles alongside Westerners to gain experience with the intent to ultimately take over.

The team will also include a number of indigenous (host country) people, usually in key management roles. As mentioned earlier, these appointments can comprise politically connected persons, rather than people who have relevant job specific experience.

Western employees of Chinese companies are mostly the facilitators of employing new Western employees. The Western facilitator is key for one to have a chance of being employed by a Chinese company, although the Chinese senior management and ultimately the most senior locally based Chinese leader will be the ultimate custodian of the decision. When a Western potential candidate is presented to the Chinese senior management, one must be meticulously prepared, as one usually only has one opportunity to impress the Chinese decision maker, who will make an affirmative or vetoed decision, which cannot be swayed thereafter.

Western colleagues are always given finite contract periods with a specific end date. Chinese business culture assumes that employees will stick around until they are relocated or dismissed, and any contract extension negotiations are usually left until the last minute. In China, employees very seldom resign, as all organizations are interwoven into the fragment of the Chinese state and upsetting your current employer will most likely cost you your opportunity at most other Chinese companies. In essence, it is a career-limiting move to upset the emperor, who is only a servant of the almighty Tiger, who ultimately makes the rules.

Chinese companies have little understanding of Western work ethics and best practices, and they often alienate their non-Chinese employees very quickly, once employed. Little do they understand that Western employees consider it their right and privilege to seek alternative employment if the Chinese company mistreats them or fails to offer promotion opportunities, not liquidate incentives, or not re-negotiate employment contracts timeously.

Once a Western or even Chinese employee has resigned, the working conditions change rapidly. The employee is sidelined in the work environment and excluded from communications and even meetings. Company service departments, such as IT, HR, and the Finance Department will fail to provide further support to resolve queries and claims.

The balance of the team is comprised of a disproportionately large Chinese contingent, mainly men, as well as a few women fulfilling some services roles, without much say or input. The bulk of the Chinese team comprises relatively inexperienced persons, who have been specifically brought across from mainland China to gain experience from the Western employees. It is made very clear to all that they are not there to work but to learn. A handful of experienced Chinese specialists, who might have had previous Western experience, are also put on the team. Then there are also one or two characters with no particular job description. It quickly becomes apparent that they represent the CPC and its investment banking affiliates to oversee the offshore investments and ultimately provide another reporting function back to the Chinese Government, which ultimately sponsored the investment.

There are numerous conspiracy theories about how Chinese companies use Chinese prisoners to do low level work on African soil (and probably on other Chinese construction sites around the world). This is a theory and likely an urban legend, which cannot be proven as the Chinese authorities have always denied this situation and no statistics are published on the profile of Chinese citizens frequenting the African shores. One theory suggests that Chinese prisoners who have only committed minor offences and are incarcerated in filthy Chinese prisons or labor camps, are given the option to work on low level, poorly paid construction sites in remote locations around the world. The expectation is hard work for a foreseeable period of a couple of years during which any criminal activity or misdemeanor will result in immediate return to China and long-term incarceration. Once the mandatory work period has been completed in a host country—possibly equated to the length of their original prison terms—they will be settled in the host country for the rest of their lives to start contributing to the global economic ambitions of the Tiger.

An interesting observation is that Chinese citizens are never arrested for petty crimes in host countries, or indeed armed robberies, rape, or murder (what I like to call citizen crimes). This aligns nicely with the theory that prisoners on 'probation' in Africa are on their best behavior, as this will open a door to a new life and relative freedom from the burdens back in China, once they have done their time.

While not necessarily associated with legally operating businesses, organized crime by Chinese in Africa and indeed around the world has a far more sinister reputation. Chinese citizens are regularly exposed and caught as part of organized crime syndicates involved in the drug trade, money laundering, poaching (both wildlife and indigenous vegetation), prostitution, human trafficking—the list being too long to elaborate here. Often, these criminal citizens are well connected—within both the Chinese government as well as the host country government officials—making it notoriously difficult to corner, arrest, and prosecute them effectively.

TEAM BUILDING

Apart from a few Chinese dinners, where exquisite Chinese dishes and copious amounts of alcohol are the order of the day, no other team building exercises or workshops were encouraged by the Chinese management team. The dinners are usually organized by the Chinese leader—who invites selected team members only—and are usually limited to a maximum of twelve people, as this comprises the maximum capacity of one round table in a typical Chinese restaurant. Both the Chinese and Western people consider it a revered privilege to be invited to such events.

Cultural alignment of the team was not seriously undertaken, except for the odd circular explaining the significance of one or other Chinese or host country public holiday or calendar event. The cultural differences were significant, but the team members never really had the opportunity to appreciate all the different intricacies of the cultural differences. Key opportunities were missed repeatedly to bring the two cultural groups closer together and thus create a conducive environment for better work output and a more functional office environment.

One tactic employed by Chinese leaders is that of talking down and belittling subordinates in a forum environment. Concerns and issues, that came to the Chinese leader's attention, were nearly always raised by the Chinese leader directly with the concerned party in a forum where multiple witnesses were present, often in the presence of sub-contractors and other outside entities. Such Western employees were talked down to, addressed with a noticeable level of disrespect and were shouted down when trying to respond to the concern at hand. It was very much always a one-way-communication from the master to the servant. Depending on whether the Western employee was still of value to the Chinese organization or already targeted for inherent dismissal, he or she might even be ridiculed in meetings for things outside his or her control and apportioned with the full blame.

Being in the right did not encourage Chinese work colleagues to jump to one's defense or provide support otherwise, and any Western work colleagues quickly realized the importance of following suit. Trying to defend one's credibility and professionalism resulted in a wrathful anger outburst with more abuse being hurled in the same direction. It became clear that the end of this employment period was fast approaching its zenith. One must realize that self-defense, if successful, will make the leader lose face, so once you try to defend your credibility or professionalism, he might well retaliate even if not immediately.

This behavior was also sometimes observed in one-on-one Chinese-to-Chinese interactions in the office environment, but never in formal meetings. As these discussions were always in Mandarin, it was difficult to follow. The body language clearly demonstrated the Confucian master/servant relationship interface. When one enquired after the event what it had all been about, neither affected Chinese party would elaborate, dismissing the question with a light nervous laugh or just staring at one without commenting at all.

Where any employee is seen to have double-crossed the Chinese mantra, it can result in instant dismissal without the employee suspecting it in the least. Seemingly double-crossing Chinese values—often not recognized as serious offences in Western culture—could include:

- Disagreeing with the Chinese leader in a forum, which would be seen as the Chinese leader having lost face
- Not implementing direct Chinese instructions even if conspicuous
- Criticizing under-performing Chinese co-workers
- Or having suggested a politically sensitive viewpoint that might offend either the Chinese or the host country indigenous political mantra of the day

In some instances, outside political affiliates in government circles have asked for the removal of employees who might have dabbled in a political no go zone. In order for the Chinese organization to demonstrate their partisan allegiance to the host country political cronies, they will honor such a request. It is not about one's professional ability and contribution, but much more about a survivalist mentality in a yellow sea of complex interpersonal engagement rules and unwritten behavior regulations, if one wants to remain employed. Typically, non-challenging, subservient sycophant interaction results in the best chances at corporate longevity in the Chinese work environment, but goes right against the fundamental principles of Western professionalism.

OFFICE SETUP

The office plan layout appears to be completely random, with no single department sitting entirely in one designated area. One or two departmental Chinese team members are always placed randomly around the offices.

While working for the Chinese organization, one of the Western leaders decided to organize the office layout logically, only to have it reversed by the Chinese leader as soon as he realized what had taken place. The reversal decision hinged on three issues, (1) that the Chinese leader was never consulted and more importantly, (2) that he didn't make the decision, and (3) that the Chinese informers were no longer dispersed strategically around the office.

An open plan layout is preferred with only the managers being allocated closed offices.

THE TIGER MAKES THE RULES

Initially, the Western managers try to manage the office like a typical Western corporate office setup, but quickly discover that their Chinese colleagues do not follow their instructions; Chinese colleagues receive instructions from another source and their decisions are ignored. This phenomenon can be attributed to the parallel Chinese management structure that has been put in place and operates silently, reporting directly to the Chinese decision maker—typically, the most senior Chinese representative who has relocated to the host country.

All business and project progress and issues will be reported to the Chinese leader, often via the informal parallel Chinese management structure and so official meetings become a formality only. Often the Chinese leader might join these meetings randomly to inform the office manager or departmentmental leader of a decision taken, when the very meeting was called to debate the issue and make an appropriate decision. The decision making power of Western managers specifically is quickly eroded, much to their frustration. Chinese decisions are not debatable in a meeting forum, as then the Chinese leader relaying his decision to the office team, would be losing face, a fatal scenario for the challenger of the decision.

The office management descents into a team of subordinates following instructions. Teamwork breaks down as trust dissipates, the Western people not quite knowing who on the Chinese team reports what about whom to the Chinese leader. Of concern is that some Chinese colleagues will report on information gathered that does not constitute their field of expertise and so the gathered information is incorrectly reported to the Chinese leader, creating additional consternation.

Different rules applied to the Chinese team and the non-Chinese team. The Chinese team worked fixed office hours whereas the non-Chinese team worked as long as was needed. The Chinese team members slept on the job in full visibility of their Chinese and Western superiors. As this is normal accepted practice in China, the Chinese managers never challenged this behavior and the Western managers did not dare to challenge the status quo. The Western team members would not engage in such practice by default as it's seen as a dismissible offence according to Western work practices.

The Chinese colleagues received transportation to and from work. Chinese lunch packs were supplied to the Chinese colleagues only. The Chinese team members observed Chinese national holidays while the Western team observed the local host country public holidays. While the pros and cons of applying different rules for different cultural groups can be debated, this segregated operational approach did affect the output efficiency of the office.

New Chinese team members just appeared—after familiar colleagues were shipped back to China without any notification—and were never formally or informally introduced to anybody on the team. While the Western team members found this behavior absurd and even rude, the Chinese colleagues were certainly not fazed by this. It appeared that new Chinese team members might have even been acquainted with many of the existing Chinese team members (Guanxi working) as their ease of communication and interaction was easily observable in the workplace. Leave dates or rest and recuperation dates are not communicated to the team until just before departure. This all leads to a rather ineffective office environment, where the operational efficiency is severely curtailed by a dysfunctional Western–Sino team setup.

Working for a Chinese organization is like playing chess. Everybody becomes your opponent and you need to anticipate every political move in order to avoid annihilation. Often, as a Western employee—even in a designated management role— you end up being no more than a pawn, and the mighty Chinese Tiger is king, even on this foreign chessboard in a foreign country. The odds are always stacked against you and you need to make your next move carefully. Different rules apply to the different sides playing on either side of the cultural divide across the invisible battle line.

VALUED EMPLOYEES

While the importance of an employee's wellbeing in the work environment is continuously promoted as part of the company values, Chinese company employees enjoy relatively few privileges. Company celebrations, such as safety achievements, or achieved production targets are limited or not celebrated at all. Issued IT hardware can be outdated and is not upgraded regularly. Stationery choices are limited, requiring employees to supplement their requirements. IT support is poor, resulting in employees not having effective access to their work desktop or laptop for days on end. Parking may not be allocated to all employees, resulting in employees scrambling for a few available parking bays. Transport to and from the airport may not always be available, or if available, not flexible to suit all travel itineraries. Organized company transport may not arrive timeously, which could result in missed flights or meetings. Workstations often don't have LAN connection points or plugs; desks and chairs may be inferior and could often be crowded with multiple employees being crammed into limited office space and workstations. Other employees may use your workstation during periods of absence.

On one specific project in Africa, the lack of concern for the employee's wellbeing was accentuated in the design of the contractor camp at the construction site. The contractor camp was generally frugal with limited recreational facilities, cramped rooms, basic canteen meal plan options, and limited means to explore the immediate surroundings and sites. It was up to the employee to entertain him or herself in an isolated and remote environment. No gym was provided and only a basic social gathering area was created containing a single television and basic bar facilities and a single basketball court was provided for a contractor camp that catered to more than four thousand residents.

Shuttles to the nearest town were provided once a week on a Saturday, which could be made use of on a rotational basis—in other words not as one pleased. Grievances were poorly addressed. Management and worker living quarters and facilities were combined—some senior managers had to share rooms and use common bathroom facilities. Private vehicles had to be parked outside the camp and the camp community was not allowed to venture beyond the camp perimeter after hours, unless special permission was granted. Likewise, access to the camp was restricted after hours unless special arrangements had been made. While such strict controls might be considered typical on Chinese construction sites, this was alien to the non-Chinese and specifically Western team members.

MEETINGS

"A thousand cups of wine do not suffice when true friends meet, but half a sentence is too much when there is no meeting of minds."

—*Chinese Proverb*

Numerous meetings are held on a daily basis, taking up much time and impeding on constructive work. Everybody seems to participate in meetings, whether they were invited or not. The mechanisms of the meeting are discussed in more detail in Postscript Chapter 1 (Chinese Business Culture, Etiquette, and Behavior in the Work Environment).

What becomes apparent in meetings is that the motions of the meeting are being obliged, but no conflicts are raised, actions debated, or decisions made. As already perpetuated, it is seen as impolite and rude to challenge any feedback given by a Chinese colleague or indeed a Chinese manager in a meeting forum, even if wrong, as this will lose him or her face (although one seldom encounters a Chinese female in a managerial position).

Western team members are not used to taking a passive role in a meeting environment. Initially, they challenge and question as well as try to advise typical project or operational practices, as per their field of expertise and experience. These bouts of advice are politely ignored and often not even minuted. The meeting environment is used as a platform by the Chinese colleagues to relay messages and decisions taken by the Chinese leader, often given in the form of a 'suggestion' rather than a direct instruction. If the Western colleague does not implement the suggested way forward, then he or she is politely reminded in the next meeting.

Thereafter, the Chinese colleague or colleagues will transmit the suggestion more forcefully, by cornering one in the office environment (one-on-one) and then backing up the 'suggestion' with a rather forceful email (written in perfect English—the question always beckoned who in the Chinese organization was the original author of such an email). The Western colleague eventually starts realizing that the suggestion was not a suggestion after all, but in fact an indirect instruction coming from the top Chinese management. It is expected that the Western colleague implements the 'suggestion' rather than questions it.

Specific types of meetings often digress from its intended purpose, e.g. Steering Committee meetings turn into a Progress Meeting. The same topics can be discussed at numerous different meetings taking place in close succession, often with exactly the same audience. Challenging this status quo is futile and detrimental. Key Western managers are invited to key meetings such as executive meetings, steering committee meetings, and board meetings. Depending on the level of passivity or challenge displayed in these meetings, the Western colleague could be uninvited as quickly as he or she was invited.

An example of this occurred during my employment with a Chinese organization. One of my non-Chinese colleagues attended the first few board meetings, before being mysteriously left off the meeting invite list without any further explanation. It transpired that this colleague was challenging the board meeting discussions, in the light of his in-depth organizational and project knowledge. This challenge in an open forum was clearly unwelcome.

INFORMATION MANIPULATION

It became apparent that data provided by the team was manipulated in the board papers to suit the audience to whom the information was presented. Any information request was always communicated down the Chinese management structure and one of the junior Chinese team members then would request certain information from a senior Western colleague without the proper brief or context. Ignoring such a request was futile, as the request would be made time and again, one quickly realizing that the request was actually coming from higher quarters. The information was then interpreted, re-analyzed, recalculated and manipulated by the Chinese team, and presented to the Chinese leader in a format that would suit him.

Often, the Chinese leader would challenge Western team members by presenting data and statistics that were factually incorrect. It would take painstaking effort to convince the

Chinese leader of the real data. Nevertheless, manipulated data more often than not became official once they had been embedded in board packs distributed not only to the board members but also to the chairperson and no doubt the CPC back in China.

COMPANY VALUES

Chinese corporate setup appears to be sound at face value. Procedures and processes are usually put in place, even if late, to facilitate the work output. Cultural events of all ethnicities are observed while Chinese cultural events are celebrated with enthusiasm. Training programs are introduced. The company values, selected by the executive and based on typical Western standards, are widely published and rolled out to all. While the organization strives to officially implement and follow the HR guidelines and values, this is not the case in practice. In fact, the values published seem to be the values that are least followed. No measurement and feedback are done to assess the gaps of actual values being practiced in the workplace compared to desired values, nor are plans put in place to change perceived 'wrong' behavior. It is expected that the company employees will merely follow and live these company values.

Typical company values may include Transparency, Honesty, Teamwork, Responsibility & Ownership, Open Communication, and Trust. However, many of these values are never practiced in the company environment where political maneuvering and manipulation leads to mistrust and misalignment. It is a case of 'the values have been published so that means the company employees are following them'.

Chinese colleagues often blatantly flout the rules of engagement at no perceived detriment to themselves. Clearly, they are following instructions from above, as it is a well-known fact that Chinese subordinates will never act out of their own accord. In direct contrast, the non-Chinese team members are given very little space to maneuver in and non-compliance could have detrimental consequences, even leading to dismissal.

WORK ETHICS

The saying "blood is thicker than water" applies rather aptly in the Chinese work environment. While in a Western environment sub-contracting companies and service providers are held accountable against their contracts, a Chinese company will assist a Chinese sub-contracting company if they find themselves in a spot of bother. Assistance may be in the form of advice, management intervention, or monetary support. Ultimately, almost all Chinese companies are parastatals that report to one parent company, namely the Chinese government. Therefore, the failure of one Chinese company would be seen as a failure of all Chinese companies (which would shame the Chinese state as a whole). It was interesting to observe that Chinese companies that are already established in the host country would always be receiving some or other portion of the available work.

One Chinese company would never experience feast while one of its sister companies was in a state of famine. The in-country Chinese structures ensure that all Chinese companies will receive enough work to remain profitable, even if that means intervention in the procurement process to achieve this objective. Non-Chinese sub-contractors are not assisted in this manner and their contractual obligations are strictly enforced.

Chinese companies are forever hosting Government delegates from the host country, neighboring countries, or high profile visits from mainland China. Frantic preparations will be planned down to the last detail for weeks in advance to suit the specific audience and meet the political agenda not only of the Chinese company but also of the visiting party. Such visits are carefully orchestrated to impress the visiting party at the highest level. The company participants are carefully selected to create the impression that a Chinese team, supplemented with indigenous expertise, is executing the local investment and operation.

Many of the Western expatriates will not be asked to participate in the visit and are requested to remain out of sight while the dignitaries are receiving a tour of the facilities. This of course creates the impression to the visiting dignitaries that Chinese expertise alone can deliver multi-billion-dollar investment projects in the remote location and that indigenous expertise are being readily employed to supplement their teams. In reality, the Chinese investors rely heavily on Western expertise to implement their projects as the Chinese teams do not necessarily have the technical knowledge or local experience and the availability of indigenous expertise is severely constrained in these Third World environments where the projects are implemented.

PROCUREMENT

A Chinese procurement team typically controls the procurement process in a Chinese organization. Enquiries had to always include mainland Chinese suppliers or Chinese contractors. Some of the contractors were conveniently established in the host country, making the adjudication process far easier. Chinese bidders often missed the target price by a mile but then resubmitted an unsolicited bid after tender closing, citing that they had miscalculated the submitted cost or forgot to add certain costs in. The unsolicited cost had to then be considered during the adjudication process, a practice not typically encouraged in a Western procurement process.

The Chinese management often pushed the office team to reconsider Chinese suppliers and contractors for award. Typically, a third of all awards went to Chinese suppliers and contractors. Ensuring that Chinese contractors had an opportunity to receive work from the Chinese owner company can certainly be justified on the basis that the project was funded with Chinese money. The concern is how this award is achieved by covert manipulation. The challenge came more in integrating the Chinese suppliers to comply with the local standards. This regional procurement process is carefully coordinated at a national (host country) Chinese management level operating above individual organizations and companies and requires logistical savvy and good forward planning. The procurement and distribution of Chinese manufactured goods for the consumption by and use of Chinese companies and nationals in the host country is carefully planned and executed.

An interesting observation is that Chinese companies tend to import everything and anything that can be sourced from China. The local economy is only supported as a last resort. At one operation, even Chinese wheelbarrows were imported rather than sourced from the local hardware store. Even their favorite Chinese delicacies for the Chinese workforce are imported in bulk by a Chinese 'wholesaler' who will then distribute the items to the different Chinese organizations set up in the host country. Certain Chinese fresh produce is eventually cultivated in the host country for exclusive consumption by Chinese patrons in the numerous Chinese canteens that have established themselves in the host country.

African indigenous artifacts and souvenirs are bought, carefully studied, and then re-produced back in China and imported into Africa to be sold by Chinese hired African or even Chinese hawkers to tourists for cheaper than the locals can afford to sell it for. Such practices of local market manipulation, monopoly and eventually leading to monopsony, are conveniently overlooked by local authorities who are usually given some hush money to let such practices thrive.

A network of Chinese operations is carefully set up, operating across business boundaries and is being supported from corporate management level right down to the informal sector. The Chinese Tiger operates as one entity rather than individually competing operations trying to outdo each other. Clearly, such a coordinated approach is sanctioned, supported, and facilitated at Chinese government level. Importation of agricultural goods is not impeded by import restrictions or import duties, as would typically be the case for private businesses importing exotic agricultural products.

While Chinese companies will initially use in-country ship chandlers, clearing agencies, and transportation companies, it does not take long for them to understand the local best practices, which then prompts them to set up their own companies to handle the import and export requirements for Chinese companies. Again, the local industry is eventually bypassed, putting pressure on the local economy. And the host country authorities will happily grant the necessary permits to these new Chinese companies as, after all, the Chinese Tiger has looked well after its newly acquired cubs, when these were vulnerable and without sustenance. The peril of the local economy is far less important than the newfound Guanxi with a new and all-powerful friend and partisan.

In some African countries, product from illegal artisanal mining operations is directly bought and either beneficiated locally by 'legal' Chinese operations or shipped directly to China. Local host country authorities do not consciously or effectively curtail these practices. An intricate network of artisanal suppliers, Chinese buyers, Chinese transportation companies, and Chinese clearing agents makes it difficult to control this unofficial route of getting processed and unprocessed commodities to mainland China. Such practices appear to be supported by Chinese corporates, rather than being condemned. Because Chinese corporates are closely associated with the governments of the host country, authorities are reluctant to intervene.

In some African countries, the artisanal mining activities are under the auspices of high-ranking government officials, including presidential guards, the military, or intelligence services. Any intervention would be considered futile, as these organizations have direct parliamentary protection and further provide direct government protection to the illicit Chinese organizations operating in this environment. It is a well-known fact that it is notoriously difficult for private mining concession holders to remove artisanal miners from their mining concession areas, running up against government departments and local police resistance around every corner. Cooperation can only be achieved if the benefit to such government institutions surpasses the benefits bestowed by the Chinese operations. And this is often a non-achievable option, as Chinese operations are typically parastatal in nature and therefore have direct access to Chinese government funds.

Custom-built solutions were typically not offered to non-Chinese customers until the early 2000s but Chinese businesses are now starting to offer complete solutions to potential customers across a wide spectrum of products. However, this solution driven approach clashes directly with the Chinese cultural psyche, which does not encourage initiative, intuition, decisiveness, and broad based out-of-the box thinking. It becomes notoriously difficult to get a Chinese organization to interpret and provide the desired customized product to a Western specification. While Chinese organizations will enthusiastically indicate that they can provide any desired solution at the desirable price and accelerated time compared to a Western company, the interaction becomes rather rigid and the Chinese organization will develop a 'fixed' solution, once the contract is put in place, making it difficult to optimize the output.

Western organizations are mesmerized by the favorable pricing and conditions on a fixed price basis, but often are very disappointed when the final product is handed over, as it is often not to the desired Western standard. Western organizations are often quickly 'blinded' by the low price and fast track delivery promises, which trump quality and proper specification requirements.

While Chinese organizations are known to deliver against

the agreed price and on time, the product quality and durability are often compromised. To circumvent this problem, many Western companies have set up their own procurement offices in China, or they use reputable procurement organizations, to sift out the quality suppliers from a sea of unqualified and short-lived Chinese manufacturers entering the lucrative global market arena.

Of course, Chinese organizations are compelled to support the Chinese supply chain, with a large chunk of Chinese investment funds for offshore projects never leaving China. This is not unlike Western organizations, which can also be compelled to buy specific products where Export Credit Agencies have provided export financing. The major difference lies in the fact that Western companies are free to select the most suitable suppliers whereas Chinese companies are required to select specific products from specific companies, so that all Chinese suppliers over time benefit from the different Chinese investment funds.

One seldom hears of Chinese parastatal organizations that have gone into liquidation due to lack of work. The Chinese economic mill will ensure that all Chinese organizations will survive during good and bad global cyclical events.

For assignments and projects outside mainland China, Chinese organizations are master strategists. While certain host country laws and regulations specify local content, the Chinese organization procurement processes and contract awards are strategically manipulated, to ultimately give some of the contracts to specific Chinese organizations—even if host country suppliers or other global companies can produce the desired product better and cheaper.

While elaborate procurement procedures are put in place and need to be strictly adhered to by the team, the management does interject strategically to steer the output into the desired direction. The corporate team will be reminded of who the desired Chinese supplier is; late bids or revised bids will be considered at the insistence of the Chinese management and Chinese bidders who seem to already have pre-existing close relationships with selected Chinese team members. However, the procurement coordinator must still fulfill the tendering process in a transparent and detailed manner, even if it is the clear intention that a specific Chinese contractor is to be awarded the work. When this procurement behavior becomes apparent in the market place, non-Chinese and specifically Western companies often decline to bid on tenders.

In one specific instance, a Western Project Manager working for a Chinese owned company was tasked with implementing a project in the jungles of central Africa. For such a daunting task, it was critical to identify the most suitable engineering company to design, engineer, procure, and construct the intended operations optimally. After half a year of planning—, which included preparing the detailed project scope of work and design criteria to supplement the tender document—the Chinese leader accused the individual of wasting the company's resources. For the Chinese leader it was obvious that is was only necessary to appoint a Chinese company, which would then build the facility on a fixed price basis on time and within budget. The Western Project Manager's division was liquidated and the project delivery responsibility given to the operations department which was already operating a mine for the company in Africa.

The implementation strategies and concepts of Western educated persons versus Chinese educated persons could not be further apart than far-flung galaxies on opposite sides of the universe. Nevertheless, the accountability remains the same, should the final product not be to the expectation of the Chinese organization; heads are bound to roll when productivity targets cannot be achieved due to misunderstanding the target deliverables in the first instance.

Ironically, Western client organizations are initially more than willing to sign poorly defined contractual scopes, underestimating the astuteness of Chinese service providers and supply companies. Chinese organizations will deliver exactly and only what is specified in the scope. If the Western company demands additional work to be done at no additional cost, then the Chinese organization in question will either continue with the original work or just stop working, until the money is forthcoming.

But Chinese client organizations will hold Western service providers and suppliers to the contractual deliverable requirements. If a product is poorly specified in the contract—for example if the contract states that a Western company should provide a fully functional product with a specified throughput—but design parameters and battery limits have been poorly specified—, then that is what the Chinese organization anticipates to get. This is irrespective of what the accumulated cost for the supplier will be due to unforeseen scope changes or broader scope requirements.

It is therefore always advisable to prepare a detailed contractual scope and specify every deliverable detail to prevent any disappointment. Chinese negotiators are notorious for misunderstanding scope requirements and failing to include them in contracts. Contracts must always be read carefully before agreeing and signing them to ensure all requirements have been adequately captured. Postscript Chapter 1: Chinese Business Culture, Etiquette and Behavior in the Work Environment, includes more insight into this topic.

In summary, the Chinese procurement web extends far beyond the corporate requirements of a single company, forming part of an intricate web of procurement practices that extend far beyond the borders of the host country—all the way back to mainland China and beyond.

COST MANAGEMENT

A Chinese only team carefully monitored the project and office costs, and only a few of the non-Chinese senior team members were informed of the project and corporate cost status. The Chinese management did not readily share cost information and as such, the office team could not gauge the actual costs against budgeted costs. If one needed to order something for the office, this was done 'blindly', hoping that the Chinese leader would consider it necessary and approve the purchase requisition. Towards the end of a budget year, one had no inkling of whether equipment and services could still be acquired or whether the budget cost value had been exceeded.

Various senior Western employees on the Finance team were always under surveillance. A Chinese deputy was assigned with the unofficial duty to inform on the Western manager's performance to the Chinese leader. These deputies seldom participated in day-to-day business activities, only involving themselves at their pace and intensity. Western senior managers were not allowed to make independent decisions; instead, they had to defer all decision making to the Chinese leader.

Many senior Western Finance managers felt so restricted (and frustrated), that they terminated their contracts prematurely. This probably suited the Chinese organization perfectly, as their overall strategy appears to be to phase out the non-Chinese employees when completion target and milestone dates are approaching. At that point, the Chinese team takes over to demonstrate their 'effectiveness' in having delivered the final product.

In a modern project environment, technical and commercial information should not be separated. Information about costs should not be withheld from the design team, but this is exactly what happens in a Chinese project environment.

A Chinese-only team usually does the highly complex project commercial adjudications, and few non-Chinese team members get to see the outcome of a commercial adjudication. The technical adjudications are done in isolation, normally by Western professionals, and the final selection is then rubber-stamped by the Chinese leader himself. This stringent cost management principle—requiring different teams to often work in series rather than in parallel—impacts directly on schedule and additional resource costs. This does not appear to bother the Chinese management, who expect the team to stick rigidly to the cumbersome Chinese cost evaluation process, which is based on Chinese business principles and not suitable for a Western business environment.

DEADLINES

Once a written commitment has been made to achieve a certain target outcome against a target date, an all-out effort will be made to achieve this objective. Missing a deadline in the Chinese business environment is seen as a gross act of negligence. Additional resources will be piled onto the assignment, working 24/7 if necessary, so as not to miss the target date. After all, missing a completion date can have dire consequences for the responsible Chinese parties, ranging from withholding salaries (until the assignment has been delivered), to being demoted, to being sent back to China to do a mundane back office job. The dire prognosis compels Chinese employees to make every effort to achieve the objectives as well as pretend that the objectives have been met. Facts and figures are manipulated to make it look as though all is on track; schedules are never forecasted to reflect the true delays; and not a word is uttered at meetings about the true state of affairs. In most cases, the immediate Chinese leader—who is ultimately responsible for the outcome—is right in on the action.

Once the target date comes around, the Chinese team will claim either that the assignment has been completed—even if this is not the case—or some Outsider, (person or organization) will be blamed for the delay. That entity will be duly punished (dismissal or penalties liquidated) and then all will carry on beavering away at getting the assignment across the finishing line as quickly as possible, targeting a newly (only orally) agreed completion date. It's a cat and mouse game of making sure that the people making the rules are told what they want to hear, rather than what they need to hear. This pretence can be maintained right through the different operating echelons, as each business level of responsibility has yet to answer to another boss, who could implement punishment directly on them failing to meet target dates.

Elaborate schemes are devised to feign completion. A poly(ethanol) project in China was running behind schedule, but the Western contractor was asked to sign the construction completion certificate seven months before actual completion, so that the client management could advise their chairman that official completion had been achieved and that any ongoing site work was merely working off some outstanding punch list items. The Western company used this opportunity to agree that no penalties would be liquidated after signature date.

In another example, an elaborate photo shoot was undertaken for a product apparently made in a processing plant, where the actual 'product' was bought from another supplier and brought to the plant for the occasion. Any ongoing construction work was feigned as working off punch list items and the real product was only realized a year later. While this behavior can be seen around the world—certainly by Western companies as well—for Chinese organizations the consequences of not achieving targets are far more severe and long lasting than in Western business environments.

DISBURSEMENT CLAIMS

The claiming of personal expenses incurred on behalf of the company was notoriously difficult. A complicated Chinese based online administration system was used to submit claims. The system was not user friendly—many of the instructions were in Mandarin—and rather time consuming to fill in. Once submission requirements were mastered, many claims were never paid out; the Finance Department cited additional information requirements—information that was never in existence in the first instance. So the claim reached a stalemate point of non-processing and then died a slow death.

One exemplary example involved a Western employee picking up the tab for an approved team building exercise, but then failed to receive his money back. The company had updated the claim policy after the event had taken place, making it policy that no claims including an alcohol component would be processed (and the Chinese are consumers of large quantities of this elixir). Suffice to say, further team building sessions faded into oblivion, as it was impossible to secure an advance sum of money or a company credit card to fund such events.

BRIBERY AND CORRUPTION IN THE WORKPLACE

This is always a contentious topic, and for obvious reasons any bribery and corruption practices are done clandestinely and are generally poorly documented. Chinese people are well known for using the back door (see Chapter 5 – Guanxi) to get things done. In Chinese culture, being innovative and making use of Guanxi is not necessarily viewed with the same vilification as it is in Western operations. If one can do something cheaper or faster, and get away with it by having paid somebody to open certain doors, then such innovation should be commended and not condemned in the Chinese mind-set.

While working for a Chinese organization, many of the team members working in the office had entered the country on a tourist visa, still awaiting their delayed work permits. One day the Chinese contact person in the host country received a warning from the Immigration Department that an immigration raid was imminent. No doubt, a favor had now been returned, which allowed the Chinese colleagues to timeously leave the country. The contingency plan that was openly discussed (in the hour of need) was to pay somebody in the Immigration Department a 'consulting fee' to accelerate the issuing of the work permits. In a Western corporate environment, such talk and action would constitute a serious breach of ethic boundaries.

In another example, one of the Western engineers working on the Chinese client team helped one of the Chinese subcontractors on site to implement a fixed price-processing unit. He assisted with trouble shooting and problem solving on a construction job. The Chinese team desperately needed the help as their Chinese standards and specifications did not align with the local standards, causing endless installation problems and severe delays. After some weeks of assistance, the Western engineer was approached by the Chinese contractor HR representative and offered a brand new iPhone, as a token of appreciation for his efforts, the HR representative emphasizing that the engineer should not construe this as an act of bribery. This type of reward is not typically seen as above board by Western ethics standards, and the Western engineer naturally refused the thank you gift several times while the Chinese HR representative persisted. Ironically, it is customary in Chinese culture to refuse a gift several times before accepting it, so the HR representative probably did not even realize initially that the Western engineer was genuinely refusing the 'bribe/ gift' offer (also see Postscript Chapter 2: Chinese Cultural and Traditional Revelations – Giving Gifts).

CHAPTER 12

THE WALL

"For this reason the gentleman will employ a man on a distant mission and observe his degree of loyalty will employ him close at hand and observe his degree of respect. He will hand him troublesome affairs and observe how well he manages them, will suddenly ask his advice and observe how wisely he answers. He will exact some difficult promise from him and see how well he keeps it, turn over funds to him and see with what benevolence he dispenses them, inform him of the danger he is in and note how faithful he is to his duties. He will get him drunk with wine and observe how well he handles himself, place him in mixed company and see what effect beauty has upon him. By applying these nine tests, you may determine who is the unworthy man."

—*Confucius*

For the last 3000 years, the wall around China has played a pivotal role in Chinese culture, behavior, spirit, psyche, as well as China's interaction with other cultures. A wall of some sorts has always kept the Chinese population in and the 'barbarians' out. Influence from the outside world was limited to bloody skirmishes, trading with countries that could supply China with the necessary raw materials, as well as limited encounters with people during the seafaring excursions by the great mariner and explorer Zheng He at the start of the fifteenth century. Shortly after Zheng He's 1000 ship strong fleet departed the shores of China, The Chinese Ming dynasty (1368 – 1644) imposed full isolation from the rest of the world. This isolation was continued by the Qing dynasty (1644 – 1912) lasting until the late eighteenth century when King George III sent the first 700-person strong British trade mission to China to initiate the tea trade (Lovell, The Great Wall, Page 1).

Chinese people as late as the nineteenth century viewed foreigners as barbarians who could offer Chinese civilization very little. According to idealized Chinese diplomatic conventions over one and a half millennia old, foreigners were allowed to visit China only as inferior vassals bringing tribute, not as political equals, and certainly not as representatives of 'the most powerful nation of the globe' as the British confidently saw themselves. It was Chinese custom to prescribe a number of regulations to foreign diplomatic envoys, specifying how they had to engage with the emperor. This included group size, length of stay, how often one could see the emperor, and of course the number of prostrations required of the foreign envoys. The British spent weeks debating the diplomatic protocol with the Chinese, on which the two parties could never agree. A particular sticking point was the kowtow, a complex bowing ceremony with the head touching the ground, which the British representative refused to do unless a Chinese official of equal rank would kneel before a portrait of King George III. This was refused, as the Chinese emperor was the ruler of 'all under heaven' and therefore his subjects could never agree that foreigners had equal authority. After months of wrangling, the Emperor ordered the reduction of rations, to put pressure on the British delegation (Lovell, The Great Wall, Page 4, 5).

This first diplomatic engagement between China and a foreign entity ended in a stalemate. Two years later, the Dutch embassy did not achieve much more diplomatic gain, even though the Dutch ambassador kowtowed without hesitation. The Dutch were insulted by being put up in a stable and were given food that had already been partially consumed.

Chinese officials received impressive gifts with indifference and viewed it with amusement. The Emperor made it clear that China had never valued ingenious articles, nor did they have the slightest need for British manufactured items. Seventy years later, when British and French soldiers entered Beijing, the British gifts were discovered in a stable, unopened. Because of these early spectacular diplomatic failures, the world has always viewed China's impervious cultural wall with suspicion.

This figurative wall of isolation in many ways has shaped the modern China of today. The modern Chinese wall can be viewed from two angles, namely the physical, psychological, mental, and political wall controlling the behavior of all Chinese citizens when interacting with other cultures; and secondly, the various controls created by the Chinese system to prevent Chinese people from discovering the world and prevent the world from discovering the inner workings of China.

MEETING FOR THE FIRST TIME

When engaging with Chinese companies for the first time, the feeling of a controlled environment becomes immediately prevalent. The Chinese delegation will all move to the far side of the room, sit down in unison with the most senior person seated in the middle of the group, facing the entrance of the room. Junior team members will fan out to either end in order of importance. Everybody is dressed similarly and holds a similar posture. The Chinese delegation impersonates a Wall, sitting silently, firmly, and imposingly, facing the unknown entity on the other side. Any polite banter and chatter initiated by the Western meeting attendees, fades away before the meeting even commences.

A Chinese translator, who only engages with the most senior Chinese delegation member, facilitates these highly formal discussions with the Wall. Even if some of the Chinese delegation team members speak English, all dialogue will be from the most senior Chinese representative via the translator to the most senior Western company representative sitting directly opposite him.

Sometimes, it becomes apparent that the Chinese senior representative can actually speak English, yet he chooses to converse in Mandarin through the translator. From the onset, it is difficult to establish and build a relationship. Subsequent meetings don't fare much better, as the Chinese wall of humankind remains impervious to an elusive golden key that unlocks the Chinese psyche and start establishing bridging relationships.

Meetings are always very formal and topics are discussed frugally. There is little room for light chatter, casual talk, or informal engagement after the meeting. The stiff atmosphere leaves one exhausted and unsure what will present itself behind the Wall at the next encounter.

STERILE OFFICE

When working for a Chinese company, one enters into a sterile environment. The work environment seems devoid of positive energy and atmosphere. One is not officially introduced to the Chinese colleagues already on the team. There is no induction or onboarding process and there is no opportunity to be shown around or familiarized with the new environment. Western and local celebrations are not encouraged in the office environment. The leader celebrates Chinese festivals and public holidays with some eateries and a short speech in one of the boardrooms. It feels like a forced environment with little or no spirit and pizzazz. There is no coagulation of sense and purpose, no unification of people and teams, as well as no merger of concepts and beliefs.

While an attempt is made to align the team at rare Chinese dinner get-togethers, such dinners are only to be organized by the Chinese leader, who also then dictates the conversation. These formal dinners are stiff and tense, and the Chinese leader controls the formalities and discussion topics for the evening. The Chinese leader will often use the occasion to extract work information out of the Western colleagues by asking loaded questions for which one may not necessarily be prepared. The invisible barrier stretching across the table like a silent Wall is clearly palpable on such occasions.

STRANGE RELATIONSHIPS

As is in the nature of the Western business culture, one forms relationships and socializes with sub-groups of the team. However, trying to engage with one or two Chinese colleagues on a social level is near impossible. The Chinese establishment frowns upon Chinese people socializing with Western people. Instead, any social engagement needs to comprise an organized event to which the entire Chinese team is invited.

One peculiar incident took place, which highlights a moment when this antisocial doctrine presented itself in its crudest form. After an organized workshop, one of the Western colleagues offered to drive one of the Chinese colleagues home. On route, the Western colleague suggested dinner before going home, and after dinner, the Western colleague duly dropped the Chinese colleague off at home. The next day, the Chinese colleague advised the Western colleague that he was seriously reprimanded for having socialized on his own with a Western colleague and therefore he could not risk such an engagement again, as he might be summoned back to China for disorderly behavior.

Don't try to socialize with Chinese colleagues on an individual basis, as it will be at the expense of their well-being. Any socializing should rather be undertaken with the whole Chinese team, even if not all non-Chinese team members can attend.

IN THE CLOUD

In China, Internet access is limited and social media is restricted. Google and Facebook are not only banned but also not even accessible, having been blocked outright by the Chinese authorities from being streamed. Internet usage is randomly screened and if people are found to have visited prohibited sites, the punishment can be severe. This random policing has instilled a fear in the population who use the

Internet very cautiously.

In China, there is a good chance that banned Internet sites will not even come up in the search, but the situation is different outside China. While the Chinese company IT department restricts access to some social media sites, it is far more difficult to block all undesired Internet sites, which run into thousands. In China, this can be done at a government level, but outside China, this is not possible. Any Internet restrictions need to be imposed at company level by the IT department who don't have the resources and time to implement all the desired restrictions over a short period. The only effective control is to monitor Internet usage randomly. This situation creates a dilemma for the Chinese colleagues, who become rather reluctant to search for information on the Internet as they might mistakenly come across a banned Internet site that is now readily accessible in the expatriate environment.

Even searching for words or phrases that could imply a search for banned topics might attract the undesired attention of the control police. So a rather peculiar conundrum has presented itself where Chinese colleagues will rather request Western colleagues to provide information readily available in the cloud, than do a Google search for the information themselves. After all, the search engine Google is banned in China.

As of September 2015, around 3,000 websites were blocked in mainland China (excluding Hong Kong and Macau) under the country's policy of Internet censorship (Wikipedia, Websites blocked in mainland China). Some of the most prominent blocked sites include any Google affiliated products, Facebook, You Tube, Dropbox, Twitter, Yahoo, Wikipedia, Instagram, many Western newspapers and news broadcasting sites, blogging sites and pornographic sites.

OWNERSHIP

Committing views and decisions with pen to paper will capture one's state of mind at that very time for eternity. Thus, communication in the oral format is preferred over the written word. Email communication traffic is generally low from Chinese colleagues and if emails are written, they cover superficial topics or just pass on information. In the same vein, minutes of meetings are either conspicuously absent or very light in content, avoiding capturing any opinions and decisions made during the meeting. By not capturing decisions in writing there is a lesser chance of blame being assigned to individuals when things go wrong. A paper trail is non-existent. This phenomenon presents itself right throughout the organization—both horizontally within departments and vertically up the Chinese management structure. This lack of transparency presents a serious obstacle in effective business and team management.

It is strongly recommended for Western colleagues to record any decision in writing to avoid any shifting of blame into the wrong direction. When it comes to finding a guilty party, it is unlikely for Chinese colleagues to point out any transgression that might have been undertaken by one of their colleagues, but will rather allot the blame to their non-Chinese colleagues (the principle of Guanxi plays a big role). Having the records of decisions taking previously will come in very handy now.

THE BLAME GAME

Chinese business culture has a strong blame culture. When things go wrong, somebody must be found guilty. It is more important to apportion the blame to somebody than actually resolving the issue. Often, the person found guilty has long since been dismissed, while a solution is still being sought for the problem.

Rather than getting the responsible Western person to sort out the problem, the Chinese prefer to resolve the problem themselves—even if they don't understand the technicality of the problem. Problems can be deliberated on for weeks or even months before a plausible solution is identified. They reluctantly listen to any suggestions from Western colleagues, but typically do not consider it further for implementation even if the Western colleague is the best-suited candidate with the right technical background to resolve the issue at hand. Once a problem has come to the surface, the capability of the responsible party is no longer trusted.

In one case, a technical solution for a bad design of a small project component was deliberated on for more than seven months. As a result, this insignificant work modification started to impact on the scheduled overall completion date. The logic of delaying an easy decision for a mediocre problem that then spirals into the key issue of focus until it ultimately starts delaying the entire undertaking, is not comprehensible in a Western work environment.

When the error is traced back to a Chinese colleague, the situation is handled quite differently. Firstly, the issue is not publicized, but the Chinese team will rather try to resolve it below the radar. If the problem comes out in the open, it is normally downplayed and dismissed by the Chinese leader as though it does not have such an impact or relevance in the greater scheme of things.

An example of the blame game presented itself on a petro-chemical construction site in China where Chinese contractors executed the Chinese-owned project. The Chinese client had employed three Western engineers to assist with the project implementation management, but the project was running dismally behind schedule.

The client management team called a meeting one Saturday morning, with all the contractors as well as client team members present. The meeting quickly transpired into blame being apportionment to the three Westerners, who were accused directly of having delayed the project. They were criticized for not understanding the high quality of the Chinese procedures and processes being used and not being accustomed to working in a quality environment for a quality company.

Three engineers were the cause for a workforce of hundreds of Chinese not achieving the desired outcome. Of course it was futile for the three engineers to defend themselves and try to argue their position of innocence.

The Tiger has grasped his prey firmly in his claws, playing it like a cat cages a mouse and any wrong move to escape the Tiger's proverbial claw could lead to a fatal swipe of annihilation.

KNOWLEDGE IS POWER

Most cultures have used the principle of 'Knowledge is Power' as a manipulation tool for millennia. However, a more transparent management style has been adopted in the West over the last twenty-five years. This heralded a business culture that welcomes the sharing of all (or at least most) knowledge. It is considered a key requirement to ensuring that every employee, from junior positions right through to senior management, is empowered with the latest information in order to make the most resolute decision in the best interest of the organization in order for it to flourish.

This key management principle has however not yet instilled itself in Chinese organizations, where any knowledge is closely guarded by individuals and used to manipulate people's behavior. In Postscript Chapter 1, I discuss the covert management of traveling arrangements in detail, citing a good example of the use of this outdated management tool to control people's behavior and expectations.

In essence, withholding knowledge from people prevents them from planning their work and their private lives, which keeps them in a state of suspense and expectation. It renders them unable to execute their next progressive move. Knowledge is only shared with relevant individuals or groups of people when it benefits the bearer, but not necessarily the receiver. Knowledge that would impact a future event is withheld until the event imposes itself. At that point, the knowledge is shared to manipulate such an event in the best interest of the bearer, especially if it relates to something that is usually more difficult to foresee and control long in advance.

Sharing of knowledge can also create expectations or anticipations, which might not be able to be fulfilled or accommodated down the line. It is therefore best—in the Chinese work environment—not to create such expectations or anticipations in the first place.

This behavior is probably best explained with the following example, which I personally experienced.

As part of my work assignment, I had to spend some time away from home in a foreign African country, where the project was being implemented. As such, I needed to get a work permit. I duly submitted my details and my Chinese employer then submitted my application to the host government Immigration Department for processing. Months passed and I was eventually told that my application was unsuccessful. That was that, and I assumed that I would no longer go to site in the foreign country. Some four months later, I received a frantic call to come to site. I gingerly pointed out that I didn't have a work permit, but alas, the work permit was sent to me within hours. Closer inspection revealed that the work permit had been granted within 3 weeks of application—in other words, some eight months earlier.

Clearly, the Chinese management withheld such information from me, as I was not yet required to go to site. Advising me of the work permit application success would have created an expectation from me that I would go to the site in the near future. The Chinese management kept their options open as to whether I would be needed on site or not. While I resolved that I would not be going to work on site in the African country—which impacts on all sorts of things like planning family vacations, joining a gym, and even enrolling in a study course—, the Chinese management assumed—as is typical in China—that I would not have planned anything. After all, I didn't know what their plan for me was in the first place.

My Chinese management team found the fact that I could

not make myself immediately available to go to site inexplicable. I first needed to make personal arrangements. To add insult to injury, it turned out that the work permit letter did not suffice when I arrived at the foreign destination—although the Chinese-led HR Department assured me that it would—but the work permit still needed to be issued.

To avoid instant expatriation back to my country of departure, I was compelled to pay the hefty work permit fee on the spot. I was never able to claim this cost back from my employer. Not only was I given the necessary information very late, but also the information shared by my Chinese employer was vague and misleading. The Chinese corporation expected me to unearth the multiplicity of requirements and deal with this amplitude of issues at short notice if I wanted to remain in their employ. The choice was mine and mine alone, with no corporate support to back me up.

Another example of this behavior manifested itself during contract negotiations. After an initial interview, don't expect any further discussions for a few months. Then, without any prior warning, a draft contract will be suddenly issued and the applicant will be pressured to agree to it. The final client contract signature will only be initiated a few days before one is to commence work; sometimes it will be done after one has started working.

This behavior leaves one in a state of suspense to whether the contractually agreed terms will indeed be honored. When the contract completion date nears, a contract extension negotiation—while being intimated for months—only starts in earnest one to two weeks before the contract expiration date. The Chinese organization will feign great disappointment when one is no longer available beyond the original contract period, because one has in the meantime sought a new employment opportunity, due to the Chinese employer's lack of decision-making action.

In the Chinese corporate environment, Chinese employees will patiently await instruction about their next assignment. In a Western culture, Western employees will evaluate the situation, gauge the opportunity, and make a decision on their next move, dependent on whether the company confirms their requirement, preferably in writing, well before the contract expiration date approaches. Otherwise, employees might explore and engage in alternative employment opportunities.

Chinese organizations have great difficulty when they want to terminate one's services. The organization would lose face if they didn't renew your contract, especially if you are considered a valuable team member. In order to justify the termination, a case for dismissal needs to be concocted. It becomes quite obvious when an affected Western employee becomes a target for systematic 'attack'; he or she will be harassed for poor performance, challenged for information not under their direct control, and questioned by management on trivial issues that are usually resolved at lower functional levels. It is a targeted 'attack' with biased 'findings' to justify a dismissal or contract termination.

However, the reason for these targeted challenges is never shared with the employee. Instead, the employee's direct superior is asked to notify the employee of his immediate dismissal or otherwise the contract is simply not renewed. Interestingly, at this point in time, trust levels hit an all-time low and many Westerners start fearing that their last paycheck might not be forthcoming. In some cases, these payments are indeed delayed until HR and Finance Departments can no longer ignore the employee's incessant pestering.

Other manipulative behavior is applied by withholding important information—such as confirmed travel itineraries, accommodation details and meeting attendance requirements— until the last minute. In some instances, the Chinese management changes travel itineraries and the affected party is only notified at the last minute. In one such instance, a Western employee, realizing that they were not traveling to the airport, politely reminded his Chinese host of his flight departure time, only to be told that his return flight home had been re-scheduled to the next day as he was required to attend a function that night.

Flights might be booked at short notice, departing on a weekend to attend weekend meetings. Attendance is not negotiable.

Here Western and Chinese business cultures diverge significantly, as after work time is typically sacrosanct in Western culture; in Chinese culture, your time belongs to the company and you are expected to be accessible 24/7 for company and country. It became evident that once in the employ of a Chinese organization, they owned you.

This does not only pertain to one's availability, but also to interactive behavior, the Chinese superior owning relationship, the relationship demeanor, and relationship hierarchy. Chinese superiors quickly enforce a master-servant relational dependency, typically practiced in Chinese culture according to Confucian harmonious behavioral traits. Information is shared on a need-to-know basis, which quickly escalates the frustration levels of Western employees who are more used to working in an open and transparent communication environment where corporate work relationships are established quickly across the different functional levels with all team members.

Western employees in roles of responsibility are typically contractually incentivized against target objectives. Promotional objectives might also be set. Now as we have seen already, typically non-Chinese employees are likely to have a finite employment period planned for them without their prior knowledge. While they believe that they are building towards their next rung in their career ladder, it was never the intent by the Chinese organization to pay the incentives or promote the employee. By the Chinese company maintaining an air of expectation, the non-Chinese employees will contribute enthusiastically and professionally—right up to the point of premature contract termination, which curtails any further hope of incentive liquidation or promotional opportunity.

Non-Chinese employees need to anticipate that their Chinese employer will try to plan their exit date strategy and must make their own plans. When the signs of your imminent dismissal become evident, quit before you are fired. When the end game approaches, the playing field becomes nasty. You can avoid it by resigning and moving on in your own time. The remuneration is typically favorable, so you will want to optimize your employment period, but do not overstay your welcome. It is a delicate game of cat and mouse.

BLOOD IS THICKER THAN WATER

Chinese clients are renowned for supporting their Chinese sub-contractors in times of need—be it financially, materially, or with expertise. It is the duty of the Chinese client to look after Chinese sub-contractors and service providers, as ultimately all the Chinese companies work for the Chinese state. A Chinese client will bail out a Chinese contractor financially, if necessary. He will allow poor workmanship to slip through and ignore safety concerns and HR issues. If such poor workmanship is challenged by a non-Chinese entity, then the situation is usually vehemently defended, not only by the sub-contractor management team, but also even by the client management team, who will cite communication and interpretation issues as the main harbinger of the dilemma.

The Chinese government expects helping Chinese contractors. They don't bestow the same treatment on Western contractors and service providers, who will be continuously scrutinized for poor delivery of services, creating a conflict with the Wall, and measurable tension between the different contractors operating on the same construction site. Even if a Chinese client appoints a non-Chinese company to act on their behalf to manage a Chinese contractor, the Chinese client will side with the Chinese contractor rather than his appointed representative.

LET'S TALK

Communication represents one of the biggest barriers between Chinese and Western cultures. Apart from oral communication presenting a barrier—even if both parties communicate in the same language—these opposing cultures have very different ideas about make use of transparent communication tools.

Communication in the Chinese business culture is typically one way and from the top down. Communicating from the bottom team echelons up the hierarchy of importance is generally not tolerated. Instructions will always come from the most senior person and will be passed down the chain of command. The next person not fully understanding the origin—nor the context, or the reason of the instruction. The instruction will be carried out in silence and the collated findings absorbed back into the entangled plethora of uninformed souls, swooping the carefully packaged bundle of data up the proverbial ladder of importance, as though it were their own creation. The originator of the information will never understand the purpose of the requested work, who requested the work and where his or her carefully assimilated creation will ultimately end up.

This approach has a distinct upside in that it ensures that the author of the information will always give his or her best effort, as the audience might be super critical, and this might then single him or her out as an under-performer. The downside is of course the fact that information is not prepared fit for purpose and so time and effort could be wasted in preparing the work.

SPY VERSUS SPY

There are always proverbial ears on the walls in a Chinese business environment. One is always under the impression that somebody is listening in to one's conversation. I have experienced this many times during debates with one of my colleagues. Glancing around, one quickly realizes that the

Chinese colleagues in the immediate vicinity would stop working and concentrate hard on the discussion going on. In some instances, they would move closer to the vicinity of the conversation. On some occasions, they would interject themselves into the conversation, forming part of the conversation circle but not necessarily partaking in the conversation. If issues and concerns were noted in the discussion, one could be assured of a call from the Chinese leader not too long after the conversation had ended.

Even more concerning was the suspicion that emails, telephone calls, and meeting rooms were monitored. This would align well with a Communist mode of operation, where secrecy and confidentiality are not tolerated. On too many occasions, Chinese colleagues or the Chinese leader would conspicuously query issues shortly after the same topic was discussed telephonically or in a meeting venue.

The monitoring situation can be used to one's advantage by elaborating on targeted content for an invisible audience, anticipating that the message ultimately ends up in front of the intended target audience. This approach was especially effective with emails, where information was not only conveyed to the target audience in writing, but it also formed a permanent record for future referencing.

WE ARE ALL ONE

Having one's own opinion—especially if it's not aligned with the Chinese leadership—can be detrimental to one's corporate well-being. In a Western environment, it is normal for people to investigate and explore options as well as query previous decisions and calls made. There is no harm in raising one's concern or opinion in a meeting forum for further discussion and analysis by the greater team.

In the Chinese business environment, it is atypical for the team to question anything. After all, the Chinese leader has ultimately made most of the decisions. Questioning any decisions would therefore result in crossing knifes with Mianzi, and more importantly with the leader himself. This would be a fatal mistake. No individualism is tolerated, but rather individuals survive in this environment by clinging to a group mentality. And to change the opinion of a group of people at the same time is a rather futile exercise, as individuals can hide behind a group mentality (all exuding the same 'Wall of Thought'), and therefore do not need to have an independent viewpoint or undertake any intuitive thinking. The enforced herd mentality syndrome provides a buffer for survival within the larger Chinese organizational structure.

THE WALL OF THE EMPEROR

There are many differences between what Westerners consider good leadership styles and a Chinese leader's leadership style. The two most profound differences from my experience are that Chinese leaders talk but do not listen and blame but do not take ownership or responsibility for any failures. The Chinese management is very inaccessible, having isolated themselves not only physically (on a different floor in the office or behind a number of secretaries), but also being very unapproachable.

Chinese leaders often come across as arrogant, non-engaging, unaccommodating, and sometimes outright rude to any 'intruder' of their space. There is a distinct barrier between the Emperor and the serfs. The Chinese serfs know how to deal with problems by employing the age-old tool of Guanxi. But non-Chinese colleagues don't have the necessary relationships with the Chinese team members with whom one could resolve such issues. The only approach is to take the issue directly to the Chinese leader, if any resolve might be achievable. And herein lays the dilemma, the Chinese leaders maintain a strong buffer between themselves and the outside world. And if your Guanxi with the leader is in any way tainted (he does not approve of you), then it will be near impossible to resolve issues or implement actions going forward.

Different Chinese leaders are often responsible for different areas of the business, so knowing who the correct person is to approach for your specific problem is rather important. Just by approaching the wrong leader, everybody is bound to lose face—you, the incorrect reader, and the person you should have approached. How could you not have known his all-important position of responsibility? And the leader must be approached with benevolence and tact; otherwise, your mission will fail dismally before it has even begun.

If you manage to slot in a session with the leader, he will in all probability decide on a solution and action going forward which might not be what you had in mind. However, his word is final and it would be futile to raise the issue again, or try to counter the proposed solution, or resurrect it again at a future date in a different forum with a different leader. That would be committing an unforgivable injustice that could cost you your corporate life in the Chinese corporation. You would have committed a serious Guanxi crime in the eyes of the beholder.

It is best to remember that if you should realize that the leader's solution is headed for probable failure, you are not to correct him. If you try this approach you will in all likelihood be ignored, maybe side-lined in future, belittled at the next meeting in front of all (probably on an entirely different non relevant matter), or worse, potentially lose your job. Let it be, but make sure you safeguard yourself (should the leader's solution invariably end up failing) by documenting the decision made, even if only confirming the leader's decision in an email back to him. The leader will never take responsibility for the failure, but will seek to blame someone else.

EPILOGUE

Rushing through yet another airport, it is impossible not to notice the red lanterns and Chinese posters with gold Mandarin writing and symbols dotted around the departure area. Chinese national day is a few days away and the airport is abuzz with eager travelers returning to loved ones for this most important of all Chinese holidays. The seating areas are overflowing with parents, children, workers, business people of all walks of life, presenting a cosmopolitan profile of everyday life in China.

Pondering my journey of discovery with a people and land so foreign and far away with its own being and values has been a revelation. I compare it to traveling into the cosmos for the very first time, making new findings and observations, and slowly piecing together the essence of their existence. Invisible threads connect the people to a common identity and a web of intrigue and suspense; one constantly tries to learn the Tiger's every move—its character, its moods, its values and what makes it survive today—only to be able to conquer tomorrow.

This book presents an outside view of perceptions and interactions with Chinese people in a working environment outside China; a space rather foreign and hostile to people who only started being exposed to the rest of the world after the Cultural Revolution, a mere 35 years ago. Encountering the Chinese being for the first time, whether it is its people or its systems or the country is certainly as daunting an encounter as would have been for those souls stumbling across new lands and people during the great voyages of discovery. No doubt, the encounter is as petrifying for the Chinese counterparts, who generally have not experienced much of the rest of the world and who can speak theoretical English but have not lived the living language.

The journey of discovery seems to teach one something else about this ancient culture and its people on an ongoing basis. This learning process appears to be never ending, irrespective of how much one tries to delve into their psyche. The Chinese are a guarded people with whom it is notoriously difficult to forge a relationship. As highlighted previously, relationships with non-Chinese people are not encouraged and one indeed gets the impression that Chinese people who have formed some sort of bond with non-Chinese persons, get relocated back to China rather quickly and often at short notice.

The journey of discovery is often plagued with frustrations due to misunderstandings, miscommunication and simply because the Chinese people are obliged to dogmatically stick to their creed and culture. Trying to open the door of relationship building and bridging the cultural divide becomes a self-curtailing experience, typically terminating in frustration, disbelief, and anger.

It will take years, if not decades, for Western and Chinese cultural beliefs to forge into one melting pot of understanding, alignment, cooperation, and progressive forward thinking. This should not be surprising, when one acknowledges that the Chinese people have really only been exposed to the rest of the world for a short time period in the millennia of history. The Chinese culture with its elaborate traditions is one of the oldest in the world, having changed little over time, despite the many upheavals and many emperors who ruled and are still ruling this land. Any significant changes cannot be expected to happen in our immediate lifetime and therefore it is so important that non-Chinese people, but specifically Western-ers, make all the effort to understand the Chinese better. I hope that this book has helped pave an easier journey not only for corporate, but also for ordinary people who want to understand and know the Tiger better.

People from different backgrounds will carry on the jour-ney of discovery on a daily basis, forming the fibers of connection between cultures from very different worlds, and create a fusion of cultures with new hopes, dreams and beliefs.

My exposure to the Tiger has been an interesting journey of discovery and learning. And the more one is exposed to the vibrant Chinese culture, the more one learns and wants to learn. The figurative vessel of knowledge will probably never be filled, as China but also the rest of the planet evolves in an ever-changing world of how people act, think, behave, and challenge each other.

My flight departure is announced, and once again, I depart the African continent on a journey of new discoveries, unknown challenges, and building a further link in the chain of cultural merging which will ultimately tame the Tiger in my perception of reality. The influence of the Tiger on the rest of the world has been significant in the last three and a half decades, having left its mark on every corner of the world and culture of each continent. Never again will the world be the same in times to come, as the Tiger continues to discover the unknown, perhaps nurtures, perhaps conquers places and people that appear as strange and alien to the Tiger as the Tiger appears to the people being discovered.

POSTSCRIPT CHAPTER 1
CHINESE BUSINESS CULTURE, ETIQUETTE, AND BEHAVIOR IN THE WORK ENVIRONMENT

Dealing with Chinese companies can be downright intimidating. The Western World understands little, if anything, about Chinese business culture and etiquette. Any engagement is usually viewed with some level of trepidation. It starts with huge Chinese delegations including one speaker (the most senior Chinese representative), an interpreter, and a very slow exchange of communication between the Western party and their Chinese counterparts.

Usually, formal business meetings leave one unsure of the way forward at best and rather deflated at worst. Although one initially feels that one has agreed on most issues, be beware that in fact there is very little agreement evident in future meetings or subsequent engagements.

A Western sub-contractor presented their claim to extend the project completion date for one of the large Chinese implementation projects in Africa and reached an agreement with the Chinese leader. A few weeks into the time extension period, the Chinese leader stated that there was no agreement on the new completion date and he requested the service provider to resubmit their proposal for project completion, as he did not accept the earlier completion date and wanted them to improve on it. They then submitted several new dates, but received the same reaction from the Chinese leader every time.

None of the various new completion date recommendations were ever accepted by the Chinese leader until the project eventually finished without a planned date having ever being agreed upon. This typical example demonstrates that there is actually never agreement from the Chinese. They always leave one in suspense and anticipation and there are always unresolved issues to be contemplated. These unresolved issues leave Westerners anxious while the Chinese use the high entropy environment to their best benefit, not revealing many unknown aspects of doing business in 'Chinese', knowing that it makes Westerners very uncomfortable.

It quickly becomes evident that Western and Chinese business cultures are light years apart and it often appears as a daunting task to find a mutually workable partnership, going forward. Indeed, agreeing contractual relationships or partnerships often appear unachievable and in many instances never come to fruition.

This section provides a precise summary of Chinese business culture, etiquette, and behavior in the work environment. The intent is to have a stand-alone chapter that provides a quick reference section without having to read the whole book to get an understanding. For this reason, some of the behaviors already described in preceding chapters are repeated here for completeness of this chapter.

I have differentiated the business culture into two distinct categories, namely 'Formal Engagement Behavior', and then I will delve into 'Individual and Group Social Behavioral Trends' in the workplace.

FORMAL ENGAGEMENT

Very Formal

Chinese business people always behave in a very formal manner, not coming across as loud or bombastic or indeed laughing at trivial jokes typically shed by Western business people (with the intent to loosen the tension and start building relationships). Casual Western talk is often acknowledged with a courteous response, but questions are never comprehensively answered, giving one the feeling that the question was not understood (English communication barrier). It soon becomes evident however, that only the designated leader of the delegation is entitled to talk (see Communication below).

The Chinese delegation will all individually briefly shake hands with the non-Chinese delegation, while handing over their business cards at the same time. Typically, the presence of the non-Chinese person is acknowledged with a brief hello in Mandarin (*"ni hau"*) and nodding of the head; however, names are not exchanged, something that is typical in a Western business environment.

Business Cards

Business cards are handed over between all meeting attendees by holding the business cards in both hands while handing it over (of course standing up). Business cards should always be handed over to the most senior Chinese representatives first. Likewise, a junior employee should hand over his/ her business card from highest to the lowest ranking Chinese delegate. The process of exchanging of business cards can take some time at the start of the engagement before the formal meeting commences. Never slide your business card across the table or just bend over the table to give it to your Chinese counterpart. This is considered inappropriate business etiquette.

Put the Chinese business card into a box or container of value, but not into your wallet or purse and definitely not into your trouser or shirt pocket, as this is considered an insult.

Ideally, your business card must display your company name, your title, as well as your qualifications. If some of this information should be absent from your business card, then mention it on introduction, which is a bit more cumbersome when meeting a large Chinese delegation. Some people suggest that one side of the business card displays the information in Mandarin, as a sign of respect. Remember that Chinese business people always have one side of their business cards written in English, fully appreciating that most non-Chinese people cannot comprehend a single Chinese symbol, never mind written text.

Body Contact

Physical contact must be avoided, as Chinese people are not fond of being hugged, embraced, or even lightly tapped on their backs. While during discussions—and especially negotiations—Chinese people will come right into your personal space, the act of touching and patting is not encouraged or welcome. On rare occasions, one's Chinese host might direct you by pulling you on your sleeve. However, even this gesture is not welcomed, especially when the Chinese host's sleeve might be tucked at.

Communication

Formal communication during business meetings is generally cumbersome, being channeled through a formal translator (brought along by the Chinese delegation) even if individual Chinese group members have a good command of the English language. The Chinese team leader, in many cases the most senior member of the Chinese delegation, will be the only person communicating via the translator with their non-Chinese counterparts. The rest of the Chinese delegation will not utter a word, unless directly asked to contribute by the Chinese team leader. And then he or she will only express the bare minimum to-the-point contribution in English, directed at the non-Chinese delegation or in Mandarin to the translator for relay to the non-Chinese delegation.

The Chinese team leader will immediately answer any questions by the non-Chinese delegates—even if directed to a specific person—via the translator. Ironically, this is often where the realization comes that the Chinese team leader can at least understand English, as he might immediately respond to the question (asked in English) in Mandarin to the translator before the translator had the opportunity to relay the question back to the Chinese team leader in Mandarin. This splurging out by the Chinese team leader is probably to demonstrate that he is the Chinese authority to be conversed with, rather than starting meeting discussions with any of his subordinates.

During meeting breaks or caucuses, Chinese delegates will superficially respond to gestures of the non-Chinese delegates. Small talk is normally responded to with a light laugh and acknowledgement only. Detailed informal discussions are rare during formal meetings, especially during the first few engagements.

Meetings

Corporate meetings are planned well in advance, and are normally attended by a large Chinese delegation, consisting of a leader (normally the most senior Chinese delegate), a translator, and an array of specialists. It is very common for many of the Chinese delegates not to be able to speak English at all. As already mentioned, typically the Chinese group leader engages formally in Mandarin via the translator, even if his command of the English language is good. This is usually done to accommodate the non-English speaking Chinese group members.

It would be advantageous to have a Chinese-speaking person, but preferably a Chinese person as part of your team. This will enhance the communication and build bridges faster. This person would also in all likelihood have a much better understanding of Chinese cultural aspects, engagement behavior, etiquette, bureaucracy issues, legal issues, as well as probably having some kind of Chinese business network in place. It was interesting to note that even where Chinese people did not know each other personally, the fact that they came from the same region, studied in the same city or at the same university—even if years apart—immediately created a connection.

It is considered appropriate business behavior to give each other company brochures and company paraphernalia when meeting for the first time. Sometimes the Chinese delegation will even bring a gift to the first meeting, as a token of appreciation and respect. Western companies are normally ill prepared for the gestures of Chinese pleasantries and exchanges presented at such meetings. It would go a long way if Western companies made the effort to understand the Chinese delegation that they are about to host and prepare decorations, eateries, and beverages accordingly. When meeting with Chinese companies in China, the host will always ensure that there will be plenty of eats and drinks, appropriate for a Western palate.

Meeting dates must be carefully considered to not coincide with Chinese national holidays, especially *Chinese New Year*, *May Day*, as well as *The National Day of the People's Republic of China*. It would also be worth considering meeting start times and dates to coincide with Chinese lucky numbers and to avoid dates that represent unlucky Chinese numbers (see Postscript Chapter 2: Chinese Cultural and Traditional Revelations). Color and numbering symbolism influences Chinese behavior and interpretation significantly.

Chinese delegates should be met in the car park or company foyer and then be personally escorted to the meeting facility. The chairperson or host of the meeting should be waiting in the meeting room and welcome all the guests in order of importance on arrival. Business meeting etiquette even requires that the most senior Chinese delegation representative enters the room first on arrival with his entourage following in order of importance. One should not arrive late for a meeting, as this is considered an insult to Chinese business people. Should one be late, then one should apologize humbly for one's 'tardiness'.

In the day-to-day office environment however, it is often the case that the Chinese colleague will arrive late at meetings and any requests or pleading to attend meetings punctually will often fall on deaf ears—much to the frustration of the Western meeting participants or the Western meeting organizer. If however the meeting is organized by a Chinese senior company representative—and especially if it was organized by the Chinese leader—the Chinese subordinates will ensure to be at the meeting on time.

The Chinese delegation leader will always assume the seat facing the room entrance as well as directly opposite from the most senior delegation representative of the other party attending the meeting, as the meeting will in essence be a discussion between the two of them and very little other group discussions will take place. After everyone has been seated, but before the meeting properly commences, there is usually some brief superficial small talk. Previous Chinese encounters or visits to China would be considered appropriate topics.

One should always come across as positive and one should never discuss environmental issues, human rights, or international politics even if not inferring directly to China issues. These topics are generally taboo for a Chinese citizen to engage in, even if in a social or casual encounter.

A meeting agenda should be agreed in advance, as Chinese will plan their meeting approach carefully, with a specific purpose of what needs to be achieved. This will also stress the importance of the meeting and the topics to be discussed, which will ensure that the Chinese company sends the appropriate persons to the meeting. This will also guide the meeting proceedings and prevent the event from being hijacked to achieve ulterior motives, normally not understood or anticipated by the non-Chinese delegation.

Having set up the meeting, issued the agenda, and prepared for the meeting, it is still no guarantee that the meeting will take place. Frustratingly, Chinese companies will calculatingly only confirm their meeting attendance a few days before the planned date or even only on the day of the meeting, to keep the counterparts guessing and to create a sense of anxiety even before the meeting commences. When the Chinese company has arranged the meeting, it is likely for one not to receive the meeting date and location confirmation until shortly before the meeting takes place. It is also unlikely to receive an agenda unless the Western company forces the issue.

During the meeting, the Chinese delegation will enthusiastically nod their heads and make affirmative utterances. This does not imply that they agree, but merely that they are consciously listening to what's being said. In a Western business environment, affirmative verbal and physical reactions would typically indicate that your counterpart understands, acknowledges, and agrees with your point of view.

It is not recommended to interrupt the Chinese speaker during the meeting. Chinese meetings are highly structured and interjecting beyond a quick remark is considered inappropriate and rude. Also, don't put anyone in a precarious situation by repeatedly asking him or her to provide information that they seem unwilling to share. And remember never to challenge a Chinese person directly, as doing so will make them feel embarrassed and they will lose face in front of their colleagues.

Try not to look into your Chinese counterpart's eyes during discussions, especially during meetings, as it is considered offensive. Westerners of course prefer looking one in the eye as this confirms that one is absolutely committed to the discussion and that one is hearing and listening with one's eyes. When the

Chinese listener or speaker tends to glance away while in conversation with you, you might assume that he or she is not really listening. You might assume that their inner thoughts have drifted off to other issues. This behavior would be considered arrogant and aloof by Westerners.

You can see that the simple act of eye contact during communication engagement is vastly different in Chinese and Western cultures and this immediately creates anxiety and mistrust between these two cultures early in their engagement. Anything interpreted during the meeting as an offence or insult (we are talking about the behavioral and interpersonal issues here) will put a dampener on the meeting and the meeting can probably be considered as having been a failure.

Prepare well for the meeting and understand the audience that you will be facing, as you can be assured that the Chinese delegation has not only prepared meticulously for the meeting, but has also studied your organization and probably the people they will encounter. They will try to delve into a tremendous amount of detail—even at the first meeting encounter—by asking many detailed questions, giving the impression that they have prepared well for the meeting. This is typical. The Chinese delegation will try to get as much information as possible from their meeting hosts, but at the same time ensure that they don't give away much information. Many reciprocated questions will yield only vague responses from the Chinese delegation. Initially, this is interpreted by the non-Chinese meeting delegation as merely a language barrier and communication problem. Ironically, in these situations, many Westerners voluntarily share even more knowledge, trying to explain their comments in even more detail to help the

Chinese delegation to better understand the subject, as after all, English is not their easiest mode of communication.

Lastly, the Chinese delegation expects that a formal presentation be given by the Western organization, often required to be presented in both English and Mandarin. It is best to have the Mandarin reciprocating the English text on the slides, but if this cannot be done, the translator will meticulously translate everything in tandem. This can lengthen presentation times considerably, as translated text is often then countered with another question in Mandarin via the translator back to the presenter or his superior. Such presentation sessions can be very taxing on the Western team, but does not seem to stress the Chinese delegation even if the allotted presentation time is grossly overrun. The Chinese delegation seem to prefer the structure that a presentation brings to a meeting, and they then have something tangible from the meeting that they can share with their home office team.

Seating Arrangements

The Chinese party will always sit facing the door (even if this means that their backs will be towards the window). Chinese consider this good Feng Shui (the Chinese philosophical systems of harmonizing everyone with the surrounding environment—see Postscript Chapter 2: Chinese Cultural and Traditional Revelations). The non-Chinese delegation will normally allow the Chinese delegation to take their seats as such.

The Chinese team leader will always sit in the middle of their seating arrangement with the team members taking their place to his left and right in order of importance from highest to lowest. The Chinese team leader often assumes by default that the non-Chinese delegates have arranged themselves in a similar fashion on the opposite side of the table.

The Chinese leader will take his seat first, with team members then taking their place to his left and right in order of importance from highest to lowest.

Greetings

Formal meetings commence with a handshake and slight nodding of the head. Typically, the Chinese counterpart will say *"ni hau"* (hello) as a matter of course, while the non-Chinese counterpart generally only nods his/ her head, not sure how to respond correctly. Unlike in Western engagements, where it is common to say, *"How are you?"* and *"It's a pleasure to meet you"*, a Westerner tends to avoid such trivia with consecutive meetings, as the Chinese counterpart rarely responds in the anticipated way. The handshake should be firm, but not vigorous (often preferred by some Western cultures, showing a sign of confidence and dominance), as dynamic handshakes are usually interpreted as posing an aggressive stance.

Chinese give their names as surname first followed by their first name, unlike in the Western way of name followed by surname. Westerners will be tempted, after some time, to call Mr. Li Yang for instance by his name Yang, but this is not recommended. Always stay formal and call him Mr. Li, or if he is a junior member, address him with his full name, i.e. Li Yang, but never just Yang.

Informal meetings are still considered formal engagements, even if meeting by chance, say in an elevator or a corridor. As such, the same introductory rules apply. Importantly, Chinese women are greeted in the same manner as men, with a firm handshake, unlike in the West where women and men don't shake hands in an informal environment, but only greet and acknowledge each other orally; although this Western behavior is also slowly subsiding, the introductory handshake between opposite sexes has become more commonplace.

Body Posture

Always appear calm and collected, minimizing excessive movement, especially with the arms. Chinese people do not use their arms to communicate or make gestures, something encouraged in the West to use as an additional nonverbal communication tool. All movement must be made in a controlled manner. One's body posture should be upright, and movement must be formal, which will be interpreted by the Chinese as being in control, which affords respect.

Negotiations

Negotiating with Chinese nationals can be a daunting affair from the onset. Negotiations generally are conducted formally, either in person or via formal communication lines, such as email. The first meeting could be with a senior Chinese representative, but the negotiations are quickly seconded to a junior team member, with no direct access to the decision maker. This prolongs the negotiation process by having to negotiate via a 'go between'. Typically, negotiations become drawn out affairs that can take weeks or months.

Such negotiation tests one's patience, diplomacy, tact, and endurance capabilities. Never express frustration, hostility, and anger during negotiations. One should come across as in control and indifferent to the possible outcome of the negotiation. Once the Chinese negotiating team notices that you are uncomfortable, they see this as a weakness to be exploited. The Chinese counterpart often does not respond back for weeks. This may be due to them negotiating with a competitor at the same time or because the Chinese decision maker is not yet confident enough to make a final commitment. The first move to take negotiations to the next level will always be initiated by the Chinese negotiating party. Any prompting, reminding and enquiring generally falls on deaf ears, which can lead to frustration and impatience, seen as weaknesses in the eyes of the Chinese.

When negotiating away from one's normal place of operation, e.g. such meetings taking place in China, then negotiation resolution is usually stretched out, the Chinese negotiating team attempting to use one's imminent departure constraint to their advantage by slowing the negotiation progress down or even stalling it. It is typically anticipated by Chinese negotiators that their non-Chinese negotiating counterpart will be pressed into a rushed decision, due to time constraints.

Likewise, the Chinese negotiators stall negotiations until after hours, assuming that their non-Chinese counterparts are tiring and will be rushed into a decision, favorable to the Chinese.

Typically, any pre-negotiation meeting could involve dinners and other forms of entertainment, a calculated move by the Chinese negotiators to 'soften' their negotiating counterparts up. This entertainment could continue during negotiations until a deal is agreed or negotiations stall.

Chinese negotiators can be ferocious in their approach, varying from silent treatment to sheer psychological intimidation to get the other party to oblige with the needs of the Chinese company.

In Chinese culture, people who negotiated well are respected. People who are weak and can be easily manipulated are despised. However, there is a fine line between standing one's point of view, and being seen as inflexible and obstructive to the purpose of the negotiation in the first place. Chinese companies always have a clear strategy in a negotiation. There will always be one chief negotiator as part of a team of Chinese negotiators. Chinese culture encourages the use of patience and trepidation to force their opponents into an unwanted commitment. Chinese people despise perceived arrogance, threats, or anxiety in a negotiation.

The primary objective of a Chinese negotiator is to get his counterpart to concede on a number of issues, with at least one or two to be considered major concessions. This will make him feel like he has achieved a good negotiation position. Therefore, it is important to start with a negotiation position that can accommodate a few concessions.

During the initial stages of negotiation, the Chinese negotiators come across as humble and show deference. This is a planned tactic to make the non-Chinese negotiators think that the Chinese negotiators are not strong, not confident, and vulnerable. This will let the non-Chinese negotiators' guard down and even possibly compel them to help their Chinese counterparts to negotiate a fair deal.

As a strategy, one should never threaten to walk away from a negotiation but rather put a counter offer forward. Walking away is seen as a sign of giving up and weakness. You will be pushed to the limit of wanting to walk away but stay in the negotiations as this will earn you respect.

Contracts

As mentioned under *Negotiations* it will take patience, resilience, and time to eventually agree the contract terms and conditions. Then comes the tedious task of compiling the contract, proofreading, and signing it. Too often, the contract details, normally always compiled by the Chinese, do not reflect the negotiated position. A number of contract revisions are required to ensure that all contractual points are correctly reflected. The Chinese colleagues might claim to have agreed a different position during the negotiations, and they will want to re-debate and sometimes re-negotiate certain contractual points during this phase of contract finalization.

Most alarmingly, new non-negotiated contract conditions can appear in the contract. Thus, it is imperative that every draft contract is scrutinized from top to bottom to prevent any surprises. I have been exposed and made aware of a number of situations where the final hardcopy contract, ready for signature, had changed terms and conditions. Attention to detail during this phase of contract finalization is therefore of paramount importance. If possible, one should insist on being the custodian of the contract document, allowing one to control the changes.

Once the contract has been signed though, Chinese organizations will honor the contract conditions rigidly. While disbursement payments are sometimes not actioned, salaries and contract interim payments are typically paid on time and regularly. The negotiated position for professionals is normally at fair value when compared to the market place. I have not heard many Western professional complain about having been outdone on their remuneration packages. The same cannot be said for semi-skilled or unskilled workers, where I have personally come across many dissatisfied people in the work environment, complaining about being underpaid, and not being paid regularly.

Patience

Having now read the above sections on Chinese business culture, etiquette, and behavior in the work environment, it crystallizes one's primary attribute required to deal with the Tiger, namely the skill of patience. Without patience, one will not survive the grip of the Tiger, which slowly reels you in like a fish onto a baited hook. And once you have taken the bait, the Tiger will not let you go easily. He now owns your attention, respect, and tolerance on his terms. And more than anything, the Tiger has the patience of a lifetime. Nothing, but nothing will speed him along to close out anything. Usually, you will be forced to agree to the Tiger's position, when you eventually realize that it is impossible to sway him your way any further. One should guard against losing one's patience, as this will achieve nothing, in fact only weakening one's position.

Formal Chinese Dinners

While this item could easily subscribe to the next section on 'Social Behavior', it does warrant description here, as dinners are usually always a formal affair, following a formal ritual and participant behavior.

While meetings are held at square tables, Feng Shui requires formal dinners to be taken at a round table, immediately creating harmony between dinner participants. Nobody will sit down until the most senior Chinese representative has seated himself at the head of the table, which is always the chair facing the door or open area. He (or she) will then advise who will sit at his or her left and right, usually the next one or two most senior persons in the room, preferably somebody from the non-Chinese dinner guest list. Dinner patrons, in descending seniority, irrespective of whether Chinese or non-Chinese, will then be asked to take their place at the dinner table to either side of the host. This ritual continues until the most junior dinner guest usually ends up directly opposite the most senior person (and usually also the host) on the far side of the table.

The table will always be filled with patrons. There will always be the next most senior Chinese team member on stand-by and ready to join the dinner party. Seldom will a table have gaping holes filled only by empty chairs. The only time this happens is if the Chinese host specifically wants to restrict the audience to hold an important meeting or discussion. But typically, work matters are never discussed at dinner engagements in detail, although some loaded questions might be—seemingly casually—asked during the course of the dinner to extract information, especially when the first bottle of Mao-tai has flowed.

Before dinner commences, the host will announce the first of many toasts, normally, the glasses being eagerly emptied for the next round of toasts, for which one does not have to wait long. The host will initiate the dinner festivities by either dishing up for himself or offering the most senior invited guest an opportunity to start dishing up. The more important the dinner guests, the more exotic the dishes will be. To honor an important guest, he or she will be given the first choice of some exotic meat dish, which is likely to be something strange and never before tried 'delicacy'.

Chinese food is delicious, although not always for everybody's palate. The more important the guest, the more exotic the dishes become, especially the protein laden delicacies. The main meal consists of meat, chicken, duck, and seafood dishes with the complimentary steamed and sautéed vegetable selection. Food is brought in abundance, the table never appearing to be low or devoid of dishes. If the table should ever empty of dishes, then the host will be losing face. There is always an opulence of waiters and servers in the near vicinity, ensuring that everyone's needs are abundantly taken care of. The dishes are placed on a central movable console (a Lazy Susan), which can be rotated around by anyone wanting to help themselves to a specific dish or dishes. Only chopsticks are provided, and clumsy handling by non-Chinese patrons attracts Chinese laughter of astonishment. Chinese are appreciative if a Westerner has mastered the art of eating with chopsticks, so one may want to practice this beforehand.

Generally, the food from the dishes is scooped into one's own bowl with one's own chopsticks. This takes some getting used to, especially by Western guests, helplessly observing chopsticks going from bowl to mouth to dish. Only on rare occasions will the Chinese host order spoons for dishing, to accommodate his own preferences or to acknowledge to some extent typical Western dinner practices. But importantly, none of the other Chinese dinner participants will initiate such action, leaving it up to the host to decide.

Accompanying the dinner will always be tea and alcohol, the stronger the better. The host generally decides on what strong liquor will be consumed for the night. The host will select the wine, which does not necessarily pair with the dishes about to be consumed. The tea drinking ritual is known as 'yum cha'. Tea is brewed at the table and cups filled again by one of the Chinese dinner guests as soon as one's cup is empty. Red wine is always a popular contender, all at the table being encouraged to consume some form of alcoholic beverage. Non-drinkers are singled out for further convincing. Chinese culture observes that alcohol will ultimately loosen the tongue and the truth will thus be spoken. Non-drinkers then surely have something to hide. Only a medical excuse would be acceptable, but not on an ongoing basis. At Chinese dinners, one invariably is obliged to drink. Refer to *Ganbei* further on in this chapter to get a sense of the Chinese drinking ritual.

One invariably ends up overeating (and over drinking) as every dish brought to the table reveals a new taste, bursting with flavor. The more common meats come out first with exotic meat and seafood arriving later. Invariably, one fills up and cannot eat any further. One gets the sense of non-accomplishment as the table is still filled with ample food. Observant restaurateurs will bring out a large bowl of rice, considered a filler, and therefore left for last. Predictably, the rice goes mostly unconsumed. The next and last course brought to the table is freshly cut fruit. Again, the satiated feeling having registered with most patrons leaves the fruit dishes generally untouched.

It would be considered an insult not to complement the food. This is not very difficult unless one totally despises Chinese cuisine. It is more important for the host that the food is complimented than holding a meaningful dinner table discussion.

Every dinner is a celebration. The food becomes the medium, communicating the host's good wishes and the joy of the celebration (People.wku.edu). Finishing with a clean plate is perceived to mean that you were not given enough food and is construed as an insult. Reversely, not selecting to eat a certain dish, even if the dish appears to be unappetizing, is taken as an insult that the food was not good enough. It is recommended to politely eat a small amount, especially if the host insists that you try out that very special dish.

When you have managed to conquer the dishes and can eat no more, it is time to lay your chopsticks on the chopstick rest. Placing the chopsticks parallel on top of the plate or the bowl is considered to bring bad luck. Pegging your chopsticks into the contents of the bowl is considered rude. It is not advised to suck or lick the chopsticks ends and do not drop the chopsticks, as this brings bad luck. Unlike Western culinary culture, the bowl can be brought to the mouth and the food can be scooped into the mouth with the chopsticks. (Wikipedia, Customs and etiquette in Chinese dining)

Leaning over the table or other patrons is quite acceptable. Food left over (food that has not been consumed) must be placed in a specially provided dish, but should never be left in one's own bowl. Nobody will object to slurping, belching, and the occasional act of flatulence, as these are all signs of the guest having appreciated the meal. In fact, to most Westerners,

Chinese come across as lacking table manners, but to Chinese this is quite normal behavior. The use of toothpicks is quite acceptable as long as the mouth is covered with the free hand.

Individuals will smoke at the table before and after the meal. Where local laws disallow indoor smoking, the pleasure is taken outside. Usually patrons who are also smokers wait for the host to get up for a smoke and then join him. When smoking, it is polite to offer everybody in your company a cigarette.

Unlike in most Western countries, leaving a tip at the end of the meal is generally considered an insult in China. Most government operated hotels and restaurants prohibit acceptance of tips. The Western habit of tipping is however slowing infiltrating the bigger cities, having created an expectation with the younger service personnel.

And that concludes dinner. As soon as the last person has satiated him or herself, the Chinese host gets up, all follow and the dinner is concluded. Atypical to Western behavior, no socializing, small talk, coffees, and desert drinks are taken after the physical eating part of the dinner has been concluded. All shake hands with thanks bestowed onto the host and one takes off as quickly as one has arrived at the venue.

Business Dress Code

Chinese men wear dark suits and ties to business meetings, while women wear equally conservative dresses or suits in subdued colors. Blouses must have high necklines (Etiquette in China, Business Meeting).

This dress code does reciprocate Western standards largely and therefore Western meeting participants are usually appropriately dressed for Chinese meetings by default. However, when dealing with African businesses and government institutions, the African dress code comprises bright colors, loose clothing, or even caftans. As Africa is such a lucrative find for China, there is no doubt that a bit of cultural imposition is generally tolerable, and any disgust or astonishment will be kept under the collar.

Bright colored clothing is considered inappropriate in Chinese business culture, and flamboyant jewelry should be avoided. Women—especially those who are taller than their hosts are—should wear very low heels or flats, and reserve high heels for formal receptions hosted by foreign diplomats only.

How to Address Chinese People

For business purposes, and in line with traditional acceptable standards, it is always preferred that Chinese nationals be addressed with respect. Chinese people view formality as a form of respect, which is why it is important to address them correctly from the very first meeting. Always use their official titles, such as Doctor Chen, Chairman Wang, or Director Li. In non-professional settings, you may address a person by their family name—Mr. Kim or Mrs. Chen. You can only use a person's first name if you have known him for many years.

Since Chinese family names come before the given name (Western first name), it is probably a good idea to ask which is the family name. The given names of individuals who were born during the Cultural Revolution tend to carry political meaning. The Western informality of addressing a person by their given name tends to be strongly resisted. Maintain your professional distance and allow your Chinese counterparts to address you by your formal title (New World Encyclopedia, Chinese Surname).

Chinese colleagues prefer using the same standard when addressing a Western person, namely calling him by his full names, i.e. name, and then surname in the order that it is written.

According to New World Encyclopedia, when a Chinese woman marries, she usually keeps her maiden name, using her husband's last name only in formal situations. When dealing with government officials, always use their official titles.

Never refer to or address a Chinese colleague as *'comrade'* or *'tóngzhì'*, which also means homosexual in Mandarin.

SOCIAL BEHAVIOR IN THE WORK ENVIRONMENT (INDIVIDUALS AND GROUPS)

Greetings

Chinese don't seem to pay much attention to the mannerism of courtesy casual greetings in the work place, especially on arrival or departure. When greeted with a *"Good Morning"* or *"Good Bye"*, they will always respond in return but it is unlikely for them to initiate the greeting rituals. It is common for Chinese colleagues to leave the office punctually at closing time and walk out of the office on masse without uttering a single word.

Communication

In the work place, it is likely to spend the whole day in the same office without exchanging any words. Communication is only initiated if specific information needs to be shared or extracted. Small talk is seldom initiated by Chinese colleagues although they will respond with light laughter and a brief acknowledgement to small talk and light banter initiated by their non-Chinese colleagues.

During debates and discussions on a one-to-one basis, Chinese people push their point of view, taking little cognizance of what is being said by the other person. They will insist on repeating their viewpoint or 'request for information' several times, irrespective of the other person disagreeing with the viewpoint or advising that such information is not yet available. Clearly, the communication has been initiated to fulfill an instruction that has been received via the invisible Chinese management structure and that therefore a confirmation or affirmative answer needs to be extracted and communicated back up the Chinese management structure. For the Chinese not to come back to the Chinese team with an outcome would be interpreted as a failure which will lose the entire Chinese contingent operating within a specific team echelon, face and credibility.

Discussions can quickly end with the Chinese counterpart losing interest or unable to contribute further in the conversation.

Social Engagement

Chinese do not readily engage in small talk. Most discussions are conducted in a formal manner. It is unlikely for them to divulge a lot of information about their private lives. Chinese will respond when asked personal questions but often responses are limited to a few syllables, and even only simple yes and no answers.

Chinese do like to show one pictures of their child and are fiercely proud of their offspring.

Unless formal arrangements are in place, it is of utmost difficulty to socialize with individuals after hours. Any engagements will be at group level only or one-on-one formal dinners with a Chinese superior if he (very unlikely to be a she) specifically invites one. Chinese are not encouraged to spend too much social time with non-Chinese work colleagues. If one ends up in a social one-on-one situation, the Chinese person will often curtail the social chatter very quickly by not engaging in vigorous discussion or debate. In some instances where questions are considered politically loaded or require an opinion debate, these are only responded to with a chuckle or light laughter.

An informal one-on-one discussion will attract other Chinese colleagues to stand around and listen in, once such engagement has been noticed by them. One does get the distinct feeling that one communicates with a Chinese group structure at all times, rather than individuals. A Chinese colleague will never provide an opinion unless technical and factual in nature.

Decisions

Decisions will not be provided readily by a Chinese colleague, often requiring a decision request to be sent in writing before receiving a decision response after a lengthy waiting period. A decision needs to go up the Chinese reporting line. The head of the organization will generally make the decision that is passed down the ranks again to be shared with the person from whom the request came.

Speaking English

Chinese appear to be specifically selected to work outside China because of their proficiency in the English language, although their command in English is not interpreted as good by Western standards (yes, Western people couldn't be bothered to learn any Mandarin, expecting Chinese people to just be able to speak English). Seldom is a Chinese employee assigned to a project outside China if he cannot speak English. In the rare case that the necessity arises for a Mandarin only speaking specialist to be required on assignment outside China, he is provided with a fulltime Mandarin-English translator.

Most Chinese working outside China thus have a good command of the English language but do not necessarily have the confidence to communicate openly in a forum. A significant communication barrier is that the oral English language is sometimes interpreted literally, the figurative meaning not being comprehended at all. This can cause significant communication breakdown, as a Chinese person will always acknowledge any received communication in the affirmative. Only after some time does one realize that the Chinese colleague did not clearly understand what was being said, as some actions stemming from the discussion are not in line with what was being communicated.

Writing English

As Mandarin and English are structurally and fundamentally based on very different grammatical principals, the written English language becomes a linguistic challenge for most Chinese. The first attempt is often difficult to read and comprehend, requiring significant re-writing. Thus Chinese colleagues often shy away from writing reports, minutes of meetings or other general written documentation in English, consciously avoiding commitment to producing written text.

While Chinese colleagues are appointed in lead positions in the work place, they will delegate any writing requirements to their non-Chinese subordinates whenever possible. Non-Chinese colleagues in turn tend to not question this further, even feeling it professionally necessary to assist, even if not credited with such work.

Chinese feel uncomfortable to communicate in writing, preferring to communicate orally. Chinese do not like to commit themselves in writing (and orally for that matter), especially if decisions or directives need to be recorded.

Meetings

Chinese will participate readily in meetings. Usually invited Chinese colleagues will invite additional Chinese colleagues to participate in meetings, without notifying the meeting organizer. It is often the case that the meeting venue is inadequate in size because of the number of 'uninvited' participants joining meetings.

During meetings Chinese participants mostly remain silent, taking vigorous notes but not contributing to the discussions, although they will have the occasional breakaway conversation in Mandarin (easier for them and probably also useful, knowing that no Westerner can understand). When asked what was discussed a mere 'nothing important' will be uttered and the meeting will continue. They do not consider this to be rude, but use this strategy tactically to discuss issues amongst themselves.

Even leaders will listen rather than question or participate unless they have specifically joined the meeting to instruct a decision, or want to challenge the team on a specific issue. Often a sub-ordinate non-Chinese colleague is expected to chair the meeting on behalf of his Chinese superior and produce the minutes of the meeting.

Email

As described earlier it is not in the nature of Chinese culture to communicate in writing. The written word is a commitment and future evidence of such commitment. Thus, email communication is limited on a needs basis only. Often no response is received in writing to an emailed question or request for information, but rather the information is shared orally.

Again, the impression created is that Chinese nationals do not feel comfortable writing in English, but careful analysis clearly reveals that the concern is around the commitment such a written email will create, rather than the lack of command of the English language.

Also, it clearly appears that emails are screened and as such, the perception is that any written communication could be used negatively against individuals. The business culture hinges on suspicion and distrust, which in turn has created an evasive and non-committal business culture. Within a team environment, they will quite frequently only communicate with the Chinese team members in Mandarin and keep Westerners out of the communication loop.

Where emails are indeed used for communication (beyond the Chinese communication circle), the content is found to be short and factual only. Often the same information is re-sent by multiple Chinese colleagues to the same recipients, even if such recipients were included in the original mailing list. And such emails are forwarded without further instruction or directive, leaving the recipients dumb founded to what the intent of the email was and what further actions are to be taken. Often photos of products or received goods are circulated without reference or instruction, leaving the reader perplexed to the purpose of receiving such an email.

Internet

Most Western search engines and social media sites are banned in China (e.g. Google, Facebook, WhatsApp etc.) so it is not surprising to see Chinese nationals in the workplace being rather reluctant to use the internet. Chinese authorities randomly screen search results, and any misuse of the internet is potentially punishable with heavy jail terms. Mistakenly typing in the wrong spelling could potentially be a life changing experience. As a result, Chinese colleagues will not be tempted to go online, even waiting for a non-Chinese colleague to return to his workstation and searching the necessary data on behalf of the Chinese colleague. At this communicative inter-junction, all sensibility of understanding disappears rapidly, and non-Chinese colleagues out of sheer frustration will eventually initiate the search themselves from their own workstations, only to ultimately end up passing such information back to their Chinese colleague.

Civil Behavior

Chinese mannerisms tend to be considered anti-social in a typical Western environment. While cultural behavior should be considered with a fair degree of tolerance, it often becomes difficult to become indifferent to the lack of socially acceptable idiosyncrasies, especially in the confines of an office.

In the work environment as at 'after hours' social functions, it is rather common behavior for Chinese nationals to resort to loud burping, letting wind or clearing their noses. Such behavior is often considered bad behavior and socially unacceptable in especially Western working and social environments. Non-Chinese people can take offence to such characteristically Chinese behavior, sometimes being outright repelled to the point of repugnance.

Eating Habits

Chinese nationals are fierce Chinese traditionalists, a fact that becomes poignantly evident when it comes to cuisine. If a Chinese meal is presented, it will be consumed with gusto. A Chinese restaurant in the immediate environment of the office is sought out and frequented, or Chinese leftovers are brought to work.

Lunch is eaten at the same time every day. Chinese colleagues will congregate in an empty meeting room, an office, or at a desk to consume their feast between social exhortations.

Even on rare occasions when Chinese and non-Chinese colleagues get together for a meal, the restaurant of choice typically serves oriental and usually Chinese cuisine. Western food is typically considered unappetizing, not nutritional enough, or downright unhealthy. More to the point, Chinese are likely not to want to be seen by their colleagues enjoying foods of other cultures, as this might be considered rather unpatriotic.

Food is consumed ferociously in a social environment. Food is scooped into the mouth at high speed, and quickly grated in an open mouth; it's not unusual to see some food particles to spill out of the mouth again. Larger food is pulled apart, the teeth giving the impression of being used like cutting devices. The whole appearance can be rather unappetizing to an uneducated person, especially if coming from a typical Western type cultural background. The chopsticks are also used to spoon food out of common bowls, making the whole meal experience even more unappetizing for some non-Chinese patrons.

Food choices, considered exotic by Chinese nationals, are often considered noisome and even offensive in the eyes of the non-Chinese patrons, consisting of many types of meat dishes, including endangered species, not typically consumed in other countries. To be seen not to enjoy these exotic dishes is considered offensive by the Chinese host.

Chinese dishes can emanate some rather exotic aromas, not normally associated with delectable cuisine outside China. Such interesting smells may linger around the office for some time after lunch, normally resulting in some remarks of interest by non-Chinese colleagues. Different types of spices and herbs as well as garlic can result in strong aromas, which remain for some time after meals in the affected areas, of course something that is no longer typical in modern open plan office environments where consumption of food is encouraged in canteens, office restaurants or dedicated eating areas.

In some work environments the Chinese colleagues are allocated their own kitchen and canteen services. Alternatively, Chinese team members deliver prepared Chinese meals on a daily basis to the office for consumption by Chinese team members only. Non-Chinese work colleagues are not privy to such benefits.

Ganbei

If Chinese let their hair down in one habit, then it is the consumption of copious quantities of alcohol. Ganbei translates into English as *"to drink a toast"*. Alcohol consumption after work is of great social importance and getting drunk is a sign of trusting your Chinese host by letting your guard down. Unless you have a valid medical reason for not consuming alcohol, you will be considered with a degree of distrust and suspicion for not partaking in a drinking frenzy around a dinner table.

Alcohol is consumed in a rather formal manner, usually involving hard (distilled) liquor (like Mao-tai and 'wu liang ye') as well as red wine. Alcohol is not savored, but rather swilled down quickly. A host's representative quickly refills any empty glasses.

The Chinese have a little nasty habit of toasting a non-Chinese guest one-on-one, where each Chinese colleague will toast the guest specifically and drink with you, while the rest of the Chinese delegation only pretends to drink. The next Chinese dinner patron will initiate a toast with you, and before you realize it, you have consumed ten or so drinks while they have consumed only one each. This ritual is emphasized by the Chinese dinner patron coming up to you, you also standing up and him or her then proposing a toast with words along the way of *"Mr. [first name only], I propose toast to you; nice working with you; bottoms up Mr. [first name]"*, while moving right into one's personal space. One is so consumed by the immediate action, that it is difficult to also effectively pay attention to the alcohol consumption of all the other patrons (who cleverly disguise their participation effectively).

Without fail, Western patrons often fall victim to an excessive bout of 'forced' drinking during their first experiences of Chinese dinner rituals, but soon become bolder in politely declining too many toasts coming their way.

Patriotism

Chinese nationals behave in a typically Chinese fashion, even if they have been exposed to a Western environment for years. Remarkably, some Chinese colleagues, who had lived in the West for more than a quarter century, were still as traditionally Chinese in their behavior and mannerisms as a Chinese national who had never left the Chinese mainland. Dress code, culinary desires, interests, and outlook on life are noticeably China-centric.

It clearly comes across that behaving in a non-Chinese way is frowned upon and could even lead to one's demise. Westerners should guard against befriending a likeable Chinese colleague, as this will lead to his/her demise. Always keep your distance, as the one you get along with or you like to befriend is likely to be sent back to China. During my tenure with a Chinese organization in Africa, a number of Chinese colleagues, who did build bridges and engaged more socially, usually ended up being sent back permanently to China even if their assignment wasn't completed yet.

Typically, Chinese people clearly don't want to be seen adopting or adapting to Western culture and behavioral patterns.

Personality

Seldom does one come across Chinese individuals with unique personality traits or uncharacteristic behavior, or an atypical Chinese demeanor. It appears that all Chinese nationals behave alike, think alike, and act alike. One gets the impression that outrageous or individualistic behavior is not socially acceptable. One is led to believe that individual behavior correlates with unique personalities, and to be unique implies individualistic thinking and behavior, something that is not encouraged in the Chinese nationalistic culture. The tall grass catches the wind—adopting a mass behavior trait makes it far more unlikely for one to be singled out. One's superiors choose one for future greatness; individuals don't try to become great by marketing their individual strengths, intellect, and wisdom.

Office Hours

Chinese attend work according to strict working hours, usually from seven thirty A.M. to five P.M. with a ninety-minute lunch break at noon. Lunch away from the workstation takes about fifty minutes and the Chinese colleagues will then return to their workstation for a nap lasting about forty minutes or so. However, it is not uncommon for Chinese colleagues to also sleep during work hours. This is completely acceptable in the Chinese business environment while extremely unacceptable in the Western business environment. There seems to be no limit to how long a sleep-in at work is tolerable, but generally, it doesn't exceed an hour.

Further, Chinese colleagues are expected to work for a few hours every day in the evening, after already having completed a day's work. It is not uncommon to receive emails during the dead of night.

One interesting observation is that after five P.M. at least two Chinese colleagues remain at work and typically only leave when the last non-Chinese colleague leaves. The two random Chinese colleagues always get swapped out with other colleagues every other day. It is clearly a mechanism to observe the work patterns and output of non-Chinese colleagues.

Trust

Trust is closely linked to Guangxi (also see Chapter 5). To indicate in any way one's mistrust of a Chinese colleague is socially unacceptable even if he or she has previously displayed signs of mistrust towards you. Questioning a Chinese colleague about a precarious situation or putting him on a spot in a meeting forum is despised. Yet Chinese colleagues will do exactly that to non-Chinese colleagues and think nothing of it. To falsely accuse a non-Chinese of something or surmise his or her incapability or perceived inexperience in a forum is however not frowned upon. Refer back to Chapters 3 and 4 to get a better insight into this phenomenon.

Generally, Chinese are very mistrusting of non-Chinese colleague's capability, experience, and expertise. Even if the Chinese colleague is not proficient in the subject at hand, he still insists on providing input from his or her irrelevant background. He will normally just insist on providing specific input if he is being pressurized by his Chinese chain of command to do so. This input is then often ill informed, as he will provide it regardless of whether he has knowledge on the subject or issue. This can lead to frustration with the Western team members, as progress is often hampered. Contrary, if a non-Chinese colleague requests help or requires input from a Chinese team member, it is rarely given, as the instruction must come from the Chinese chain of command.

Decisions are never taken at the time, but are referred by the Chinese colleagues up the Chinese chain of command. Decisions taken by non-Chinese in forums initially appear to receive approval, but are mostly referred up the Chinese chain of command to the Chinese leader, and then are challenged days or even weeks after the decision has already been implemented.

It quickly becomes apparent in the work environment that there is a distinct 'Them' and 'Us' management approach. Chinese colleagues appear to be wary of non-Chinese expertise and capabilities and thus check everything in parallel and question any conceivable information, irrespective of how trivial it may appear to a non-Chinese work colleague.

To emphasize such mistrust, hard drives on individual workstations are auto-linked to the server where they are very likely to be screened. Emails, telephone calls, video conferencing calls and key meeting rooms as well as offices are in all probability monitored and screened, creating an environment of mistrust not only between Chinese colleagues but also between Chinese and non-Chinese colleagues as a whole.

Further, Chinese work colleagues will confidentially report to their Chinese leaders on work progress and issues as soon as such information becomes apparent. The Chinese management will then question the non-Chinese colleagues at the earliest opportunity on issues that are 'fresh off the press' and still being dealt with 'on the ground'. The Chinese management will also then overwrite any proposals or decisions taken in the meantime by the work teams trying to resolve the issues. In short, the work teams and team management are often disempowered to deal with issues effectively and constructively at the lowest common denominator level, as the senior Chinese management team will involve themselves very quickly with such issues, i.e. people are not empowered to manage their areas of responsibilities. Ultimately, that then leads to team leaders not assuming accountability, as they are not allowed to make the necessary decisions to ensure efficient work progress. This vicious cycle of classical mismanagement quickly leads to an environment of mistrust and significant inefficiency in the work place.

Aloofness

While Chinese colleagues always come across as friendly and generally carry a smile on their face, they do tend to keep interactions short and to the point, coming across as not really wanting to engage for too long with the non-Chinese colleagues. Their behavior smacks of a certain level of aloofness and a degree of arrogance. This can possibly be attributed to their lack of English skills, which discourages general chatter and social interaction in the first instance. The lack of effort made to socially interact with non-Chinese colleagues does become apparent. Tea breaks, lunch breaks, and after work socializing happen very seldom, unless formally arranged beforehand. It is very likely for one to end up at the same establishment for lunch with separate Chinese and non-Chinese tables. One does get the impression that the Chinese colleagues prefer sticking to themselves. Initially a lot of effort is made by non-Chinese colleagues to integrate the two cultural groups. Ultimately, such efforts lead to futile grounds and the efforts are gradually abated and ultimately abandoned.

Chinese Management

In a Chinese company environment outside China, a significant number of Chinese colleagues supplement the work teams. The ratio can be as high as six to one. Designations of Chinese work colleagues are often fuzzy at best and their role in the team structure is often not clearly understood by non-Chinese work colleagues. Chinese team members come and go, and are regularly replaced without such team dynamics being shared with non-Chinese colleagues. Newly arrived Chinese team members are seldom introduced to everybody.

The Chinese team members work directly for 'invisible' Chinese leaders, any direct reporting lines to non-Chinese managers being a formality only. Chinese colleagues will seldom follow instructions given by non-Chinese managers, despite always acknowledging it—the work is just not done, and eventually the non-Chinese manager will undertake the work him or herself in order to avoid missing deadlines.

A separate parallel unofficial Chinese team structure—not published or advertised—exists in the work environment, taking instruction from a separate non-visible Chinese management team. The Chinese work colleagues hold separate progress meetings to which no non-Chinese team members are invited. The details of the meeting discussion are then not shared with the non-Chinese team members afterwards, even on request. This often leads to friction in the work environment, especially between the non-Chinese and Chinese management teams.

The Communist Factor

The Chinese team will always include a high-ranking communist party member. While this is not widely advertized, his role is normally one of non-descriptive observation and work execution. The individuals can be easily identified, generally not partaking in the day-to-day job management functions but sitting in on many meetings. They also tend to not readily engage with the non-Chinese team members, but hold many impromptu meetings with Chinese individuals or engage all his or her compatriots in Chinese only meetings. During the lifespan of the interactive engagement between the Chinese and non-Chinese organizations, this party representative position might be filled by numerous individuals, the previous incumbent disappearing back to China as quickly as he arrived.

Traveling for Chinese

Traveling is strictly categorized according to rank and status. While a CEO may enjoy the pleasures of first class transport and five star accommodation, subordinates will have to do with far fewer amenities during their business travel. Anything from living out allowance, entertainment allowance, housing allowance, to mode of transport is strictly controlled according to one's position within the Chinese organization and status in the CPC (Wikipedia, Communist Party of China).

Depending on file and rank, Chinese work colleagues are expected to share accommodation while traveling or when on offshore assignments. There will be many sharing an apartment as well as cooking and cleaning duties. In one specific example, a senior engineer and his wife shared their apartment with one of the young single engineers. Western people would not tolerate such practices. Chinese communes and canteens also started springing up in the towns and suburbs where the Chinese businesses were established, for which normally a suburban house was acquired and converted. I had the privilege to be invited to these communes and canteens on a number of occasions.

On one occasion, we had lunch at one of these communes, which from the outside appeared to be a normal double story, three-garage home. But appearances can be deceiving. We entered through one of the garages, which had been converted to a kitchen, featuring a huge wok (which would have never fitted into a normal Western style kitchen anyway). The open plan dining room and lounge in the main house had been filled with long plastic tables and plastic chairs of all colors and sizes, extending onto the covered patio, which in total could seat thirty people.

The kitchen in the house appeared to be unused. I casually enquired about how many people stayed at this commune, and was rather surprised that it housed some twenty-four people at the time, in a home that probably featured four bedrooms only.

On another occasion, I ate at one of the Chinese canteens, a converted one story, and two-garage suburban house. The open plan lounge and dining room were filled with a number of round dining tables, the walls were adorned with shelves, filled to capacity with Chinese crockery and chopsticks. Numbered stickers adorned each shelve. On enquiry, I gathered that the Chinese patrons each had their own set of crockery and chopsticks, which they would use. The shelves housed approximately sixty-five sets. They could eat three meals a day at the canteen, the prices being heavily subsidized, probably by the various Chinese companies operating in town.

The Chinese meal prices were about one fifth of the prices at the local restaurants in town, clearly encouraging Chinese patrons to eat at the canteen. The canteen was effectively a private venue, not open to the public. In both cases, it appeared that the local municipality provided the necessary authorizations for these restaurants and hotel-type accommodations to operate in residential zones.

On relocation from China, some of the Chinese individuals will find themselves in a foreign country without a work visa for some time, while the company tries to obtain their visas. In a Western environment, one decides on your own safety and abides by in-country legislation and an individual will not enter a country unlawfully and work without a work visa, regardless of your company's stance on the matter. Chinese people, however, will work without a visa.

There was an instance when the Chinese office team just did not arrive for work one day and the Westerners were wondering what the matter was. Later that day, the Immigration Department visited the office only to find no Chinese present. The Chinese had gotten wind of the upcoming immigration visit and received instructions to stay home for the day. The next day, they were back at the office as if nothing had happened and it was business as usual.

The frequency of travel back to China for a well-deserved rest and recuperation period depends on the rank of importance in the organization as well as communist party status of the Chinese colleague. A high-ranking Communist Party member in the HR department approves traveling. The incumbent, having submitted a travel request to go back to China, is often notified only days or even hours before his or her flight departs. A similar scenario is played out for permanent transfers with the incumbent sometimes only advised that the transfer to another office site is permanent after having departed, or close to departure from the current office.

Depending on rank and status, some Chinese colleagues can bring their families with them to the country of assignment; however, many Chinese are not entitled to this luxury and have to endure long periods away from their families.

Leave and Relocation

Chinese work colleagues are subjugated to a complex traveling code. Depending on rank and status, Chinese team members are subject to different cycle times for their eagerly awaited return trips to the homeland. More senior or politically affiliated team members may return to China once every 2-3 months. Junior staff and persons not closely associated with the inner (political) circle can often wait up to 10-12 months before a return trip is approved.

In some instances, some of our Chinese colleagues became parents while away from home, the child being born back in China. No paternal leave was granted. When leave was taken, typically a trip turnaround back home took two to four weeks, again dependent on the person's rank and status.

Typically, the Chinese individual will submit a leave request, subject to approval by only one or two senior Chinese managers. This then becomes a waiting game, with some Chinese colleagues being notified only on the day of departure. All traveling arrangements are taken care of by the 'system' and traveling details are provided to the individual very close to the time of departure. While leave is requested for a certain date, often the individuals wait for weeks or even months for the leave to be approved for a period well after the requested traveling date. This does not seem to faze the Chinese colleagues, who will happily wait for extended periods to get an opportunity to see their families again for a short time.

Permanent relocation to another office or back to China is handled in much the same way, where Chinese employees often only find out days before the approved traveling date that they will not be returning to the same office. Some Chinese colleagues will only be advised that they will not be returning to work (in the host country) once they have arrived back in China. Such individuals will travel with a suitcase full of clothes and nothing more to the next destination. Their acquired wealth has to be brought to them in drips and drabs by colleagues to the new location, as and when the opportunity arises.

Of more concern is the fact that due to the late approval of traveling requests, nobody is notified until a few days or hours before departure of the imminent traveling arrangements of Chinese co-workers, which makes it difficult to effectively manage team interactions and team effectiveness. Notification of traveling arrangements is given only to the individual traveling, so a superior often only finds out about the travel arrangements after the individual has in fact departed.

Traveling for Non-Chinese

All traveling request are approved only at the highest Chinese management level. The most senior Chinese leader in the organization ponders on and ultimately decides on the necessity of traveling. Typically, such travel approvals or rejections are left until a few days before the due date, making it notoriously difficult to effectively plan and manage the tasks and the business in general. Team managers are not allowed to approve travel requests. While team members or team managers can initiate travel requests, these must be carefully motivated and traveling is never guaranteed to be a fait accompli. In some instances, team members have embarked on their business trips without having been notified of their final destination or accommodation arrangements. The management of people's behavior, by withholding information and not being transparent, plays a significant role in the Chinese business management behavior.

The Chinese Way

When encountering Chinese for the first time, it very quickly becomes apparent that the Chinese culture is hugely different when compared to typical Western business practices. For Chinese to operate outside China they need to be proficient in two things, namely command of the English language and having a sound understanding of Chinese work practices and the Chinese business culture. The Chinese system is profound for ensuring that each citizen works in the interest of the Chinese nation and according to the Communist Party mantra.

Stereotypical Behavior

When engaging with Chinese people, one very quickly develops an impression that the behavior is very much stereotyped. Every engagement brings out a very similar interactive body language as well as oral responses by different individuals. Discussions are normally to the point and do not delve off the topic at hand. The typical non-Chinese interpretation of this behavior is to associate it with a communistic system that discourages individualism and outspoken personality traits. Conversation is normally limited to work related topics and small talk before or after work quickly dulls into silence. Any sensitive topics as well as politically related discussions, related either to China or even office politics, would not entice any response from the Chinese counterpart. In other words, a certain repetitive type of behavior and engagement is observed across a broad spectrum of the Chinese populace, without fail.

It is a well-known fact that stepping out of line curtails one's rise into the Communist Party. Any deviation it not tolerated, be it behavioral, professional or in one's private capacity. This requirement encourages individuals to stick to expected behavioral norms. And this becomes rather challenging in the work environment as Chinese colleagues will stick to procedures and processes to a tee, not prepared or encouraged to deviate for one instance, so as not to jeopardize their good standing within the Chinese organization, with their Chinese colleagues (who could report their behavior back into the system), or indeed with the CPC.

It has been observed that Chinese colleagues, not adhering to strict Chinese behavioral patterns, are unambiguously sent back to mainland China. Atypical behavior would include getting too acquainted with non-Chinese colleagues, not following procedures and processes correctly, challenging authority, and not agreeing with the Chinese views expressed even if incorrect.

Business Practices

Typical Chinese business practices are worlds apart from what is considered progressive twenty-first century business management, especially in Western type companies. In essence, Chinese companies conduct business in the very autocratic and task driven manner, with no transparency and empowerment of functional managers in the team. Agreed processes cannot be changed even if it would result in a more efficient and effective overall outcome. Vertically integrated management is non-existent with subordinates not allowed to challenge any viewpoints and instructions coming from the top down. In fact, the Chinese leader becomes a functional 'expert' in all areas. He will often lecture his management team in their areas of competency and in particular on how to do their jobs to an extent where it becomes embarrassing, to say the least. But it would be futile to challenge the contents of the incorrect lecture, as the leader will not let you off lightly for making him lose face in front of the other perplexed team members.

While not being openly debated, it is apparent that Chinese companies could be open to engaging in bribing government officials, suppliers and anybody else who might benefit the Chinese Tiger. It's a murky path, best not to get close to or to become too aware off, as the Chinese Communist representative sits right around the corner. Moral positioning on this topic is discouraged, if one does not want to endure potential un-pleasantries. Challenging the Chinese way is an ineffectual exertion, not ending in one's favor or fortune.

Racism

It is a well-known fact that Chinese tend not to be that tolerant of non-Chinese people. Typically, Chinese see themselves as superior and more intelligent when working with other nationalities. Chinese people tend to 'talk down' to non-Chinese persons and do not take the points of view of non-Chinese people seriously.

Chinese people are purported to particularly dislike black people. There have been numerous observations of black workers being treated badly in the work environment in Africa. Complaints have ranged from working people too hard, physically assaulting them (burning people with cigarettes to get them to work), groping female workers, and not paying salaries at the end of the month. Many workers are too afraid to report such incidents to their superiors (often Chinese) or the authorities, as they fear losing their job. When reported, these incidents often do not get properly investigated nor is action taken against the perpetrators, except perhaps for a nonchalant warning.

While Chinese people do come across as very courteous when one engages with them for the first time, over time some Chinese people, normally those in positions that are more powerful, can become a bit more antagonistic and disrespectful towards non-Chinese people. This is rather prevalent when one does not agree with their viewpoints. Initially interaction is very harmonious but when one has to deal with issues on the ground and conflict situations need to be negated, then the stance of the Chinese colleague or colleagues can abruptly change towards non-Chinese colleagues. The voice will be raised, which can go over to shouting with a definite decree of arrogance, talking down to their non-Chinese colleagues. Untrue accusations can be made in-line with not working in the best interest of the Chinese company, disrespecting the Chinese leader, as well as wasting the Chinese company's money. While all this is a tactic to get the non-Chinese colleague to 'bend over' and be intimidated into the Chinese way of thinking and decision making, the interaction between the two groups of very different cultural backgrounds, suggests a strong sense of Chinese superiority being perceived by the Chinese over other ethnic groups.

It must be said that similar behavior has been observed between Chinese colleagues especially when a more powerful and politically superior colleague engages with one of his compatriots. While the essence of the discussion is difficult to interpret, the body language and verbal expressions can be clearly interpreted as superior bullying.

The noticeable difference between the Chinese colleagues and Western colleagues is how the recipients respond. While Chinese colleagues will generally accept the verbal aggression from their superior Chinese counterpart, Western people tend to respond defensively and in an orally challenging manner, which only adds fuel to the fire and typically these arguments end in a stalemate situation with the Chinese colleague walking away, mumbling loudly in Mandarin with gestating arms flailing through the air. The Chinese colleague is sure to report the encounter to the Chinese leader. He is also likely not to engage with the affected Western colleague for quite some time, expecting some type of apology, as he believes that the trust and his face have been tarnished. After a few days, the anger subsides and it's back to business as usual. However, the incident will never be forgotten by the Chinese colleague and will be held against the challenger for the duration of them having to work together. The Western colleague is in effect marked, and once he or she has a number of incidents and perceived underperformances against his or her name, it could quite well be used silently against him or her to terminate the employment.

At official engagement level, the image portrayed to the world is one of cooperation and harmony. Chinese Government officials have now been wooing and entertaining African governments for decades in exchange for access to commodities, access to land, access to lucrative business deals and of course the resettlement of Chinese citizens to the adopted host country. At political level, these relationships appear to be very healthy, with portraits of host country presidents, other influential political figures, and official Sino-Africa engagements adorning Chinese offices, Chinese factories, and Chinese canteens. Key management positions in the Chinese organizations, operating in the host county, are filled with local, politically connected people, irrespective of their ability to be able to do the job or not. It's a matter of political strategy to achieve the objectivists to secure long-term commodity supplies from host countries. It can be seen as an economic colonialization of the third world countries coming with all its glory of superiority, domination, and exploitation.

Honesty

Because Chinese people are soft-spoken, courteous, polite, non-aggressive and don't overbear in early encounters, one can quite easily assume them to be honest, transparent, honorable and respectful.

However, there is a different side to Chinese nationals that only becomes apparent with time of having got to know their psyche somewhat more closely. Everything a Chinese person does in his or her life is for the better good of the Chinese Tiger. Their actions and decisions, while they may appear one sided to a Westerner, are on closer analysis, made to ultimately benefit the machine that is China. This has always been the case over thousands of years of Chinese existence. After all, if one is seen not to act in the best interest of the Chinese state then one could quickly become a casualty statistic. So it is not so much about loyalty, but rather a survival strategy. The CPC plays a large part in rolling out the communist party expectations to its citizens, right down to the hawker, street sweeper, and peasant. One just does not disobey the behavioral requirements of the Chinese state.

One should not be surprised when one starts understanding the modus operandi of the Chinese industrial machine. Contract negotiations can be stretched out to the extreme, just to negotiate another few hundred dollars off the bottom price. It has been observed that contract conditions in final agreed contract templates have been subtlety altered when the document is presented for final signature. While in the West this is interpreted as sly behavior, in the East this is considered clever negotiating tactics. When confronted the Chinese negotiator would not even blink an eyelid, quite happy to start negotiating that changed condition in his organization's favor right there at the signing ceremony, claiming that this was how he had understood the outcome of the negotiations.

While in Western countries a very transparent procurement

process is encouraged, as ethics and honesty in the workplace is paramount to one's own corporate longevity, Chinese organizations will be quite happy to manipulate procurement processes to ultimately award selected work to Chinese contractors. Sharing of closed bid costs to Chinese contractors and accepting late bid submissions are considered quite normal behavior, while in a Western work environment this would immediately cast a shadow of doubt on the tendering process.

It is also quite normal for Chinese colleagues to twist the truth in the work environment to suit their own objectives. For Chinese natives, it is quite normal to consider paying a bribe to an official to get out of a sticky situation, e.g. not having a work permit, a traffic offence, visa requirements etc.

While all these behaviors can be considered as clever business practices, they heavily cross into the dark space of ethics, bribery, and corruption, so taboo in a Western working environment.

Chinese companies will be quite happy to delay payment to non-Chinese contracting companies, for no given reason. And Chinese companies will delay or underpay their local host country workers, citing under performance and dissatisfaction as the main reason. In countries like South Africa, Botswana and Namibia the labor law does largely protect the worker, which is however not the case in many other African countries. Even in Southern Africa there have been cases where workers have taken the Chinese contractor or company to the Labor Court however, the case was squashed or the case file mysteriously disappeared, it being strongly rumored that the Chinese employer paid a healthy bribe to the official dealing with the case. It's a well-known fact that African government officials can be easily bought over with some money or by extending some favors. In many ways, Africa is therefore the perfect hunting ground for commodity hungry China.

Loyalty

As mentioned previously, Chinese citizens are fiercely loyal to China, to the Communist Party of China, and to each other. This could be more out of anxiousness, fearing prosecution, than it is being a proud and upright citizen. Chinese loyalty will go to the extreme, from defending a Chinese colleague in the workplace, a Chinese citizen in the street or defending Chinese culture and business practices. Patriotism and nepotism are not a new concept in the world, however modern work practices encourage employing somebody for their intellect rather than their skin color, belief, affiliation or conviction. This practice however has not manifested itself in the Chinese work environment, where Chinese citizens and family members are readily employed, irrespective of their ability to do the work or having the necessary experience.

The Chinese management will take the side of Chinese opinion, sometimes openly distrusting the position of the non-Chinese employee. It is typical for a Chinese organization to favor Chinese suppliers and contractors, even when working in the remotest part of Africa. Between organizations, there is a fierce loyalty, being induced at government level that compels one Chinese organization to insure the interests of other Chinese organizations, where it can directly influence the outcome.

Chinese clients are known for protecting failing Chinese contractors by bailing them out financially, assisting them with equipment and 'confidential' information, and openly allowing them to underperform without applying any penalties. The same treatment is not given to non-Chinese service providers, suppliers, and contractors who will be pushed to deliver beyond their contractual agreement and will be hit for every contractual penalty. Failure by one Chinese company will be the failure of all and this could have a detrimental outcome for the most influential Chinese people, associated in any way with the durability of the Chinese modern business policies of securing strategic commodities to feed the Chinese industrial beast and ultimately dictate the world economy.

Favoritism

Favoritism goes hand-in-hand with loyalty. As can be seen in many parts of the world people tend to favor their own kind when it comes to business, but also when it comes to cultural engagements and social rendezvous. The Chinese people are no different. Their kind and creed will be favored in key appointments, unless it makes more sense to appoint a local Government affiliated patron for political reasons.

As highlighted previously, family members are favored in appointments. Children of Party representatives, known as Princelings, are very influential and will be accepted without question to any appointed position. Princelings are very influential, as one or two of their parents hold prominent ranks in the CPC.

Blame Culture

This behavior has also been previously elaborated on in Chapter 9: The Angry Tiger. When something goes wrong, somebody needs to be given the blame. Typically, all other entities are wrong, except Chinese, even if the fault can be confidently apportioned to a Chinese person. Chinese will go to any length to defend their kin. Typically, 'facts' are concocted that will point the finger to a non-Chinese person, who might have been involved on the fringes. Typically, concerns are elevated to the Chinese leader via the unofficial Chinese management structure, and the leader will then take up the issue and apportion the blame to some unlucky candidate.

Chinese colleagues are known to spy on their non-Chinese colleagues and if there is any reason for concern, rightfully or not, this will be elevated to the Chinese leader who will directly take up the concern with the affected party. Western work colleagues often complain that they have been merely employed to take the fall when something goes wrong. In many cases Westerners appointed in management roles, are never allowed to exude their authority especially on the Chinese team members.

As soon as somebody is blamed and possibly dismissed, the delay can be explained, and would suffice for the Chinese senior management and board members. Usually, a Chinese team is then appointed to resolve the issue, and 'save' the day.

One for All and All for One

This book has spent a lot of time on describing the common Chinese psyche that exists across most of its citizens. Individuals behave in a similar fashion, a stereotype behavior encouraged by the Chinese state's communist mantra. The Chinese system does not encourage individual opinion, initiative, intuition, or individual leadership. Not behaving as 'one', would attract immediate attention from the Chinese leadership as well as the Chinese Communist Party appointees interspersed throughout the team.

There is a strong hierarchical consciousness, with every individual understanding and honoring his place in the team and the greater China. There is little ambition from individuals to better themselves by standing out as overachievers. Rather, the system dictates when one is up for promotion or recognition. One has a better chance of moving up the career and political ladder when doing exactly what is prescribed by the Communist system. Of course, these rules do not apply to all, especially if you're politically connected.

Chinese people are renowned for receiving instructions from a superior and passing instruction down to a subordinate, with some lowly paid junior ending up doing the work. Instructions are followed and not questioned. Chinese subordinates will always be in agreement with their superiors, irrespective of what the work request is. The Chinese cultural, business and state psyche ensures group behavior rather than individual prospering. In this way, groups of people can be controlled much better.

Entropy

While Confucian Harmony, Mianzi and Guanxi have dictated the Chinese culture for many decades, ironically in the workplace it is not favored when that there is not a stir or some element of anxious excitement in the air.

The work output and workflow are continuously being interrogated and analyzed by the Chinese management team. Requests for redundant information are made repeatedly.

One's ability to execute the work effectively is also being questioned by analyzing the minutest work details at senior management level. It is not uncommon for a Chinese leader to immerse himself into a technical detail, of which he is not a master or has very little knowledge of, and questioning the issue at hand. Questions will follow a path of more and more detail being asked for until the recipient cannot possibly answer further. Failure to answer all detailed questions will result in the Chinese leader putting the recipient's capability into question.

Unrealistic deadlines are set without consultation and if deadlines are missed, the responsible party will be pestered for this information relentlessly, irrespective of whether such information can be produced or not. A subordinate should never be in a position of control. His motives and output will be questioned at random. A subordinate should be kept on his or her back foot at all times. Creating an environment of high entropy is seen by the Chinese leadership as pushing individuals to operate at the maximum output, even if expectations become unrealistic. Chinese leaders like to emphasize the role and responsibility as follows, *"If a Westerner is late, he loses his job. If a Chinese person is late, he will go to jail"*. Operating within the Chinese framework is not easy—especially if you do not understand the Chinese business culture.

Sexism

Women don't have much status in Chinese day-to-day life. While women are given equal status in the business environment, especially in government-controlled companies, they are not necessarily given equal opportunities. Expatriates Chinese business appointees are predominantly males. The very few females brought over from China usually end up with mundane clerical jobs in the office, even if their job title might imply otherwise. Their opinions are not valued in meetings and generally they have to behave in a rather conservative way, which includes not speaking up, not interjecting in discussions, dressing conservatively, and generally not to be noticed in the office environment. The same is expected of non-Chinese woman. Chinese women are not expected to drive a car, drink alcohol at functions or engage in loud social activity (once alcohol has been consumed copiously). It is also frowned upon for Chinese woman to socialize with men, especially non-Chinese men.

POSTSCRIPT CHAPTER 2

CHINESE CULTURAL AND
TRADITIONAL REVELATIONS

Selected sections of this chapter have been compiled with researched information obtained from knowledgeable sources.

Chinese cultural and traditional values define the Chinese 'every day' behavior, from greetings to business decisions. Chinese people are heavily influenced by Chinese myths, superstitions, beliefs and values. Chinese culture is as old as it gets. The Chinese had been decades ahead with their inventions, compared to the rest of the world and on the back of their prospering society, they also created an intricate cultural aspect to their society. The dynasties and emperors were steeped in culture and traditions, which shaped the Chinese nation of today. While the Chinese culture and traditions were heavily suppressed during Mao Zedong's era, with many Chinese historic artifacts and writings having been destroyed, especially during the Cultural Revolution, these traditions have come back since China's social and economic enlightenment after Mao's death.

In this chapter, I highlight the most important Chinese cultural and traditional practices, that non-Chinese people are bound to be exposed to quite regularly in dealings with China, Chinese companies and Chinese people. The purpose of this chapter is to give the reader a feel of what influences Chinese behaviors and mannerisms when engaging with Chinese people, both in a social as well as business environment, but it will not make you an expert just yet. Yet understanding the basics of these traditions and cultures, so vital in the personal as well as business life of every Chinese national, will help you a long way in engaging more successfully with every encounter. The power of these important influencing factors of the Chinese psyche must never be underestimated.

I have taken the liberty to reference material from internet research, where appropriate, finding that a number of topics being addressed have been well researched and therefore, I would not be able to present the information any better. Some additional research is recommended after you have finished reading this book, should you desire a deeper appreciation of Chinese culture and traditions.

I recommend that you research Chinese culture if you wish to have a successful working relationship with any Chinese company. Don't expect the Tiger to change his stripes to accommodate you. You will have to be on top of your game and armed with information, foresight, strategies, plans, and backup plans; or you will be pulled apart by the Tiger.

As mentioned in Postscript Chapter 1, this Chapter is also intended to be a standalone, quick reference section. Therefore, some of the traditions and cultural aspects have already been touched on in previous chapters, and are briefly repeated here for completeness of this chapter.

PUBLIC CONDUCT

Chinese people are generally very friendly and fascinated by Westerners visiting their country. One is often asked to pose for photos in front of famous sites, like the Great Wall or the Forbidden City. A Chinese stranger will engage enthusiastically with one, despite the language barrier. The friendly banter often has hidden purpose in the form of yet another pose with this stranger for a sought-after photo opportunity.

Chinese are known for inviting Westerners into their homes for a dinner, even if the acquaintance was only made recently, and it is a great privilege for a Chinese man to introduce his family to one. He will brim with pride, smiling from ear to ear on such occasions. I have been personally introduced on a number of occasions to some of my work colleagues' wives and children late at night after a business dinner. The family had waited patiently outside the restaurant for our dinner to conclude.

Handshaking is common in China. Initial presence is acknowledged with a nod of the head before a gentle hand-shake is made. Vigorous handshakes are considered as a sign of rudeness. Bowing is seldom used except in ceremonies. When joining a large group of people, it is common for all to clap. This is a sign to welcome you. You should return the gesture.

Expansive hand gestures and facial expressions should be avoided. Chinese people do not speak with their arms and hands and consider any excessive use of these extremities during conversation as annoying. This can be difficult for Western people who have from an early age learned to express themselves not only orally but also physically. A consciousness is required to abstain from coming across as over-busy.

Do not touch a Chinese person during conversation or any other time. Especially older people and people in positions of authority do not like to be touched by strangers.

There is a heavy emphasis on repressing one's emotions in a public environment. Therefore, one does not see a lot of smiling Chinese people.

Members of the same sex may hold hands in public, seen as a display of friendliness. Public displays of affection between opposite sexes are frowned upon.

It is considered unacceptable social behavior to put your hands into your mouth, bite your nails, remove food from your teeth, pick your nose, or scratch in your ears. However, exuberant burping, continuous sniffing, open-mouth yawning and flatulence in public are not considered offensive. Until recently, spitting was an acceptable social behavior but has now been curtailed by the imposition of heavy fines.

Jumping the queue is very common in China. Pushing and shoving to prevent losing your place in a queue is also common, but patrons will be rather offended if somebody else pushes in front of them.

While conversing in Mandarin is enthusiastically encouraged by the Chinese, using a word incorrectly or pronouncing it incorrectly (subtle pronunciation differences for homophones) can exude a roar of laughter from Chinese in one's hearing vicinity, which can make one feel somewhat uncomfortable and less reluctant to try communicating using newly acquired Mandarin words or phrases. The laughter though seems innocent enough rather than willfully sarcastic.

Smoking is a national pastime for many Chinese, although there seems to be a lesser trend amongst the youth these days. A cigarette is typically enjoyed during dinner, when it is customary to join the host for a smoke either at the table or in a designated smoking area. One can join the smoker's corner, if one is a non-smoker, and this provides a useful opportunity to talk some casual business in a smaller group of people. Allowance should always be made for a few smoke breaks during meetings, negotiations, and workshops.

SIGNIFICANCE OF COLORS

Selecting the right colors to avoid any negative connotations can be quite a daunting task.

Chinese culture assigns certain values to colors. Some colors are considered auspicious and others are inauspicious. *Yánsè* is the Chinese word for color. *Sè* means emotion or 'color in the face'. The word was used on its own in Classical Chinese, and referred to sexual desire or desirability, but it was changed to incorporate all types of color during the Tang Dynasty (618 – 907 AD). The idiom, *Wǔyánliùsè*, which describes many colors, is also used to refer to color in general (Wikipedia, Color in Chinese culture).

Theory of the Five Elements

According to the Wikipedia contributors, traditional Chinese art and culture view black, white, yellow, and qing or "grue" (a mix of green and blue) as the standard colors. Each color represents one of the five elements—metal, earth, wood, passion, and water. These elements are taught in traditional physics and Emperors used this theory to select colors throughout the Shang (1,700 – 1025 BC), Western Zhou (1,025 – 771 BC), Eastern Zhou (771 – 256 BC) and Qin (221 – 206 BC) dynasties.

Black

A neutral color that corresponds with water, black, is regarded as Heaven's color by the *I Ching*, which is also known as the *Book of Changes*. According to the Wikipedia article, the Chinese believed that the Heavenly Emperor or Tian Di resided in the North Star, and they derived the saying 'heaven and earth of mysterious black' from the observation that the northern sky remained black for a long time.

Probably the most well known representation of the unity between Yin and Yang is the Taiji symbol, which carries equal parts of black and white in opposing yet interconnected parts.

The ancient Chinese honored black as the king of colors, but Lao Zi felt that five colors caused blindness. As such, the Dao School chose black as the color of the Dao.

While white tends to be associated with mourning after death and was worn to funerals depending on the age of passing, black is a preferred color for daily clothing.

Red

Red is also referred to as *Vermilion* and *Chinese Red*.

It symbolizes joy and good fortune, and is used in abundance, especially at social gatherings, holidays, and Chinese New Year. Monetary gifts are presented in red envelopes to symbolize good luck. However, because it is a symbolic color of happiness, it is strictly forbidden at funerals.

This popular color is also affiliated with the government (Wikipedia, Color in Chinese culture).

Green

Green is generally associated with harmony, health, and prosperity, according to the above Wikipedia article.

However, the Chinese also associate green hats with infidelity and as an idiom for a cuckold. Chinese Catholic bishops have been uneasy about this, as they usually have a green hat above their arm sleeves to symbolize ecclesiastical heraldry. They have compromised to use a violet hat in their coat of arms instead. Additionally, an indigo feather is used to further show their disdain for green.

White

White represents purity, fulfillment, and brightness, and corresponds with metal—gold in particular, according to Wikipedia, *Color in Chinese culture.*

However, since it is associated with death and mourning, it is used at funerals. In ancient times, Chinese people only wore white clothes and hats during periods of mourning.

Yellow

Yellow is said to generate Yin and Yang and is revered as the most prestigious and beautiful color around which everything else centers. It corresponds with earth, and is often used with red in place of gold. Yellow signifies good luck and neutrality and it often adorns the robes of emperors, as well as temples, altars and royal palaces according to the Wikipedia research.

Buddhist Monks esteem yellow, as it represents freedom from the cares of the world. As such, their garments and temples are adorned with yellow, which also happens to be a mourning color for them. It is symbolic of heroism. This is another contradiction with Western culture, which associates yellow with cowardice.

The emperor of Imperial China used yellow as his symbolic color and it remains that of China's five legendary ancient emperors.

SIGNIFICANCE OF NUMBERS

In Chinese tradition, certain numbers are believed by some to be auspicious or inauspicious based on the Chinese word that the number name sounds similar to. The numbers 0, 6, 8, and 9 are believed to have auspicious meanings because their names sound similar to words that have positive meanings. The superstitious aspect of this primarily grew out of the Cantonese Culture, but it has taken root through other dialects and regional groups of Chinese (Wikipedia, Chinese Numerology).

The following numbers are considered lucky numbers: 0, 2, 3, 5, 6, 7, 8, and 9.

Eight is considered one of the luckiest numbers in Chinese culture. If you receive eight of any item, consider it a gesture of goodwill. Six is considered a blessing for smoothness and problem free advances.

Unlucky numbers are 4, and 5.

Each of these numbers has a specific significance. Combinations of these numbers are also superstitiously interpreted.

The number 4 is considered a very unlucky number in Chinese because it is nearly homophonous to the word 'death' (pinyin sǐ). Due to that, many numbered product lines skip the '4', for example, Nokia cell phones (before the Lumia 640, there is no series containing a 4 in the name), Canon PowerShot G's series (after G3 goes to G5), etc. In East Asia, some buildings do not have a fourth floor. This can be compared with the Western practice of some buildings not having a 13th floor because thirteen is considered unlucky (cn.hujiang.com, Chinese Lucky Numbers and Unlucky Numbers).

In Hong Kong, some high-rise residential buildings omit all floor numbers containing a four, including 4, 14, 24, 34 and all

40–49 floors, in addition to not having a 13th floor. As a result, a building whose highest floor is number 50 may actually have only thirty-five physical floors (Wikipedia, Chinese Numerology).

Other numbers that should be avoided too, according to the article, include 73, which symbolize 'the funeral' and 84 means 'having accidents'. The task of understanding number combinations can get rather daunting and unless one lives the Chinese culture it will be rather difficult to fully comprehend the Chinese numbers game.

GIVING GIFTS

Gifts must always be selected with sensitivity and having some deeper knowledge of the recipient to be receiving your gift. The act of bestowing a gift onto somebody you respect or consider important has been part of the Chinese culture for hundreds of decades and is thus not seen in a negative light. Gifts are carefully chosen and it is important not to represent something negative. Even the gift color and wrapping paper color will be carefully considered (see section on *Significance of Colors* above) (USchinabiz.com, Top Ten Guidelines to Gift-Giving in China).

Ideally, gifts should be wrapped in plain red paper, as it is considered lucky. Pink, silver, and gold are also great choices, while yellow with black writing should only be given to the dead. Plain black or white gift-wrapping paper represents mourning (Wikipedia, Color in Chinese culture).

Color meanings may also differ by region, so if you're unsure, it is advisable to check with a local.

Presents are typically exchanged when a Chinese colleague

returns from mainland China, as a thank you for assistance rendered, as a token of respect to a superior—and sometimes to buy future favors of which one might not yet be aware. Gifts are not just given for the sake of giving a gift, but are always motivated with a reason, or bestowed as a small token of appreciation. Chinese people will ensure that the gift is presented in the presence of one or two witnesses, so that the gesture can never be misconstrued as an act of bribery. The gift will not be opened immediately, but rather in privacy, suggesting that the thought of giving a gift has much more bearing than the material value of the gift.

In all likelihood, the future bearer of the gift will try to find out from the recipient what he or she would like as a gift. One does not have to be too modest, as it is expected that the recipient will reciprocate with a similarly elaborate gift. However, it is important to consider the symbolism around the type of gift requested. The gift request should be at least Chinese in origin, like Chinese alcohol, silk paintings, and Chinese gadgets like fans or even Chinese tea.

It is not advisable to give money to a Chinese colleague as a gift. Thought must have been put into a gift, which must have a worth to the recipient. The beauty of the gift will be scrutinized, so presentation and colors play a significant role in this cultural exchange of gifts. Giving the same type of present more than once is considered being tardy, not having put enough thoughtfulness into the gift selection.

The Chinese will refuse a gift at first before finally accepting it, in line with Chinese tradition. You will have to continue to insist. Once the gift is accepted, one must then express gratitude for the recipient having accepted the gift. You will be expected to go through the same motion when you are offered a gift.

Never present a gift of high-perceived value to one person in the presence of others, as it will cause embarrassment. Chinese business culture observes strict rules against bribery and that can cause problems for the recipient. For that reason, it is not recommended that you take photographs of any gift giving ceremony unless it is presented symbolically to the entire organization. Gifts presented to the company as a whole—and not to an individual—are acceptable (chinesetime-school.com, Business Gift Giving).

However, it is important to conclude all negotiations prior to exchanging the gift and present it as a gift from the company you represent. If possible, explain the meaning of the gift, and present it to the leader of the Chinese negotiators. In order to prevent a feeling of obligation to reciprocate, steer away from obviously expensive gifts.

If you present an individual with a valuable gift, do so in private and only as a gesture of friendship. People of the same level of importance should receive gifts of a similar value so that nobody feels short-changed. Otherwise it may lead to relationship strains.

Wrap your gift only after you have gone through Chinese Customs, as it will probably be unwrapped.

Chinese people value symbolic gifts, such as:

- Cigarette lighters for smokers
- Stamps for stamp collectors (a popular hobby in China)
- Solar calculators
- Fine pens (with blue or black ink—never red)
- A fine liqueur or cognac

Acceptable gifts for a company include items from your

country or city, such as handicrafts, or an illustrated book.

Dinner is always a welcome gift, and since you're bound to be invited to dinner, you should probably reciprocate. Senior local officials in parts of China will host a welcoming party for you, but they may expect you to pay for it. Come prepared!

Food gifts are welcome, except at occasions such as dinner parties where food is served. You can however send a fruit basket or candy as a thank-you gift after the event.

Certain gifts should be avoided, such as sharp objects (scissors or knives) as they signify the severing of a relationship. If you do want to give those items as gifts, ask your Chinese friend or colleague to give you a few cents (the smallest amount of money possible) in exchange. The exchange of money for goods would mean that you 'sold' the item to your friend or colleague, which means it is not a gift.

Other items that should be avoided because they are associated with funerals include.

- Four of any item ('four' and 'death' sound similar in Cantonese)
- Any gifts wrapped in white, blue, or black paper
- White flowers
- Green hats
- Handkerchiefs
- Clocks
- Umbrellas
- Straw sandals
- Chrysanthemums

CHINESE NEW YEAR

Also known as the Spring Festival (Chūn jié) in modern Chinese culture, Chinese New Year celebrates the turning of the lunisolar Chinese calendar. Traditional celebrations start on the evening before the first day (which falls on the first day of the new moon between January 21 and February 20) to the Lantern Festival, which takes place on the fifteenth day of the first calendar month (Wikipedia, Chinese New Year).

According to my research, this age-old festival is signified by many traditions and myths and is celebrated wherever significant Chinese populations are found. It started as a celebration to honor deities and ancestors.

In China, regional traditions and customs determine how the New Year is celebrated. Chinese families typically gather on the eve of Chinese New Year's Day to enjoy a reunion dinner. Families will use this time to perform spiritual house cleansings in order to remove any ill fortune and to clear the way for good fortune.

During New Year, Chinese people will decorate their doors with red couplets and paper decorations, and they will light fireworks and present monetary gifts in red envelopes.

The Chinese calendar does not use consecutively numbered years, but outside of China, years are numbered starting from the Yellow Emperor's reign in the third millennium BC. Various scholars have used three or more years numbered year one, which makes 2017 equal to the Chinese year 4715, 4714, or 4654. This can appear overwhelming to non-Chinese people who very often will choose to rather ignore the more intricate details of Chinese cultural aspects.

NATIONAL DAY OF THE PEOPLE'S REPUBLIC OF CHINA

The People's Republic of China celebrates their National Day of the People's Republic of China (Guóqìng jie) on October 1. The annual celebration commemorates the founding of the PRC with a ceremony at Tiananmen Square (Wikipedia, National Day of the People's Republic of China).

The PRC was founded on September 21, 1949. The Resolution on the National Day of the People's Republic of China was passed on December 2, 1949 by the Central People's Government and declared October 1 as the National Day.

The PRC's National Day marks the start of one of the PRC's Golden Weeks.

National Day is celebrated throughout the Chinese mainland, as well as in Macau and Hong Kong. The government organizes many festivities, including concerts and fireworks shows in public places that are adorned with festive decorations, as well as public displays of portraits featuring prominent and revered leaders, including Mao Zedong.

In the Chinese work environment National Day is taken very seriously; celebrations are had in the office and the Chinese work colleagues are often given a few days off to coincide with National Day Golden Week.

GOLDEN WEEK

The People's Republic of China implemented a semi-annual seven-day national holiday known as Golden Week in 2000 (Wikipedia, Golden Week China). China currently has two Golden Weeks:

- Chinese Lunar New Year Golden Week begins in January or February
- National Day Golden Week begins around October 1

Until 2007, a third Golden Week holiday was celebrated to commemorate Labor Day, which falls on May 1.

Companies offer three days of paid leave during the Golden Weeks, and they rearrange weekends to give employees a full seven consecutive days off work.

The aim of the Golden Weeks was to expand domestic tourism in the PRC and to improve the standard of living of the people. It has provided people the opportunity to travel long distances to visit family that live far away.

EATING CULTURE

The Chinese essentially observe traditional Han dining customs in Greater China, although some of the etiquette points have evolved in the wake of the Communist revolution. From invitations to seating order as well as paying the bill, many different protocols and customs have to be followed in formal dining (Wikipedia, Customs and Etiquette in Chinese Dining).

Table Settings and Place Settings

Small groups may sit by square or rectangular tables, but round tables are preferred when it comes to large groups, as it makes sharing easier.

Traditional dining often involves communally shared dishes, and Lazy Susan turntables are typically placed in the middle of larger tables.

Place settings include:

- Small teacup
- Dinner plate with a small rice bowl (empty)
- Set of chopsticks to the right of the plate
- Spoon
- Large glass for water or wine
- Small glass for *baijiu* or *shaojiu* (a sorghum wine made from grain)

Low-end restaurants or homes may use paper napkins, provided by the diner, while high-end restaurants usually provide cloth napkins.

Formal Seating Order

Every formal dinner requires a specific seating arrangement that is based on organizational hierarchy and seniority, according to the Wikipedia article, *Customs and Etiquette in Chinese Dining*. A seat of honor is reserved for the host, who is usually the most senior representative of the Chinese dinner delegation. It is usually the seat in the center facing east or more likely facing the entrance. Guests with the highest status or a foreign guest of honor will be placed next to the host. If the guest of honor has a higher status than the Chinese host, then the guest of honor is placed in the center facing the entrance with the Chinese host positioning himself next to him or her. Other guests with high status then sit in close proximity to the seat of honor, while those with lower positions sit further away.

Courses

Although it varies throughout China, the vast majority of full-course dinners are similar in terms of the timing and choice of dishes. As Chinese cuisine can be rather complex involving many exotic meats, varied exotic spices and a wide range of greens and vegetables, I have not delved further into this topic, as it would distract from the overall purpose of this book.

Snacks

Once guests are seated, waitrons will present one or two small dishes with snacks such as salted roasted peanuts or boiled unsalted peanuts to be consumed while waiting for the food to be served.

Beverages

Most often, hosts or restaurateurs will provide tea as soon as guests are seated, and the beverage can be consumed at leisure. Refills will be offered throughout the meal and guests can verbally thank servers by saying *"xiexie"* or by tapping the table twice using two bent fingers. Additionally, copious amounts of alcohol are also consumed during dinner.

Main course

The main meal typically consists of many communal dishes—approximately one per person.

Generally, no starch is served during the main course but only after all dinner patrons are satiated—see *'Starch'* below.

There will sometimes be small bowls of white rice accompanying the main dishes, especially in Chinese restaurants located in Western countries. The dishes are typically consumed over small quantities of rice, allowing the sauces of the dishes to flavor it. Rice is not consumed separately, unless one is still hungry after all the dishes have been consumed.

Soup may be served—especially at home—as one of the dishes and it may be used to replace beverages entirely.

Starch

Towards the end of the main meal, when everyone has stopped indulging in the main dishes, waitrons will bring out a starch to ensure guests are satiated. The starch could be rice, Chinese dumplings or noodles. Chinese dumplings, also known as baozi, is a steamed bun made from yeast.

Fruits

A variety of fresh fruit, cut into smaller pieces and often beautifully presented, is served at the end of the meal after the starch course. At this point of the meal, there are very few takers—the fruit selection looking more like a table decoration.

Manners and Etiquette

Eating is an important part of Chinese culture, and guests are often treated to a dining experience. It is used as a means to grow friendships and deepen relationships.

Traditionally, the Chinese believe that good manners and etiquette bring good luck, while bad manners invite shame. While Maoist programs aimed to eradicate many traditional social practices, table manners are considered an indication of educational status.

Dinner Invites

Households may make their own rules, but customs and traditions tend to be common throughout China. Foreigners are often invited into homes for dinner, and it is not unusual for business associates to be invited to dinner. Hosts have to follow certain rules when they invite guests over, and guests are expected to adhere to a certain etiquette (Thoughtco.com, Etiquette for Visiting a Chinese Home; Wikipedia, Customs and Etiquette in Chinese Dining):

- Guests must either accept an invitation or decline, giving a specific reason. Vague excuses are considered a sign that you do not want to have a relationship with the person
- Many homes feature a rack of shoes at the entrance, and the host may meet you by the door in bare feet, stockings, or slippers. Good etiquette dictates that you should remove your shoes. You may don a pair of sandals or slippers if the host offers this or you may simply wear your socks or walk barefoot. Some households will offer a communal pair of elastic sandals for use in the restroom
- Good etiquette dictates that you bring along a gift for the host. You may invite the host to open it in front of you, but they may decline and you should not force them to do so
- Tea will be served and you will be expected to drink it. It would be impolite to request an alternative drink
- The meal will typically be prepared by the wife or one of the mothers who may not join the festivities, until all dishes have been brought to the table
- Dishes are typically served family-style, with some households providing separate serving chopsticks and others not
- You should follow the host's lead in serving yourself, but only eat when he or she eats
- Enjoy the food, as eating generously shows that you are enjoying the meal, but never finish off the last bit of any dish; this will indicate that the cook did not

prepare sufficient food. Leave a small amount of food behind

- Stay for at least thirty minutes after the conclusion of the dinner to show that you enjoyed the meal and the company

Drinking

You can consume non-alcoholic beverages and water throughout the meal, but you should take a single sip of an alcoholic beverage during toasts in a formal setting. However, when a toast is ended with *"Ganbei!"* you should empty the glass. It will typically be refilled immediately in preparation for the next toast (Wikipedia, Customs and Etiquette in Chinese Dining).

Lazy Susan

A rotating circular wooden, plastic, or glass tray known as a Lazy Susan placed in the center of the table is used to simplify the sharing of multiple dishes. When all the dishes for a specific course are brought out, they are placed around the tray. The guest of honor is typically served first, and the dishes are then rotated clockwise to the other guests. The host will usually wait for all the guests before he serves himself.

It's best not to remove the dish from the Lazy Susan, but if you have to, hold it aloft while serving yourself, and then replace it to its spot on the Lazy Susan. Try to avoid moving the tray while transferring food from the dish to your plate.

Take a small amount of food from the dish until everyone has had an opportunity to take a portion, and be mindful of the other diners when you take a second helping.

Personal Dinner Etiquette

In order to accommodate the use of chopsticks and spoons, Chinese food is typically served in bite-sized chunks, or soft enough to be easily picked apart. The following personal etiquette rules apply (China Highlights, How to Eat in China—Chinese Dining Etiquette):

- Hold your chopsticks in such a way that they are the same length and that the ends are even
- When they are not in use, place your chopsticks on the small ceramic rests provided near the napkin to the right of your bowl
- Do not allow your chopsticks to stick out of dishes upright in a way that resembles burning sticks of incense for the dead
- Do not pick at your food using chopsticks
- Do not spear your food using chopsticks
- Never chew on the ends of your chopsticks
- Do not use chopsticks to move plates or bowls
- Never 'play drums' with your chopsticks.
- Chopsticks are meant to be used as an extension of your fingers and it would be impolite to wave them around or point them at other dinner guests
- Do not use your chopsticks to pick at your teeth or something similarly unhygienic, as non-disposable chopsticks will be washed and reused
- Place both hands above the table, even when you are not using your left hand to hold a utensil

Communal Behavior

Formal meals will usually provide pairs of communal serving chopsticks or *gongkuai* that are meant only for shared dishes, and are normally longer in length and more ornate than regular chopsticks or *putongkuai* used by the patrons to eat with. There may be a set of communal chopsticks per dish or per course (World Heritage Encyclopedia, Customs and Etiquette in Chinese Dining).

Gratuities

Unless explicitly posted, most Chinese restaurants do not require gratuities. If it is required, it will be included on the bill.

Chinese restaurants in Western countries do usually expect that you pay gratuities to the waitrons (China Highlights, How to Tip in China).

FENG SHUI

Feng Shui is an ancient Chinese philosophy that harmonizes people with their environment. The term Feng Shui translates to 'wind-water'. Guo Pu explained it as such in the lost Classic of Burial, *"Feng Shui is one of the Five Arts of Chinese Metaphysics, classified as physiognomy"* (Wikipedia, Feng Shui).

Despite its wide use in China and across the world, scientists consider it a form of pseudoscience. It was suppressed during China's Cultural Revolution in the 1960s and 1970s, but has grown in popularity since.

According to the *Skeptic Encyclopedia of Pseudoscience*, the Feng Shui principles relating to living in harmony with nature are 'quite rational'; however, the non-scientific claims lack credibility.

Scientific skeptic and author Brian Dunning performed a comprehensive evaluation of Feng Shui in 2016 and concurred with the claims that it is a pseudoscience, according to the Wikipedia research. He wrote, *"There's no real science behind Feng Shui… It's also a simple matter to dismiss the mystical energies said to be at its core; they simply don't exist"*.

CHINESE MYTHOLOGY

China's historical areas are the birthplace of many myths and legends, including those related to the founding of the Chinese state and culture. Historians have found evidence of mythological symbolism from as far back as the 12th century BC, written in the Oracle bone script (Wikipedia, Chinese Mythology).

For more than a thousand years, legends were passed down before being recorded in works such as *Classic of Mountains and Seas*, or performed through song and theatre before being recorded in novels.

In the past, it was believed that Chinese mythology was partly factual, which is why many of the stories told in the study of Chinese historical culture included two versions—one historicized and another that is mythological in nature.

China is also home to many ethnic minority groups, each speaking its own language, and following their own folklore. Some have their own writing, which is filled with unique myths, as well as valuable cultural and historical information. In many cases, the same myths are relayed across multiple ethnic groups, with small differences.

You can learn more about Chinese myths in philosophical canons or imperial historical documents, such as *Book of*

Documents, Records of the Grand Historian, Book of Rites, and *Lüshi Chunqiu.*

CHINESE ZODIAC

The Chinese use a zodiac classification scheme, which assigns an animal to each year in a 12-year cycle. Like the Western zodiac, the Chinese zodiac also has time cycles consisting of twelve parts, the majority of which carry animal names. Each time cycle ascribes a person's character or life events to his or her relationship with the cycle. Variations of the Chinese zodiac are popular in many East Asian countries and in the Buddhist calendar, but there are some major differences (Wikipedia, Chinese Zodiac).

While the Chinese cycle corresponds to years, the Western zodiac is based on the twelve months of a calendar year. Unlike the Chinese zodiac, the Western zodiac does not only feature animals, but is associated with the constellations that span the ecliptic plane.

Signs

The sign of the Rat is traditionally the first item on the Chinese zodiac, followed by the other eleven zodiac signs below, retrieved from Wikipedia:

- Rat (Yang, 1st Trine, Fixed Element Water)
- Ox (Yin, 2nd Trine, Fixed Element Earth)
- Tiger (Yang, 3rd Trine, Fixed Element Wood)
- Rabbit (Yin, 4th Trine, Fixed Element Wood)
- Dragon (Yang, 1st Trine, Fixed Element Earth)
- Snake (Yin, 2nd Trine, Fixed Element Fire)

- Horse (Yang, 3rd Trine, Fixed Element Fire)
- Goat (Yin, 4th Trine, Fixed Element Earth)
- Monkey (Yang, 1st Trine, Fixed Element Metal)
- Rooster (Yin, 2nd Trine, Fixed Element Metal)
- Dog (Yang, 3rd Trine, Fixed Element Earth)
- Pig (Yin, 4th Trine, Fixed Element Water)

Chinese astrological animal signs represent how a person presents him or herself, or how others perceive them. In addition to the annual animal signs, a person is also assigned a monthly animal sign (an inner animal), a daily animal sign (true animals), and an hour animal, known as your secret animal. A person who appears to be a Goat (since they were born in the year of the goat), may actually be a Dragon internally, an Ox truly, or a Snake secretively.

The conflict between a person's lifestyle and their zodiac is known as *kai sui* or *tai sui*.

Chinese Calendar Based on the Chinese Zodiac

Four Pillars

The Chinese calendar consists of Four Pillars or Columns, since it falls into columns, much like Chinese writing. This method traces back to the Han Dynasty (210BC-220AD) and remains popular in general analysis and Feng Shui astrology (Wikipedia, Chinese Calendar).

Each of the four pillars or columns consists of a stem and a branch, with each column representing a person's year, month, day, and hour of birth. An animal and an element are assigned to each of the columns. The 'Four Pillars' can be presented as follows:

- The Year column represents a person's ancestor or early age
- The Month column represents a person's parents or childhood
- The Day column represents oneself (upper character), one's adulthood, or one's spouse (lower character)
- The Hour column represents one's children or golden age

Years

According to the Wikipedia explanation, the Year pillar represents a person's family history and background, as well as his or her relationship with grandparents and society as a whole. One can use a person's sign to calculate a person's age based on their perceived age (teenager, someone in their 20s or 40s).

For example, a teenager born in the year of Rabbit would have been 13 in 2011.

Months and solar terms

A month represents a person's childhood and parents. That is why the month pillar is often considered the most important factor in determining a person's life experiences in adulthood (Wikipedia, Chinese Calendar).

The twelve zodiac animals are interlinked with the Chinese agricultural calendar, which runs parallel to the lunar calendar. The latter contains twenty-four two-week Solar Terms. Each animal links to two solar terms—similar to a Western month.

While the lunar calendar consists of sixty years and may vary from the Western calendar by as much as a full month, the agricultural calendar only varies by one day, which begins on February third or fourth. The Tiger, which is the first spring animal, heralds the start of the lunar year. Since the signs are linked to solar months, they are also linked to seasons.

Fixed elements are those that share seasons with a sign, and it is believed that these elements impart their characteristics to the signs. The same element will apply to the hour, month, and year in addition to the sign.

Day

The four pillars calculator can determine the zodiac animal of the day (Wikipedia, Chinese Zodiac).

True animals are depicted by the day of birth. For an astrologer to prepare a chart, he or she must know the animals of your date of birth. There are twelve animals and only seven days, which means that some days have two or three animals, as shown below:

- Monday: Goat
- Tuesday: Dragon
- Wednesday: Horse
- Thursday: Rat, Pig
- Friday: Rabbit, Snake, Dog
- Saturday: Ox, Tiger, Rooster
- Sunday: Monkey

Hours

Each sign in the Chinese zodiac corresponds to the time of day. The *shichen* or large hour (two-hour period) is assigned an animal, which equates to twelve animals. Knowing the exact time of an individual's birth is key to assigning a person's secret animal, which is thought to be their truest representation

(Wikipedia, Chinese Zodiac).

The hour animal is assigned, based on the sun's position in the sky, rather than the time shown on the clock, in order to compensate for daylight savings time. Since some online systems and astrologers may already compensate for it as well—in addition to the client's own compensations—it can lead to inaccurate readings.

The hour pillar represents one's children and contributions to the world.

Animals are assigned to solar time in the following order:

- 23:00 – 00:59: Rat
- 01:00 – 02:59: Ox
- 03:00 – 04:59: Tiger
- 05:00 – 06:59: Rabbit
- 07:00 – 08:59: Dragon
- 09:00 – 10:59: Snake
- 11:00 – 12:59: Horse
- 13:00 – 14:59: Goat
- 15:00 – 16:59: Monkey
- 17:00 – 18:59: Rooster
- 19:00 – 20:59: Dog
- 21:00 – 22:59: Pig

Times are based on local solar time, rather than on standard time. One can convert local solar time to standard time by adding or reducing time based on one's birth location. London marks the central meridian of Greenwich Mean Time where standard time is equivalent to solar time (Wikipedia, Chinese Zodiac).

CHINESE CALENDAR

China's official calendar is the Gregorian calendar, but the community still adheres to the Chinese calendar, also known as the Rural Calendar, which has had a significant influence on many traditional Asian calendars (Wikipedia, Chinese Calendar).

The Traditional Chinese calendar reconciliates years, months, and days based on astrological phenomena. The Standardization Administration of the People's Republic of China issued the GB/T 33661-2017 Calculation, which is used by Chinese communities across the globe, on May 12, 2017. This calendar is the culmination of centuries of cultural evolution spanning well over one hundred variants. It is based on seasonal and astronomical factors.

This calendar lists dates of traditional Chinese holidays, and enables people to select the most auspicious days for special events, such as starting a business, moving house, holding funerals, or hosting weddings.

Solar terms are crucial components of the Chinese calendar, and each month contains up to three solar terms, according to the Wikipedia article.

As in the Western calendar, the Chinese day begins and ends at midnight. New months begin at dark or new moon, and years begin when the dark moon reaches the midpoint between winter solstice and spring equinox.

CHINESE ASTROLOGY

Traditional calendars and astronomy form the basis of Chinese astrology, both of which flourished during the Han Dynasty (210BC–220AD).

Closely linked to Chinese philosophy which follows the theory of three harmony—heaven, earth and water) it uses concepts foreign to Western astrology, including Yin and Yang, Wu Xing teachings, the lunisolar calendar (sun and moon calendars), the 12 Earthly branches, the 10 Celestial stems, and time calculation (Wikipedia, Chinese Astrology).

Background

Chinese astrology advanced during the Zhou dynasty (1046 – 256 BC), and became popular during the Han Dynasty (210BC-220AD), when various elements of Chinese culture were combined into what is now known as the philosophical principles of Chinese medicine, alchemy, astrology, and divination.

Wu Xing is associated with the five classical planets, according to the article in Wikipedia, *Chinese Astrology:*

- Venus—Metal (White Tiger)
- Jupiter—Wood (Azure Dragon)
- Mercury—Water (Black Tortoise)
- Mars—Fire (Vermilion Bird) (may or may not be associated with the phoenix which was also an imperial symbol along with the Dragon)
- Saturn—Earth (Yellow Dragon)

Chinese astrology believes that the position of major planets at birth—along with that of the sun, moon, comets, zodiac sign and time of birth—can determine a person's destiny.

Astronomers observed the orbit of Jupiter (which is associated with the constellation Sheti, and sometimes referred to as Sheti), and built the twelve-year cycle of animal signs. They then divided the celestial circle into twelve sections, which they rounded to twelve years.

Zi Wei Dou Shu or Purple Star Astrology is the practice of computing a person's destiny based on his or her birth date, birth season, and hour of birth. This system is still used in modern-day Chinese astrology.

Interestingly, Chinese constellations differ significantly from Western constellations, but like Western heavenly bodies, the stars are used as inspiration for fairy tales (Wikipedia, Chinese Astrology).

Luni-Solar Calendar

Two separate, interacting cycles combine to create the sixty-year cycle that is the lunisolar calendar. The first cycle is the ten heavenly stems, or the Five Elements in their Yin and Yang forms, in the order of Wood, Fire, Earth, Metal and Water (Wikipedia, Chinese Calendar).

The second cycle is based on the Earthy Branches or twelve zodiac signs in order of Rat, Ox, Tiger, Rabbit, Dragon, Snake, Horse, Goat, Monkey, Rooster, Dog, and Pig.

The sixty-year cycle is created as the result of the least amount of years required for it to go from Yang Wood Rat to the next iteration. It always starts at Yang Wood Rat and ends in Yin Water Pig. The current cycle began in 1984.

The zodiac animal cycle can only be divided by two, which means that every sign may only occur as Yin or Yan. Therefore, the Snake will always be Yin and the Dragon will always be Yang.

Handy ways to understand the lunisolar calendar is to re-member that years ending in odd numbers are always Yin, and those ending in even numbers are always Yang, according to Wikipedia, *Chinese Calendar*.

- If the year ends in 0 it is Yang Metal
- If the year ends in 1 it is Yin Metal
- If the year ends in 2 it is Yang Water
- If the year ends in 3 it is Yin Water
- If the year ends in 4 it is Yang Wood
- If the year ends in 5 it is Yin Wood
- If the year ends in 6 it is Yang Fire
- If the year ends in 7 it is Yin Fire
- If the year ends in 8 it is Yang Earth
- If the year ends in 9 it is Yin Earth

The traditional Chinese zodiac follows the lunisolar Chinese calendar; the years switch over at Chinese New Year and not on January 1, as in the Gregorian calendar. That means that individuals born in January and early February would carry the sign from the previous year, and therefore, placemats at Chinese restaurants and some online sign calculators may assign the wrong sign (Wikipedia, Chinese Calendar).

WORKS CITED

1worldglobalgifts.com, "International Gift Giving Etiquette – China", http://www.1worldglobalgifts.com/ chinagiftgivingetiquette.htm (accessed March 29, 2018).

China Highlights, "How to Eat in China—Chinese Dining Etiquette", https://www.chinahighlights.com/travelguide/ chinese-food/dining-etiquette.htm (accessed March 29, 2018).

China Highlights, "How to Tip in China", https://www.chinahighlights.com/travelguide/guidebook/ tip.htm (accessed March 29, 2018).

China Mike, "The Cult of Face", http://www.china-mike. com/chinese-culture/understanding-chinese-mind/cult-of-face/ (accessed March 29, 2018).

China Mike, "Confucius 101: A key to understanding the Chinese Mind", http://www.china-mike.com/chinese-culture/understanding-chinese-mind/confucius/ (accessed March 29, 2018).

China Mike, "Guanxi", http://www.china-mike.com/chinese-culture/understanding-chinese-mind/guanxi/ (accessed March 29, 2018).

Chinese Time School, "Business Gift Giving", http://www.chinesetimeschool.com/en-us/articles/ business-gift-giving/ (accessed April 29, 2018).

Chu, B. (2013), "Chinese Whispers" (pp. 113, 114, 127). London, Great Britain, Weidenfeld & Nicolson.

cn.hujian.com, "Chinese Lucky Numbers and Unlucky Numbers", https://cn.hujiang.com/n/search/numbers/ (accessed March 29, 2018).

Collins, J. (2001), "Good to Great" (pp. 17-40). United Kingdom, Random House.

Free Tibet, "Tibet's Monasteries", https://freetibet.org/tibets-monasteries (accessed March 28, 2018).

French, H. W. (2015), "China's Second Continent". United States of America, Vintage Books.

Guangzhou.chn.info, "Numbers in Chinese Culture", http://www.guangzhou.chn.info/culture-tradition/cantonese-cultures/numbers-in-chinese-cultu (accessed March 28, 2018).

History.com, "Cultural Revolution", https://www.history.com/topics/cultural-revolution (accessed March 28, 2018).

Lovell, J. (2006), "The Great Wall" (pp. 1, 4, 5, 29, 48, 49, 52, 53, 121, 126, 128,). Great Britain, London, Atlantic Books.

New World Encyclopedia, "Chinese Surname", http://www.newworldencyclopedia.org/entry/Chinese_surname (accessed March 29, 2018).

Military Wikia, "Organization of the Communist Party of China", http://military.wikia.com/wiki/Organization_of_the_Communist_Party_of_China (accessed March 29, 2018).

Moyo, D. (2013), "Winner Take All" (pp. 37, 41, 48, 52, 64, 72-73, 117-120). Canada, Penguin Books.

NPR.org, "African Elephant Population Declines By 30 Percent", https://www.npr.org/sections/thetwo-way/2016/08/31/492124724/african-elephant-population-declines-by-30-percent (accessed January 12, 2018).

People.wku.edu, "Chinese Culture and Customs", http://people.wku.edu/haiwang.yuan/China/docs/chinese cultureandcustoms.rtf (accessed January 12, 2018).

Rediff, "Bo Xilai Indicted", http://www.rediff.com/news/report/bo-xilai-indicted-for-corruption-abuse-of-power-in-china/20130725.htm (accessed January 12, 2018).

Stalin's Moustache, "New CPC Politburo takes oath of admission at site of first meeting in 1921", https://stalinsmoustache.org/2017/11/02/new-cpc-politburo-takes-oath-of-admission-at-site-of-first-meeting-in-1921(accessed January 12, 2018).

Trading Economics, "Unemployment Rate", www.tradingeconomics.com/china/unemployment-rate (accessed February 14, 2017).

The Guardian, "China Indicts Bo Xilai Corruption", https://www.theguardian.com/world/2013/jul/25/china-indicts-bo-xilai-corruption (accessed January 12, 2018).

Thoughtco.com, "Etiquette for Visiting a Chinese Home", https://www.thoughtco.com/chinese-etiquette-visiting-a-home-687432 (accessed June 12, 2017).

USchinabiz.com, "Top Ten Guidelines to Gift-Giving in China", http://www.uschinabiz.com/TopTens/ GiftGivinginChina.aspx (accessed March 29, 2018).

Wikipedia, "Belt and Road Initiative", https://en.wikipedia.org/w/index.php?title=Belt_and_Roa d_Initiative&oldid=785831347 (accessed June 16, 2017).

Wikipedia, "Cemetery of Confucius", https://en.wikipedia.org/w/index.php?title=Cemetery_of_ Confucius&oldid=780804010 (accessed June 16, 2017).

Wikipedia, "Chinese Astrology", https://en.wikipedia.org/w/index.php?title=Chinese_astro logy&oldid=783297397 (accessed June 16, 2017).

Wikipedia, "Chinese calendar", https://en.wikipedia.org/w/index.php?title=Chinese_calen dar&oldid=783297503 (accessed June 16, 2017).

Wikipedia, "Chinese Mythology", https://en.wikipedia.org/w/index.php?title=Chinese_myt hology&oldid=782035434 (accessed June 16, 2017).

Wikipedia, "Chinese Numerology", https://en.wikipedia.org/w/index.php?title=Chinese_Nu merology&oldid=777172861(accessed June 16, 2017).

Wikipedia, "Chinese Zodiac", https://en.wikipedia.org/w/index.php?title=Chinese_zodi ac&oldid=782044592 (accessed June 16, 2017)

Wikipedia, "Color in Chinese Culture", https://en.wikipedia.org/w/index.php?title=Color_in_Chi nese_culture&oldid=785913845 (accessed June 16, 2017).

Wikipedia, "Communist Party of China", https://en.wikipedia.org/w/index.php?title=Communist_Party_of_China&oldid=785499623 (accessed June 16, 2017).

Wikipedia, "Cultural Revolution", https://en.wikipedia.org/w/index.php?title=Cultural_Revolution&oldid=785830325 (accessed June 16, 2017).

Wikipedia, "Customs and Etiquette in Chinese Dining", https://en.wikipedia.org/w/index.php?title=Customs_and_etiquette_in_Chinese_dining&oldid=782537697 (accessed June 16, 2017).

World Heritage Encyclopedia, "Customs And Etiquette In Chinese Dining", http://worldlibrary.net/articles/customs_and_etiquette_in_chinese_dining (accessed March 29, 2018).

Wikipedia, "Chinese New Year", https://en.wikipedia.org/w/index.php?title=Chinese_New_Year&oldid=785707965 (accessed June 16, 2017).

Wikipedia, "Feng shui", https://en.wikipedia.org/w/index.php?title=Feng_shui&oldid=785365163 (accessed June 16, 2017)

Wikipedia, "Golden Week (China)", https://en.wikipedia.org/w/index.php?title=Golden_Week_(China)&oldid=778419406> (accessed June 16, 2017).

Wikipedia, "Great Leap Forward", https://en.wikipedia.org/w/index.php?title=Great_Leap_Forward&oldid=785254579 (accessed June 16, 2017).

Wikipedia, "History of education in China", https://en.wikipedia.org/w/index.php?title=History_of_education_in_China&oldid=785787181 (accessed January 12, 2018).

Wikipedia, "Maoism", https://en.wikipedia.org/w/index.php?title=Maoism&oldid=785367065 (accessed June 16, 2017).

Wikipedia, "National Day of the People's Republic of China", https://en.wikipedia.org/w/index.php?title=National_Day_of_the_People%27s_Republic_of_China&oldid=763909313 (accessed June 16, 2017).

Wikipedia, "Quotations from Chairman Mao Tse-tung", https://en.wikipedia.org/w/index.php?title=Quotations_from_Chairman_Mao_Tse-tung&oldid=785968228 (accessed June 17, 2017).

Wikipedia, "Websites blocked in mainland China", https://en.wikipedia.org/wiki/Websites_blocked_in_mainland_China (accessed June 16, 2017).

Wikipedia, "Trofim Lysenko", https://en.wikipedia.org/wiki/Trofim_Lysenko (accessed June 16, 2017).

Window China, http://window-china.blogspot.com (accessed January 12, 2018)

World Tourism Summit, "Doing Business, World Tourism Summit", http://www.worldtourismsummit.com/Travel/DoingBusiness/tabid/113/Default.aspx (accessed March 29, 2018).

Yvonne Yanrong Chang, "Cultural Faces of Interpersonal Communication in the U.S. and China", https://web.uri. edu/iaics/files/29-Yvonne-Yanrong-Chang.pdf (accessed March 29, 2018).

www.ingramcontent.com/pod-product-compliance
Lightning Source LLC
Chambersburg PA
CBHW022109210326
41521CB00028B/175